THE BURDEN
OF HITLER'S LEGACY

The Burden of Hitler's Legacy

ALFONS HECK

RENAISSANCE HOUSE

A Division of Jende-Hagan, Inc.
541 Oak Street • P.O. Box 177
Frederick, CO 80530

RENAISSANCE HOUSE PUBLISHERS
541 Oak Street ~ P.O. Box 177
Frederick, Colorado 80530

Frontispiece: Surveyed by two SS guards, Hitler greets a Pimpf of the Jungvolk at his Berghof retreat in Bavaria. (Lower:) The end comes for Hitler Youth members of a Volkssturm unit as they surrender to a U.S. soldier on the Western Front, April, 1945.

(Bundesarchiv, Koblenz)

Cover design by Vaughn Reichelderfer

Library of Congress Cataloging in Publication Data

Heck, Alfons, 1928-
  The burden of Hitler's legacy.

  Bibliography: p.
  1. Heck, Alfons, 1928-   . 2. Hitler-Jugend--Biography.   3. World War, 1939-1945--Personal narratives, German.   4. World War, 1939-1945--Influence.
5. Germans--Psychology--History--20th century.
6. Guilt.   I. Title.
DD253.5.H35   1988   940.54'82'43   88-6674
ISBN: Hardcover, $18.95, 0-939650-79-7
        Paperback, $9.95, 0-939650-80-0

PREFACE

The most naively fanatic members of the Hitler Youth were those still in their teens when the war ended. I was one of them.

Unlike our elders, we adolescents had never known anything but the siren song of the *Führer*. Many were so thoroughly indoctrinated that death seemed preferable to surrender. Fittingly, they were among the very last defenders of Hitler's bunker. The last propaganda photo of Hitler was taken on his fifty-sixth birthday, April 20, 1945, ten days before he committed suicide. It shows him decorating members of the Hitler Youth, some as young as 12, in the devastated garden of the chancellery in Berlin. The boys and Hitler beam fondly at each other in genuine affection, although there is no longer the slightest doubt that Germany is doomed. To the last, the boys went out and died willingly. It was a fatal bond.

Is it possible to recover from fanaticism so intense that it blurs reality and makes death less frightening than captivity? Yes, mere physical survival can accomplish that. But it takes much longer to wither the roots of such total submission if it has been induced during one's formative years as an integral part of growing up.

With the exception of conceding military defeat in 1945, millions of former Hitler Youth have never come to terms with their own involvement, beyond a self-serving admission that they were used. Some, but by no means all, are bitter about that. Thousands are now aging leaders in their fields in today's Federal Republic of West Germany, and it's not surprising that most maintain a spontaneous conspiracy of silence. Only quietly do they acknowledge that the Nazi regime did indeed commit crimes against humanity and destroy Germany's reputation as a civilized nation. There are no active neo-Nazis beyond their late 50s in West Germany today who openly reminisce about former glories. All Germans of that age have a selective memory and try to wring some personal honor from the blood-soaked rags of the past.

In my autobiography *A Child of Hitler: Germany in the Days When God Wore a Swastika*,* I describe my childhood and life as a member and high-ranking leader of the Hitler Youth. My career peaked and ended at 17 with Germany's total defeat, which I accepted only intellectually in 1945. It took another 30 years to accept it publicly and without reservation.

The Burden of Hitler's Legacy is my account of that 30-year odyssey. It complements and expands on *A Child of Hitler* by reaching from 1933 to the present. Like my former comrades who still do not talk, I once concealed details of my life in the Third Reich.

I was arrested by the French military authorities in July of 1945, but was neither charged with nor convicted of having committed war crimes. A unit of General George Patton's U.S. Third Army had captured me on March 7 while I was on furlough in my hometown. At the time, I was a *Fähnrich* in the *Luftwaffe*, equivalent to an ensign or second lieutenant in the American armed forces, and the Americans had no reason to suspect that I had been an acting *Bannführer*. In this position as district leader of the Hitler Youth, I had been in charge of my home area with roughly 6,000 members, of which 3,000 were boys.

During my benign American captivity, we remained at war for another two months. I had plenty to eat and worked as an interpreter in an American field hospital. But all that ended when the French took over as occupiers. I was arrested solely because of my rank in the Hitler Youth and threatened with immediate execution, together with about 30 other Nazis. There was no formal charge of wrong doing. It was, a captain wryly proclaimed, "Nothing specifically personal but an act of retribution for Nazi actrocities committed in France."

During that endless night of terror, I began to resent Hitler for the first time. He had conveniently chosen suicide, while I was about to die for having served him so zealously. My emotional rejection of Nazism, however, a rejection free of self-pity, occurred much later when I began to accept the evidence of the Nuremberg War Crimes Trial, which began in November, 1945 and ended 11 months later in October, 1946.

The hardest part of my awakening was my concession that our regime had indeed committed genocide by slaughtering six million Jews. The obsession to annihilate a race even transcends

---

* Renaissance House, 1985; Bantam edition, 1986.

in enormity the murder of five million other "inferiors." The tremendous suffering of our own people, which is often cited as a redeeming circumstance, cannot eradicate that burden we bore. Hitler had started the war and we had followed him.

I had to travel a long road to comprehend and accept what had happened. To insure a fresh start, I left Germany for good in 1951, settling first in Canada and moving to the United States in 1963. That was my planned escape, although I soon discovered that the ghosts of the past are not deterred by oceans and continents.

My insight culminated on February 27, 1986, in Los Angeles, when I was a guest on the "Tom Snyder Show." My debating partner was the then leader of the American Nazi Party, Stan Widek. Predictably, Mr. Widek was more interested in blaming the Jews for every calamity of mankind than in hearing my acceptance of the truth of the Holocaust. It really didn't matter to me how *he* perceived the Nazi era, but it bothered him greatly that *I* could calmly repudiate it.

When I joined the Hitler Youth as a 10-year-old in 1938, I never could have foreseen the destruction of the Germany I loved. Equally incredible to me now is that I stand next to a survivor of Auschwitz on the lecture stage, not as an antagonist or apologist but as a partner. Our perspectives of the Nazi years are so opposite in terms of our personal experience that some listeners are offended by our joint appearance. How can a victim join a perpetrator? The truth is that we both became victims, although certainly not to the same degree.

The Hitler era with its roughly 50 million casualties was much more than a Jewish tragedy. It is an indictment of all humanity, which has left me with a lasting skepticism about the innate goodness of man.

FOREWORD

World War II was the most destructive conflict in human history. The Nazi regime that began the European phase of that war was among the most evil in history. It is, therefore, startling that so few of the thousands of books published about the Second World War address the moral dimensions of this cataclysmic struggle. Fewer still are the books that examine these moral questions on a personal basis and from the German perspective. Even now, more than 40 years after the end of the war, it is difficult to recall more than a handful of books (available in English, at least) in which German participants bare their consciences.

This is the great value and the great fascination of Alfons Heck's **THE BURDEN OF HITLER'S LEGACY**. Like his earlier memoir, **A CHILD OF HITLER**, Mr. Heck's new book will no doubt impress readers as a painfully honest attempt to relate one young German's role in the cataclysm that befell his country. Anyone interested in the history of that terrible period would find Heck's account of his experiences as a teenage officer of the Hitler Youth fascinating. But the greater contribution of **THE BURDEN OF HITLER'S LEGACY** is Heck's admirable, and so very rare, attempt to confront publicly the many moral issues raised by his participation in the Nazi apparatus that ruled and defended Germany.

More remarkable still is the teaching-lecturing partnership that developed between Alfons Heck, the former Nazi zealot, and Helen Waterford, a Jewish survivor of the Auschwitz death camp. Since their first meeting in 1980--a meeting prompted by a commentary article written by Mr. Heck and published in *The San Diego Union*--these two remarkable persons have appeared together in more than 200 lectures across the United States. The effect on many audiences, as one might imagine, is electric.

For many in these audiences, the effect must also be cathartic. As described in the book's final chapter, Helen Waterford and Alfons Heck share the lecture platform. By turns, they relate their experiences, past beliefs and emotions. Ruthless candor is a prerequisite. Heck reports that he once felt compelled to admit, in answer to a question from the audience, that he would have killed Mrs. Waterford had he been ordered to do so during the war. Unquestioning obedience to any order was central to the Nazi code of discipline.

And yet, it is the Heck-Waterford collaboration that gives **THE BURDEN OF HITLER'S LEGACY** its ending sense of hope. The enormity of World War II's toll--an estimated 55 million lives and incalculable destruction--and especially the deliberate murder of millions in the Nazi concentration camps is so overwhelming as to induce moral and emotional numbness. Perhaps that is one reason why so little of the literature of World War II addresses the larger moral issues; that, and the self-evident evil of Hitler's regime. If guilt is so obvious, it hardly needs belaboring.

But here, too, Mr. Heck's book is instructive. To millions of Germans, and even some outside Germany, Hitler and his Nazi ideology hardly seemed evil at all. When Alfons Heck was caught up in Nazism as a schoolboy before the war, it seemed to him a grand adventure and, moreover, an historically justified assertion of German nationalism. Heck knew that Jews, and others deemed undesirable by the Nazis, were harrassed and eventually rounded up and taken away. He did not know of the mass murder and the death camps until the end of the war.

There is much to be said for this reminder (how many do we need?) that evil frequently comes clothed in deceptively appealing, even idealistic garb. And there is much to be said, as well, for the realization that evil is often served unwittingly by quite decent, if profoundly misguided, persons not unlike the teen-aged Alfons Heck.

What gives cause for hope is that decades after the global catastrophe that nearly destroyed them both, Alfons Heck and Helen Waterford can give testimony together in a way that demonstrates the mutual respect and friendship that binds them today. The blind hatred and murderous madness symbolized by Auschwitz are facts of human history. But so is the triumph of reconciliation that permits Helen Waterford not to hate and Alfons Heck to seek moral redemption in the honest revelation of painful truths.

As Mr. Heck notes, more generations of Germans must pass before Hitler's legacy can rest less heavily on the collective German conscience. But Germany and Germans were not to blame for all the evil committed during World War II. Alfons Heck's example of moral regeneration and his success in showing the banality of evil offers lessons for us all. Let us hope they are always heeded.

Robert J. Caldwell, Editor
*The **San Diego Union** Sunday Opinion Section*

FOREWORD

This book, and indeed the entire life work of Alfons Heck, is a unique personal statement regarding Hitler's Germany and the Holocaust. It is a wonderfully fresh and firsthand view of the Third Reich from the eyes of a believing child. It is remarkable for Heck's story-telling ability: he depicts for us the complex motives and actions of a great variety of human beings in a situation of total moral bankruptcy, finding its inevitable conclusion in the collapse and devastation of the society and the state. Yet the book's special strength lies in its unsparing honesty. Alfons Heck seeks to draw an exact picture of himself as child and youth committed to Adolf Hitler. His purpose is to acquaint our generation and future generations with what happened in those days, and to show, by faithful use of himself, his experience and his awareness, exactly how it happened.

Alfons Heck says that his major goal in this book is "to reach that one vital segment of our society, the young." Beyond question he has attained his goal. Recently my wife and I attended a lecture by Mr. Heck and Helen Waterford in a large auditorium at Penn State University. The hall was almost entirely filled; the audience consisted largely of students and other people under 25 years of age. It was extremely gratifying for us to see that at the end of their presentation the two received a lengthy standing ovation.

The importance of Alfons Heck's work transcends the dreadful history of twentieth-century Germany. Thought control, whether imposed by the state or by other groups, is today becoming an increasingly threatening presence. It is abetted by a new technology, and its particular target is the young. Alfons Heck has devoted his life to seeing that the past shall serve as a warning to the present and the future, and he has served his purpose well indeed.

Philip Winsor
Senior Editor
The Pennsylvania State University Press

To the memory of one who never succumbed to the siren song,
my grandmother, Margaret Heck,
and to my Cusanus Gymnasium school mates who became its victims.

Most of the events in this account happened 40 to 50 years ago. Nearly all of my war notes as well as my extensive Hitler Youth records were destroyed in the air raids, but I have made every attempt to reconstruct the happenings and the dialogue as accurately as possible, aided by the recollection of former colleagues and other witnesses. In a few cases, I have changed names to protect the privacy of persons still living, but in all other aspects this is a factual account of how I experienced Nazi Germany and its aftermath.

Alfons Heck

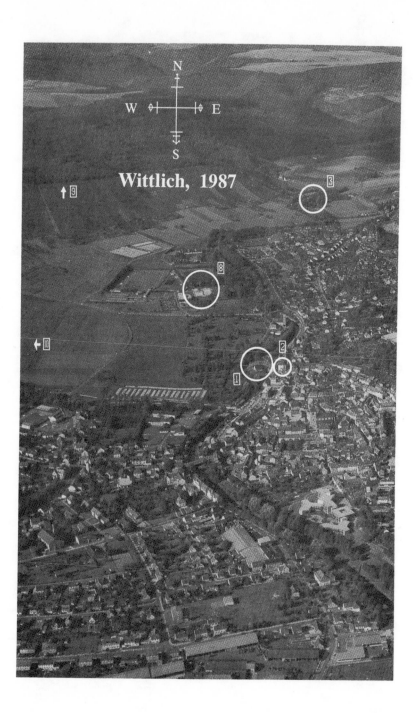

Wittlich, 1987

LEGEND

1. Heck farm today
2. Rebuilt synagogue, now a cultural center
3. Location of hut (former toolshed) where my grand-mother lived when U.S. Army arrived
4. *Cusanus Gymnasium* today
5. Former Hitler Youth Headquarters, now a school
6. Once the house of my late Aunt Ottilie
7. Plein Viaduct, blown up by *Wehrmacht* March 8, 1945
8. City Pool
9. Beginning of Eifel Mountains Plateau above vineyards
10. Penitentiary is out of photo to west

Hitler Youth Buglers or "Fanfare" Players

Chapter One:

FACING THE EVIL

Despite Germany's vast destruction, I had to see Nuremberg in ruins to overcome my nostalgia for the power of the Nazi regime. By September, 1946, when the trial of the major Nazi war criminals before the International Military Tribunal in Nuremberg ended, I was aware of most of the evidence, primarily through media reports. German newspapers were severely hampered by a shortage of newsprint and seldom exceeded six pages per issue, but one page was usually devoted entirely to the trial proceedings. It was the one page many Germans cut up for toilet paper before reading. Life during the first two postwar years was extremely precarious, a grinding daily fight for physical survival in the face of imminent starvation for millions. For that reason, few people had the inclination to read or think about the fate of their former leaders whom they now blamed for their abject misery.

Most Germans' allegiance to Hitler died with him. Never after Germany's capitulation did fanatical Nazis engage in guerilla warfare against the occupiers on any noticeable scale. Conditioned by Germany's own propaganda, Allied soldiers expected a fierce, hostile population, and were confused by the pathetic remnants of the Master Race who crawled out of their ruins, hailing their conquerors as liberators from their despised dictatorship. Much of this appearance was later proven false, however. In a survey carried out by the American occupation authorities six months after the end of the war, more than 50 percent of those questioned thought the idea of National Socialism was good, but had been badly administered. While 40 percent conceded it had been a bad idea, only 20 percent accepted Germany's responsibility for the war. So much for the notion of collective mass guilt. Despite the disclosures about the horrors of the concentration and extermination camps in particular, the majority remained skeptical about the scope of the Nazi atrocities. I was one of those.

When we in the Rhineland and Palatinate came under the French zone of occupation in July, 1945, my rather benign American captivity ended abruptly. That July day when three French soldiers drove me through the streets of my hometown clad only in tattered shorts and an undershirt, prodded by blows of rifle butts, will forever remain chiseled in my mind. Myself and the other 30 Nazis who had been been rounded up in the penitentiary were to be shot within 12 hours. The enormity of that announcement rendered me numb for several hours. I felt as light-headed and curiously detached as if I had received an injection of morphine. The public spectacle of having been beaten through the streets I once commanded seemed worse than death, although that sentiment changed as the hour of execution crept nearer. I tried to imagine what it would be like to get a bullet between the eyes, and consoled myself that the split second before death could hardly be more painful than being jammed with a rifle butt. But what if the French merely shot us in the belly?

Later that evening, a French soldier, stirred by pity, whispered to me that none of us would be killed, that we were merely hostages. I could not at first accept this supreme act of mercy, although I later counted this rough, wine-reeking enemy as the greatest friend of my entire life. I never saw him again.

My whole body was quivering as I was led out of the mass cage the following morning. Miraculously, we passed the stake before the bullet-scarred prison wall, and I was shoved into solitary confinement. When I was released 12 days later, still designated a hostage, I felt I had atoned for all the sins of my 17 years and for those of two more lifetimes as well. I had also begun to look upon Adolf Hitler as a coward who had chosen the easy way out. It was the beginning of my rehabilitation, but it never inched far beyond self-pity. The gnawing uncertainty of when the French would execute me, perhaps because a German had once ambushed them, seldom left me in my waking hours. Our security forces had often shot 50 Frenchmen in occupied France in retaliation for the death of one German soldier. The SS had eradicated the whole village of Oradour-sur-Glane when one of its regiments was fired upon by French partisans who promptly disappeared into the countryside. That *SS* atrocity had already cost the lives of many captured *Wehrmacht* soldiers during the first heady days of liberation when a whole nation looked for revenge.

After that nightmarish six months, I welcomed the denazification hearing. It was conducted by three French officers and two of my townspeople who had been classified as anti-Nazi. One, a dour shoemaker, was a Communist of long standing who had survived the concentration camp Dachau. He deserved his status as an untainted German, although that would, within a few years, become more of a liability than a virtue. The other man was a Social Democrat who had refused to join the Nazi Party, had been classified as politically unreliable, and had lost his job as a minor civil servant. His purity was suspect, because everybody in town knew he had reversed himself and even applied to be accepted as a member of the *SA* (the brown-shirted storm troops).

Even the French, who were by no means enamored of former Hitler Youth leaders, rejected the shoemaker's heated plea that despite my 17 years I ought to be dealt with "most harshly" (a Nazi euphemism for execution) on the grounds that I had been our district's last acting *Bannführer*. He buttressed his plea with the assertion that I had helped organize the last-ditch defense of our hometown, and would have ordered his execution had I been aware he were hiding in his cousin's wine cellar. I privately conceded that his argument was dangerously plausible; but to my credit, there were at least three elderly townspeople who testified that I had overlooked their disappearance from a *Volkssturm* exercise. My last order to my successor had been to head for the Rhine with the retreating *Wehrmacht*.

When the five members of the commission withdrew for their deliberations, I was under no delusions about my fate. I had become what Joseph Goebbels, our diabolical Minister of Propaganda and *Volk* Enlightenment, had accurately predicted in case of our defeat: a slave at best, subject to sterilization or the firing squad.

There was no appeal to any sentence in these early months. There was, however, a review process by military authorities who were usually so overburdened or indifferent that justice became the interpretation of the local commanders. The one I faced was proud to have been an early member of the Resistance, which became fashionable only after D-Day, June 6, 1944, when the French could be certain that Germany's demise was imminent.

Next to the Soviets, the French plundered their zone more savagely than the Americans or British. This was partly in retribution for our harsh treatment of their land, but also to demonstrate that we were now totally at their mercy. There was also the matter of French grandeur. General de Lattre de Tassigny, the first Commander-in-Chief in Germany, lived on a lavish scale reminiscent of one of the Bourbon kings. He assumed the vanquished could be reeducated by impressive ceremonies and military displays.

"We are going to show the Germans that we too can conceive big ideas and carry them out on a grand scale," he proclaimed. At one time he had 10,000 Algerian cavalrymen line his route when he bid farewell to a visiting American general. The French left-wing press became disgusted with the high living, especially in Baden-Baden, seat of the French Military Government. It estimated that each Frenchman in this once luxurious spa city consumed as much meat in one week as 55 Germans. To the French that was a mere statistic, but in many of us it evoked bitter resentment, since every German knew that neither the French nor the British alone could have defeated us. The Americans and Soviets had decided the war. They and the British, who had valiantly held out against us before the United States came to their rescue, were the victors. The French held no credibility with us because so many had collaborated with the Nazi regime. At least 11,000 Frenchmen were summarily executed as collaborators within the first few weeks of the liberation, often without trial, until General Charles deGaulle ordered a stop to the indiscriminate killings usually carried out by the Maquis.

The true conquerors had thrown the French a chunk of the spoils, unfortunately that chunk was my home province. Once, when I was pushed off the sidewalk, forced to my knees and spat upon in the face by three grinning Algerian soldiers, I tasted a genuine lust to kill, such as years of Nazi indoctrination had never been able to instill in me, even against the savage Soviets.

My knees were shaking when a submachine gun-toting soldier motioned me back into the room at our centuries-old *Rathaus*, scene of the hearing. The faces of the officers were blank, but the German Communist grinned maliciously at me. "Attention!" yelled a corporal, and I slammed my heels together, evoking a sneer from a captain. "This is not the Hitler Youth, *Herr ex-Bannführer*," he rasped in flawless German, and looked down at a piece of paper.

Every German over 18 had to fill out a *Fragebogen*, a questionnaire, and the Americans became quickly bogged down with their own zeal. The justice that was meted out in judging 13 million questionnaires was, at best, rough and ready. Few Allied officials spoke German, and fewer still understood the nuances of the Nazi rank order. The industrialists, some of Hitler's most culpable servants had, for example, never belonged to the Party. The Americans, British and French classed five categories of Nazi offenders, ranging from major war criminals to mere followers, the so-called "*Muss Nazis*" who had been under pressure to join the Party to keep or enhance their jobs. The most numerous in that group were civil servants, including school teachers and mailmen.

Since Party membership was the greatest common denominator in trying to assess guilt, I was lucky at first. I stated truthfully to my American captors that I had been too young to join the Party. In general, soldiers of the *Luftwaffe*, unlike the members of the *Waffen SS*, were not singled out for special treatment, which sometimes consisted of a quick bullet in the neck, particularly from units of the Free French Forces. To be caught with the tattoo under one's left armpit, where each *SS* soldier was marked with his blood group, meant almost certain death on the Russian Front. It was also the first sign for which Americans looked if they at all suspected a prisoner's identity.

As a 17-year-old, fuzzy-cheeked *Luftwaffe Fähnrich*, I was in little danger, especially since I spoke English, as long as the Americans didn't discover that I had been a high-ranking leader of the Hitler Youth. The French were very aware that many members of the Hitler Youth had been far more fanatical than most Party adherents. The fact that since December 1939, membership in the two branches of the Hitler Youth had become compulsory for every healthy Aryan German child of 10, was not an extenuating factor for those who rose to the

higher ranks. With advancement, we became adults, fully
accountable for our deeds. Predictably, I was denounced by an
anonymous fellow citizen of my hometown, and for me the
amnesty granted to any German under 18 no longer applied.

I had spent enough time under the French to realize the
futility of a reply when the German-speaking captain asked me
if I had any comments before the Tribunal announced its
findings. I had once lost two teeth for refusing to salute a French
sergeant with an outstretched arm and shouting instead, "*Heil
Hitler!*" I wasn't about to risk much more than that by appearing
recalcitrant. It's easy to disguise flaming hatred when the stakes
are that high. My sentence could range from years in prison to
slave labor in France, even execution, although that seemed
unlikely since I had passed that hurdle once already.

"Please consider my age," I said. "I was 17 when the war
ended, not when it began." I couldn't bring myself to say more,
and I don't think it would have made any difference. They had
arrived at their sentence before I was asked to speak. At that
moment, the only thing I regretted was that the situation were
not reversed. Chances are I would gladly have imprisoned all
five of my judges. The Communist snorted as if he had guessed
my thoughts. The presiding officer, a gray-haired colonel with a
hawkish nose watched me intently as the captain lifted the sheet
and began to read: "This Tribunal finds you guilty of fanaticism,
which enabled you to reach a high rank in the *Hitlerjugend*
despite your youth. We have no doubt that you would have
remained a dedicated, ruthless follower of Adolf Hitler and the
Nazi creed had Germany won the war."

He paused for a moment as if challenging me for a reply. So
far, the Tribunal was right on the mark. But what was the
punishment for fanaticism? I pressed my hands against my sides
to stop them from shaking. "You are sentenced to one month at
hard labor here at the garrison, restricted to the town limits of
Wittlich for no less than two years, and barred from attending
any institution of learning."

He stopped and broke into a thin smile. "Despite some
dissension, the Tribunal finds you not guilty of having committed war crimes. Your efforts on the *Westwall* were within the
scope of legitimate orders given to you." He grinned widely.
"The lives you cost were those of your comrades. While that is
entirely acceptable to this Tribunal, it might turn into a life

sentence for you. Dismissed." I clicked my heels, turned, and left, smiling at the soldier who handcuffed me to the jeep for the short ride to the garrison, formerly the home of our elite 105th Infantry.

The following month wasn't pleasant. I was part of a gang of eight prisoners, all former Nazis with minor sentences. We were treated roughly and only allowed to speak during the half-hour noon meal which was usually bread and cheese. To some of us who were semi-starved, the food alone was worth a beating. I was the only member of the Hitler Youth and by far the youngest. After the second day, I was allowed to go home at night. I didn't need to be told that I would be shot for escaping, for there was nowhere to go. Besides, I considered myself very fortunate, despite the fact that I was being treated like a felon merely for having served Germany. "I was only following orders," was the refrain used by all of us.

Nothing is less conducive to rehabilitation than harsh treatment, especially when one believes that treatment to be unjust. Usually we worked in twos, scrubbing endless tiled hallways on our knees at a lung-searing speed, occasionally prodded by a rifle butt. Once a fellow prisoner, a former platoon leader in the General or "Black" *SS*, whispered to me, "One day the *Führer* will personally thank us for our suffering." I thought he had lost his mind. "He's in Argentina," he rasped, "and he'll rise again to fight the Bolsheviks." His eyes were flickering and I turned away, shaken by his inability to face the truth.

The worst task we performed occurred during my last week of confinement. We had to excavate a mass grave of French prisoners of war who had died in a fighter bomber attack on Wittlich in January of 1945 as they were returning to their camp from a construction site. The stench of the partly decomposed corpses was so overwhelming that we vomited until our stomachs were dry. There were no guards to prod us on; they stood a hundred yards back with masks over their noses. The second day, I was reaching into the pile of corpses with rubber-gloved hands to separate them, sometimes cracking the spines with a shovel. It was a scene out of Dante's *Inferno*. By nightfall we were quite drunk, for the soldiers supplied us liberally with cheap red wine, which we not only gulped down but poured over our heads and face masks. Townspeople walking the cemetery path crossed themselves when they saw us. Months later, when I saw a documentary of the concentration camp Buchenwald (by choice and not by coercion) I immediately ran out and vomited. I knew then the stench of hell.

Nearly seven months later, I stood before the same captain who had read the sentence at my hearing. Things had taken a turn for the better. My expulsion from the *Cusanus Gymnasium*, the school which had reopened in the fall of 1945, lasted less than four months. One Monday morning, on my bi-weekly appointment with the French Military Security, I was unceremoniously handed a note by a corporal saying that I was granted permission to return to school. I was wise enough not to ask why, and I'm sure the corporal could have cared less. My visits had become so routine that he no longer bothered to greet me with "*Bon jour, Nazi cochon.*" Perhaps he realized that under the circumstances it was rather a compliment to be called a Nazi pig; there were so few of us who admitted our past allegiance, even to fellow citizens.

I was elated to be returning to school. Most important, it signified a softening in the harsh attitude of our conquerors. I spent all of my days either working on the removal of the rubble from our decimated farm or helping my grandmother and aunts prepare the fields for planting. All our animals had been killed in the Christmas Eve air raid of 1944, so we scratched the shallow furrows into the soil by pulling the plow ourselves. Every ten yards or so we rested to catch our breath, and I began to understand the punishment contained in the plan of Henry J. Morgenthau, Jr., President Roosevelt's Secretary of the Treasury, who wanted to see Germany turned into a permanent cow pasture.

I felt isolated from my former comrades, which may have been an unrecognized blessing, and I began to brood about my life under Hitler. Why had the unlimited promise of a carefree boyhood in a privileged society turned into this nightmare? Often in the early mornings, lying on my narrow cot in the wooden hut we had erected next to the remains of our farm, I tried to postpone awakening to another day. It wasn't the back-breaking labor that sapped my spirits; what bothered me more was the attitude of my fellow Germans. Our family was still much better off than most Germans, for we had our land and we would not starve to death. The magnitude of our disaster had temporarily levelled all class distinctions, something Hitler had not been able to do. The new aristocracy were those most able to survive by any possible means. For millions of women, prostitution became a legitimate and acceptable route, while their brothers or husbands either languished in captivity or hunted for the cigarette butts of the conquerors. It was the nadir of the Master Race, but it was also the triumph of a new people, a spirit which I despised at first for its craven surrender of all dignity in exchange for survival. While it may be too much to ask anybody hunting for a piece of bread to grapple with the moral issue of guilt and compliance, it astonished me that it never became a burning question for this new breed even when their bellies were full again. By now, even the most fervent former Nazis felt they had paid for their past enthusiasm with their suffering. It was quite akin to penance after confession in the Catholic Church, where even deadly sins are never fatal.

I was born into a regime which had succeeded in turning me into a fanatic, willing to die for a cause I believed not merely achievable but just--the creation of a new world order under the Nazi ideology. The tenets of this faith had never been opposed by those who influenced me as a child--my elders and educators including my priests. Since membership in the Hitler Youth was compulsory, we had no choice but to follow orders. By granting a youth amnesty, the Allies conceded that anyone under 18 at the end of the war could not be held culpable since he was a victim of Nazi indoctrination, too immature to recognize the evil of a regime venerated by so many million adults. There were exceptions, though. Members of the *Waffen SS*, no matter how young, were classed in a criminal group. Although the Hitler Youth was never indicted as a criminal organization, its higher-ranking leaders were all interrogated, and I was one of the very few under 18 accorded that dubious distinction. I deeply resented it. I believed myself entirely innocent of having committed any crimes, but curiously, the French Tribunal had found the one charge that was justified--fanaticism.

Since fanaticism is, by definition, irrational, can it be a crime? I wasn't ready to concede that in 1945. Even then I knew that there are degrees of irrationality which may range from mild delusion to stark insanity. Had I been insane? Certainly not, although some of the orders I gave or followed had not been rational. Is it rational to order a group of a hundred Hitler Youth boys, some as young as 14, to stop an American tank

column? Possibly, but not two months before the end of a war
already lost, unless one believes that it's better to die fighting
than live on in slavery. I did.

My rejection of the Nazi ideology did not occur overnight.
At first there was a feeling of wonderment that I had survived
the war. I was relieved that the pressure of constant fear was
gone, a fear I had never been able to admit to any of my
comrades. The creed of the Hitler Youth, although recognizing
that legitimate fear exists, made it taboo to discuss. It was
something one had to overcome at all costs. The threat of what
might happen if one did not subdue one's fear was highly
effective and the basis of our system of unquestioning obedience. As I rose in the ranks, I perceived only dimly that I was
becoming more visible and vulnerable. Only at the end, when I
read an order by *SS Reichsführer* Heinrich Himmler decreeing
immediate execution for any district leader who retreated
without permission, did I realize that any setback in my sector
could easily put me in front of a firing squad.

It was not uncommon for the *SS* to shoot deserters in one
part of town while the other part of town had surrendered. Most
officials made bombastic public statements of resisting to the
last breath, while packing their cars for the escape across the
Rhine. Tragically, the children were often the most stalwart
resistors. I was told by an American tank sergeant of General
Patton's Third Army that he was forced to machine gun a 12-
year-old boy because he refused to lower his bazooka pointed at
the tank. What seemed to the American to be a soul-shaking,
unforgettable event was to me routine bravery. I assured him he
had been lucky for having been faster on the trigger than his 12-
year-old adversary. I did not tell him that the boy had likely
belonged to a unit under my command.

The French captain who sentenced me had been perceptive
in gloating that I had cost more German than enemy lives. That
was precisely the burden I began to carry when I tried to assess
my wartime actions. The consensus of most townspeople
regarding my role was that I had merely become the object of
the victors' revenge. Most gratifying was the response of my
fellow *Gymnasium* mates when I was allowed back to school.
Nearly all of them had been under my command and many did
not recall their Hitler Youth service with great nostalgia, but
they understood better than any Tribunal that I had done my

best for the wrong cause. *Herr* Fetten, once our feared German teacher, said as he shook my hand, "You had better look upon this not as the result of a personal aberration, but as the inevitable conclusion to an era of madness which you had no way of evaluating."

"So, why in hell didn't you do it for us?" I felt like screaming at him. "You were a mature adult when the Nazis came to power." To *Herr* Fetten I said nothing, though, because he, at least, had not become a Party member despite considerable pressure. But that was the extent of his courage. Compared to most professors in our vaunted universities who fell all over themselves in their eagerness to embrace the new ideology, he, the high school teacher, had at least silently clung to his principles. Was that enough?

I didn't think so then, and I don't think so now, more than 40 years later. When the true scope of Hitler's regime began to mount, I watched the toll it exacted from our people, falling prey to the idea that we had been more than amply punished. As long as I lived under the French, which was, for me, far more terrifying than the *Gestapo*, it was easy to believe that we were being unjustly punished.

My return to school was, therefore, a turning point. I was no longer a hostage but was deemed worthy of a chance at what democracy had to offer. Democracy was a farce. We had merely exchanged one dictatorship for another. A common joke of that time was: "How do the Allies differ from the Nazis?" The answer: "They're more inefficient and don't speak German."

But despite the fact that our fragile press was rigidly censored by the masters of each occupation zone, the French did make a sincere effort at reeducating us. Much of that initial effort was aimed at baring the truth about the Nazi regime. The French understandably omitted any reference to their own glaring collaboration, but instead explored the reasons why a whole nation had become so enthralled by such a vicious regime. At the heart of it they saw the basic Teutonic flaw of worshipping authority without question, combined with the Master Race complex. That feeling of national superiority they understood much better than any other nation. It was one of the major reasons why France and Germany had been invading each other for centuries. There was something refined about French culture and history which we had not been able to match. We compensated by being more efficient and by bathing more often. Still, I had never been ashamed that my paternal ancestor had been one of Napoleon's officers, albeit with the good sense to settle in Germany.

The worst days of my persecution had passed with my return to school. The French garrison of 2,000 soldiers was, to Wittlich, a town of 9,000, quite overpowering, especially since the French had requisitioned the best housing. They evicted residents on a few hours notice, usually with strict instructions to leave behind everything except their clothing and some personal items. Since one third of the city's buildings had been destroyed or badly damaged, it put a severe strain on the available living space, as well as on the compassion of the townspeople who were forced to house displaced neighbors. Our family felt a certain satisfaction that our miserable hut was apparently immune from invasion by house hunters. It was part of a former *Wehrmacht* hut, quite sturdy, and we divided it into four rooms.

Since both my uncles were missing in action in Russia, I was the only male on the farm until my twin brother Rudolf made his way from Oberhausen in the British zone. He had a valid permit to visit us, and it took him seven days to travel the 200 kilometers by bicycle. He had come looking for food because he and my parents were subsisting on an official ration of 1,050 calories per day. Just half an hour from Wittlich, he was picked up by a French patrol and thrown into the same penitentiary where I had been. The reason was that he wore a GI jacket which, the French claimed, he must have stolen. On the fourth day of his incarceration he was sodomized at gun point by two Algerian guards. They gave him two packages of Camel cigarettes and threw him out on the street. It was a measure of the toughness of the times that he was able to quip that he had been paid twice as much as a woman for a whole night's stand. He also got his bicycle back.

During the three months my brother was allowed to remain in the French zone, we rarely discussed our paths under Hitler. We had grown up in separate homes--Rudolf with my parents in an industrial city, I with my grandparents on a beautiful farm. Because of my father's influence, my brother had not become as fanatic as I, but he felt just as keenly the tragedy that had befallen Germany. In a way, the readjustment was easier for him, since my father had convinced him long before the end of the war that Hitler was the curse of our country. That realization did not, however, protect him from being drafted into the *Wehrmacht,* or motivate him to desert. He shared the dilemma of millions of disillusioned Germans who continued fighting--that the unconditional surrender demanded by the Allies was nearly as frightening as the ongoing slaughter.

One evening while my brother and I were washing ourselves in the creek which flowed by our farm, we were ordered out of the water by a French patrol and marched down the street half naked, past my wailing grandmother and aunts. We had missed the eight o'clock curfew announced by a tolling church bell just as we jumped into the creek.

The soldiers placed us side by side on two chairs in the empty window of a former shoe store which now served as a check point. We were threatened with execution if we so much as lifted a finger without permission. Dead tired and ravenous from having been out on the fields all day, we were made to watch a squad of soldiers noisily wolf down its rations, which consisted of long loaves of bread with fragrant cheese, sausage, pate and an oxtail stew, all rare luxuries to us who lived mainly on potatoes, turnips, barley soup and coarse rye bread. They watched our stares with obvious glee. Finally one of them asked if we were hungry or thirsty. When we nodded eagerly, he walked over and poured half a quart of red wine over our heads while his comrades howled with pleasure. The soldiers then ordered us to sing "Lily Marlene" and "*Deutschland über Alles.*" We might have gone through the whole repertoire of Nazi songs, but a lieutenant wandered in unexpectedly. He looked at us with some astonishment, questioned a corporal in rapid-fire French and then began to bellow at his men who looked sheepish and sullen. I wasn't fluent enough to follow all of his outburst, but it was clear that he was berating them for their treatment of us. He demanded to see the report sheet of the arrest and snorted in disgust when the corporal admitted we had been seized at the sound of the warning bell and on our own property. What incensed him most was our appearance--we were still dripping from the wine. He dispersed the men with a curt command and motioned us to the food-laden table. "*Mangez s'il vous plait,*" he said politely. We dropped all pretense at dignity and tore into the delicacies. The same soldier who had drenched us with wine kept filling our glasses with the solicitude of a first-rate waiter, while the officer watched us, his arms across his chest.

When we finally quit gorging ourselves, he whistled softly in admiration for such reckless gluttony and pointed to the door. "*Allez*," he ordered in French, "I'll take you home in my jeep." When we thanked him in French for our short ride, he looked startled. My brother, in too friendly a manner I thought, told him our ancestor had been born in the Dordogne region of France in 1763, as if that would explain our textbook French acquired nearly 200 years later.

The officer held out his hand. "*Gute Nacht*," he said. My brother shook it warmly, returning the greeting, but I turned away. The man's face turned crimson, then he shrugged. "Watch the curfew, or you'll be in serious trouble," he admonished us, suddenly stern, and gunned his jeep.

Just before he turned off the light, my brother looked over at me from his cot. "This officer saved us from possible disaster," he said quietly. "Would it really have hurt you to shake his hand?"

"What the hell is the matter with you?" I yelled. "Don't go soft on me because of one seemingly decent Frenchman. There's still open season on any German and I, for one, am getting sick and tired of being threatened with execution by the bastards every time I turn around. Have you forgotten, for Christ's sakes, that the dirty swine raped you?"

"Keep your voice down," he hissed. "You gave me your word you'd never mention that to anybody, you hear?"

"All right," I said. "You know I won't, but doesn't that show you how vulnerable we all are, not just me? If that officer had been half drunk, he could have joined in the torturing of a couple of unarmed slobs."

"I don't think so," he said. "He doesn't have the *Gestapo* mentality. By the way, could you imagine a *Gestapo* officer letting a couple of prisoners feast and then driving them home? We were technically guilty of breaking the curfew, you know."

"Most of us weren't the goddamn *Gestapo*," I said, "and you know that too. I never did anything I'm ashamed of except lose the bloody war."

"Big Brother," he said softly, "there's no need to snow me. You were a prime specimen of the Master Race, ready to follow any order. You're still breathing only because that Luxembourg school teacher had sense enough to get away from you before you had his ass shot. The French know that and you know it, so don't give me this noble warrior crap."

When I didn't reply, he lit a couple of precious cigarettes and threw me one. "Maybe you ought to make a trip to Nuremberg," he chuckled, "to see your former idols in the dock, accused of crimes against humanity."

"You're crazy," I said, "unless you can convince me that humanity includes Germans too." Nearly ten million Germans had been driven out of their homes in the east, two million or so, most likely including our Uncle Albert and his family, having been bestially slaughtered by the Soviets. "Tell me," I asked my brother, "does that count as a crime against humanity, or is it merely a regrettable overreaction?"

"We started it, Big Brother," he said, "and you'd better come to terms with that or you'll gnaw your limb off like an animal caught in a trap."

With this rather bizarre analogy, my twin brother had accurately defined my dilemma. I secretly admired his detachment from an era which had been the apex of my life. I continued looking for extenuating circumstances, a sudden discovery which would explain the barbarous cruelty which had been the hallmark of the Third Reich. During his remaining two months in Wittlich, we never again talked about that night. While I was in school, he became invaluable on this peculiar farm, which consisted of land and a dozen chickens.

As the months passed, my brother's sarcastic suggestion that I visit my former idols in Nuremberg became a fixation with me. Nearly half my classmates from 1939 were either dead or still in captivity. In my class, everyone had been a veteran of the war, either as a member of the *Wehrmacht* or Hitler Youth. Yet it seemed that I alone persisted in delving into the past. All teachers who had been Party members were barred from teaching, and there was such a shortage of acceptable instructors that many classes contained 80 or more students. It was a curious sort of instruction, because the Allies prescribed it. We studied the neutral subjects, such as Latin, English, French, physics and mathematics with particular zeal, and avoided the interpretation of history like the plague, partly out of cynicism, but mostly because we were honestly confused. When we were handed our first history books, printed in France, we opened the windows and threw them out. It put our teacher into a state of panic because the French kept a close eye on the school. Following his perspiring entreaties, we compromised by keeping the books closed on our desks while he discussed art.

We were a new breed of students, immune to threats by mere professors, most of whom we held suspect as cowards anyway. If they were now so wise, why hadn't they spoken out ten years ago? Only a handful of former soldiers commanded a grudging respect. They knew that after the brutality we had witnessed, the specter of failing a grade would merely evoke amused laughter. These were new times--times when I was ashamed to eat my sandwich in front of my classmates, who were always on the lookout for something edible.

One morning the principal introduced our new French teacher to us. She was indeed French and spoke only a few words of German. After he had left, the rather attractive young lady (whose appearance only suffered because of a fairly long nose) began to instruct us briskly. We were a cold-eyed assortment of former young Nazis, clad in dyed uniform pieces, and when she began to question us about the text, we rose politely and grinned lasciviously at her enticing bosom. In less than 20 minutes she ran sobbing out of the classroom.

Only when the principal stormed at us to consider the gravity of our actions, which were surely a deadly insult to the occupiers, did we relent. Inwardly we did not regret our behavior, since we saw her as the representative of the enemy, but he appealed to our chivalry as men toward a woman. Gradually, Mademoiselle Mercier became one of our favorites. We realized the advantage of learning the language from a native, but more than that, we admired the guts she had shown by choosing us over a junior class. She also shared cramped quarters with a German colleague, when she could have demanded better accommodations at the expense of another German family.

When I finally encountered the French captain from the Tribunal seven months later, it was at the school. He had become the liaison officer of the French Military Government in matters of education. I ran into him outside the massive sandstone building with my chunk of firewood under my arm, a requirement for attending school. Since there was no coal for central heating, each classroom had a wood burning stove with a pipe leading out of the window. Half the window glass was still missing and plywood sheets kept out most of the cold. I was surprised when he greeted me by name. "*Guten Tag, Herr* Heck," he said politely and touched his uniform cap. "Do you like the new chemistry lab we installed?"

I nodded, tempted to ask him if he knew that the Americans had smashed our old lab to bits on the first day of their occupation, apparently believing it was a sinister testing ground for sadistic Nazi scientists. That seemed a bit childish, though, so I said nothing.

"May I ask you a favor?" I suddenly blurted out, startled at my own temerity.

"Certainly," he smiled, "although I can't make any promises, you understand."

"I would like permission to leave the French zone for about 10 days or so. I give you my word I'll return," I added quickly.

He arched his eyebrows. "Where to? To visit your family?"

"Yes," I replied, seeing a chance, "but I would also like to visit Nuremberg."

He stepped back and stared at me. "Trying to relive old glories?"

"No," I said, "the Trial is coming to an end and I would like to be there."

"Whatever for?" he asked, and then stopped, recognition dawning in his eyes. "You won't be able to get near the courtroom. Only Germans directly engaged in the defense are allowed to set foot in the building."

"I'm aware of that," I said, suddenly feeling very foolish. "I want to get a notion of what it's like close up. It seems so remote here; nobody talks about it."

"Maybe you Germans don't," he said, "but we do." We looked at each other silently, his facial muscles working. "*Bon,*" he said. "You'll get a travel permit valid for two weeks in both the British and American zones." He saluted and began to walk away. "Don't break the curfew again," he called over his shoulder.

And so, a week later, I forced my way into a grimy train compartment, jammed with reeking humanity, bound for Nuremberg, the city of triumph and tragedy, hoping for deliverance in a quest nobody else seemed to share.

Baldur von Schirach inspects flag bearers of numerous *Banne* at the Nuremberg Party Congress of 1938. I was there with my *Bann* 244. In his entourage are three *Gebietsführer*, provincial leaders similar to *Gauleiter* of the Nazi Party.

Chapter Two:

THE CRUCIBLE OF NUREMBERG

Today a traveler can reach Nuremberg from any point in the Rhineland in less than half a day, indulged passengers on the luxurious Paris-Vienna Express. In the fall of 1946, traversing the 300 miles from my hometown was an obstacle course fraught with danger. Most of Germany's dense rail net was still fragmented. It had been the primary target of thousands of Allied air attacks. But it was the retreating *Wehrmacht*, under Hitler's orders, that gave it the *coup de grâce* by blowing up hundreds of bridges and maintenance depots. Along the winding Mosel river from Trier to Koblenz, the destruction was complete. The debris of 19 bridges clogged the important waterway, paralyzing all river traffic, which cut the vital rail link to the Rhine and thus to the center of Germany. We had become an island.

I began my journey in a third-class passenger train of the *Reichsbahn*, as it was called until 1949 when, under the emerging Federal Republic it became the *Bundesbahn*. The first leg of the trip ended just 12 miles south in Bernkastel, Germany's most picturesque wine town on the Mosel river. Here we swarmed aboard six rickety, bullet-scarred coaches of a private line, the small-gauge, slow-moving Mosel Valley Line, called the drunkard's railroad. Before the war, the Mosel Valley Line was usually jammed with throngs of people, especially in good weather. For a few marks one could travel all day, rounding every bend of the river from the French border to the Rhine, enjoying exquisite views of the numerous castles, steep vineyards, and cobblestoned medieval villages which produce the best Riesling wines in the world. Names like Bernkastel, Wehlen, Piesport, Graach, Kröv, Cochem and Zell trigger the taste buds of thousands of wine connoisseurs around the world.

Even children drank wine mixed with water on the Mosel River Valley Line, the only German railroad where the schedule was unimportant. If somebody wanted to get off between villages, he merely pulled a cord. On crowded Sundays, a special lookout watched for the inebriated who might have fallen asleep on the tracks. The line gave the shivers to bureaucrats, but was the delight of young lovers, who waltzed slowly in the dancing car to the strains of a wandering accordion band.

There was no dancing in 1946, and wine had become such a precious commodity that few wasted it on revelry. Until 1948, the French Military Government confiscated the total wine harvest within its zone, leaving only ten percent to the vintners. That meager ten percent put even the poorest wine farmer among the privileged new class. Money could buy only the starvation rations allotted on consumer cards, but wine could be bartered for anything from butter to shoes, American cigarettes to herring.

What wine couldn't buy was freedom. Nobody on that small train, where we literally sat on each other laps, was without a special travel permit, complete with finger print. The French sealed off their zone hermetically, as if it were no longer a part of Germany. To be caught outside one's town exceeding a perimeter of six kilometers, meant instant arrest. In my case that could have led to a prison sentence or a term of slave labor in France. The French were also aware that nearly all passengers were on a barter trip, to or from another zone of occupation. Germans who could not barter or sell themselves and their labor starved. It was as simple as that. As a result, the Black Market, or "compensation" as it was generally called, was sanctioned by the authorities. By obtaining a "de-blockade" certificate, a merchant from the French zone could exchange wine for food or goods from another zone, if he were lucky, for German police, under the supervision of the French, had the authority to confiscate goods from Black Marketeers at will.

I witnessed the power of the German police at the first checkpoint on our trip. Here we left the Mosel Valley Line, crossed the river by ferry, and continued in cattle cars of the *Reichsbahn*. Before we were allowed to climb into the wagons which were outfitted with wooden benches, we had to pass a control. Four German gendarmes under the supervision of two armed French soldiers checked every fifth passenger at random for a permit and possible contraband. They merely glanced at me and my knapsack, which contained three bottles of wine, two pounds of lard, and a pound of bacon. Under my belt I carried two pounds of our own tobacco, finely cut for cigarette making. I was quite rich. Soon, a man began to howl in anguished protest. His bulging suitcase, wrapped with twine, disgorged 16 bottles of wine.

"Where is your permit, you lousy Black Marketeer?" demanded a gendarme in faked indignation, admiring the bottles which he would soon share with his comrades. "Confiscated," he added coldly, waving his arm toward the wine.

"You can't do this to me, you pigs," yelled the man, "my family is starving." He still had a paunch, rare in Germans then, suggesting that he was a *Schieber*, a profiteer, but I felt sorry for him. We were all trying to survive the best we could. Just as the gendarme reached over to pull the suitcase from him, the man lunged, grabbed the handle and shoved all 16 bottles over the embankment and onto the tracks, where they crashed.

"You are under arrest," screamed the gendarme, crimson with rage.

A threatening murmur arose from the crowd of hundreds and somebody shouted, "Leave him alone, you French lackey. Hasn't he paid enough?" The French soldiers instantly sensed the ugly mood and moved their heads toward the train. *Allez, vite, vite,*" they yelled, opening the wooden barrier, and we surged toward the train, carrying the profiteer with us. It was a small victory, but it lifted my spirits even further.

After ferrying across the Mosel once more to circumvent a destroyed bridge, we walked a mile and reboarded another dilapidated train. It was midnight before we reached Koblenz, the major center of traffic at the confluence of the Mosel and Rhine rivers. It had taken 16 hours to travel 60 miles, but from then on we made good time. Unlike the French, the Americans had an abundance of material to restore the major rail lines in their zone. We entered the American zone in the middle of the night. Half an hour inside the border was the huge railroad station of Frankfurt. As in Koblenz, only the skeleton of the vast roof remained. In the wan light of the early dawn I caught a glimpse of the city around the station. The streets had been cleaned of rubble, but many of the buildings still lay in ruins.

Masses of people, most resembling beggars in their worn

clothing, milled around on the platforms between the tracks. Teams of German railroad police spot-checked travel documents, here and there turning somebody away from the last wooden barrier. When our train for Nuremberg was announced, people began to jump across the barriers and stormed the train before it had come to a complete stop. I followed the example of some other youths and climbed in through a window. Riding on the roofs, which had been common during the first six months after the war, was no longer permitted, since trains now rolled at normal speed. Every compartment and walkway was filled with sweating humanity, but still hundreds of travelers remained behind, beaten back by the batons of the railroad police. No conductor could have forced his way through to check tickets, which were collected at the destination. We pulled out of the station parallel with a train reserved for Allied personnel only. The stark contrast between the sparsely occupied first-class Pullman cars served by white-gloved waiters, and our reeking conveyance, made it clear who was now in charge.

A few kilometers east of the ruins of Frankfurt, much of the Hessian countryside was untouched by war. This was the destination of many passengers engaged in an unending search for food. Now there was enough room to sit, and the cool autumn air swept away much of the stench. For the first time since the end of the war, I experienced a feeling of freedom, even elation, as if I were on vacation. I had forgotten how beautiful much of Germany was, and as we traveled south, crossing the Main river, my anticipation grew.

Although I was still under surveillance by the *Sûrete*, the French security police, my situation had improved considerably since that bitter day of unconditional German surrender 17 months ago. I was no longer afraid of sudden arrest, and whole days passed without my cursing the presence of the French. This journey was my first opportunity to leave their zone of occupation. Unlike other former Nazis, I had never been issued a written denazification document, ironically called a *Persilschein*, after a popular laundry detergent. I had been seized during the most dangerous period, the first weeks of occupation when revenge took precedence over justice, but once I had served my term of hard labor, I was immune from further prosecution unless I violated the restrictions. By letting me return to school, the French tacitly admitted me to the ranks of the blameless. They had followed the example of the Americans who speedily released even high-ranking Hitler Youth leaders, provided they were under 18 and passed an investigation into their former activities. Only crimes against the Allies were culpable, not military actions which had led to the death of Germans.

I knew that Nuremberg had been especially marked for devastation, but that had not prepared me for the reality. It was night when the train, overflowing with passengers, rattled into the outskirts of this most Teutonic of all German cities. Its Gothic style, embodied in the *Altstadt* (the old part of town), with its elaborate facades, splendid town hall and castle, and the massive 16th century gates, had created the wealthiest and most beautiful city in the land.

The eminence of the "free city" of Nuremberg had faded since the heady days of the 16th century, which had produced Albrecht Dürer and the *Meistersinger*. The following two centuries encompassed The Age of Enlightenment. The nobility, in particular, turned away from German tradition which it considered coarse, and aped French culture and the splendor of the Bourbon kings to such an extent that French became its language. Even Frederick the Great, who had made Prussia the most militaristic and powerful of all German states, preferred to speak French, and counted Voltaire among his friends.

Nuremberg was rediscovered after the Napoleonic era, when the power of France had faded and German nationalism began to rise under the influence of such philosophers as Fichte and Hegel. They preached the theory of a selected people, forerunners of the Master Race. After the Franco-Prussian War and the establishment of the Second Reich in 1871, Germans went on a nationalistic binge which, although it ebbed and flowed, set the tone for the next 50 years and crested in the super spectacle of the Nazi *Reichsparteitag*.

Hitler, with his uncanny ability to sense the mood of the people, selected Nuremberg as the site of the annual high mass of his regime, even before he became Chancellor in 1933. Nuremberg, like no other German city, served as the ideal foil to lend the respectability of the past to Hitler's movement when it was still considered on the lunatic fringe of radical parties. Most Nurembergers ignored the first Party rally of 1927. The Weimar Republic was enjoying a brief heyday after years of unprecedented inflation and before the outbreak of the world-wide depression. Since the government no longer saw the Nazis as any threat, it restored Hitler's permission to speak publicly again in Bavaria. The rally drew more than 30,000 marchers of the *SA*, the brown-shirted storm trooper detachments. That was fewer than previous Party rallies had drawn, a fact not lost on the newspapers.

The *Münchener Post* wrote, "The citizens of Nuremberg are happy to have the party day of the NSDAP behind them. The affair lasted for three days. The working people reacted very coolly to the Wilhelminian megalomania of the party members. The parade and review were merely a final demonstration to salvage some of the prestige."

When I saw the dark silhouettes of the first houses which lined the track, I wasn't thinking of any party rally, but tried to gauge the extent of the damage. On the outskirts, most houses were still standing. As we neared the center of the city, the gaps between dwellings grew wider. Soon, continuous walls of rubble flanked the streets on both sides, here and there broken by the ruin of a building from which a forlorn light flickered. The destruction was so complete that I didn't recognize the main station. Fortunately the freshly painted black and white sign above the platform said *Nürnberg*. I grabbed my knapsack and followed the throng toward the exits.

Perhaps because the hour was late, most of us were quickly waved through the check point. A few minutes later I stood on the station square and looked around for shelter. By the light of the moon, the buildings facing the square resembled an abandoned construction site. The smell of decaying mortar hung in the air. People hurried away quickly, some running toward a street car which had clanged into view. I saw no point in boarding it. Whatever its destination in this moonscape, there was no hotel left to which it could take me.

It was close to midnight and had become quite cool. At least the huge, plywood-sheeted lobby of the station was warm. But I was turned away at the entrance since I had not yet purchased a ticket. The ticket counters were closed. The railroad official pointed down the dark street leading into the ruins of the inner city. "About 15 minutes walking distance down the road is a Red Cross hut. You might find a corner there and a cup of rye coffee. In five hours, you can come back and buy your ticket."

"That won't do me any good," I said. "I need a place to stay for about a week. I'm on vacation."

"Vacation?" he repeated incredulously. "In Nuremberg? You must be joking. You're certainly the first tourist of the postwar era. What are you going to see? The ruins of the Third Reich?"

"Exactly," I said, "and I've got bacon. I'm from a farm in the Rhineland." *Herr* Peter Friedrich, assistant inspector of the *Reichsbahn*, told me some days later when we had become friends, that he had known from the beginning I was mentally unbalanced. But he, like any German of the time, could not resist the lure of bacon. He took me home with him.

The following morning I awoke in a tiny attic room on the third and top floor of a bombed-out building. The ground floor, once a delicatessen, was still a mass of rubble, and only two rooms were habitable on the second floor. Fire had destroyed the third floor, and one could reach the attic only by means of a ladder. The housing authorities who surveyed every property for possible living space, hadn't gone beyond the shell of the stairway. One look at the angle of the structure turned them away. If *Herr* Friedrich wanted to risk his life in the ruin of his house, that was his affair.

When I looked out of the small attic window in daylight, I saw row upon row of ruins, which made *Herr* Friedrich's house appear quite presentable. The roof was still firmly attached to the shell of the brick house. Here and there from the mounds of rubble rose thin plumes of smoke. Tens of thousands of residents lived underground in their basements, upon which their houses had collapsed. Nuremberg had become a ghostly city of cave dwellers.

My deal with *Herr* Friedrich included an evening meal limited to one bowl of soup and two slices of bread. For that I had to relinquish my travel ration coupons to his wife, whose main occupation was to stand in endless queues for the daily food allotment. All in all I fared quite well. For a pound of bacon and a quarter pound of tobacco, I had acquired food and lodging for ten days in a town where a dozen people frequently shared one dank basement room. Because of the trial, the Americans simply ordered German witnesses or members of the defense to be quartered with total strangers, no matter how cramped the conditions. The few habitable hotels were off limits to Germans.

Despite its massive destruction, the Allied War Crimes Commission had selected Nuremberg as the site for the trial precisely because it was the city where Hitler had celebrated his greatest domestic triumphs. The world over, Nuremberg was synonymous with Nazi power, as evidenced at the stupendous annual Party rallies. For more than a half million German Jews, Nuremberg stood for terror. It was from here that the regime had announced the Racial Laws in 1935, which deprived Jews of their citizenship. This startling violation of civil rights had gone unopposed by both major churches and was applauded by millions of fellow Germans. The Dark Ages had returned. It seemed fitting now to make Nuremberg the nation's city of shame.

That notion was not shared by most Germans, either in November, 1945 when the proceedings began, or on October 1, 1946, when the verdicts were announced. Burdened by a struggle for survival, the majority of Germans looked upon the trial of the 21 major war criminals with total indifference, despite the incessant reporting of the atrocities committed by their former leaders. At best they conceded that the accused deserved whatever they got because they had turned Germany into a slag heap. At worst, they dismissed the trial as "victor's revenge." These people showed no noticeable effort to come to terms with their own feelings of guilt. Instead, the accused became the convenient scapegoats for a dishonored nation.

When I asked *Herr* Friedrich to show me the way to the Palace of Justice, one of the relatively few usable public buildings in Nuremberg, he looked at me with some suspicion. "You're not a witness, are you?"

"For which side?" I smiled. "Do I look like a Nazi victim?"

"Not very likely," he said, "wearing officers' boots and a dyed *Luftwaffe* tunic." When I told him that I had come to gauge the interest of the citizens in these later days of the trial, with the verdict due any day, he shook his head.

"And for that you have spent a precious pound of bacon and a quarter pound of tobacco? Why didn't you stay home and read it in the paper or listen to it on the radio? It's all the same nonsense."

"Well," I said, "some day I plan to become a journalist. This trial is an important part of our history and I want to be able to recall the atmosphere surrounding it."

"*Mein Gott*," he said, "I wish I had your problems. My son Tristan is a prisoner of war in France, my poor wife lines up for food all day, and my daughter sleeps with Ami soldiers for nylon stockings and cigarettes, which she gives to me for Black Market barter. And you have come here to soak up atmosphere! Are you shell-shocked?"

"Would it help you to know that I was a high-ranking leader of the Hitler Youth?" I asked.

"Not in the least," he said. "That's your problem. I myself never joined the Party, despite the hoopla here in Nuremberg. That's why they made me an assistant inspector last year."

"Wasn't there any pressure on you to join the Party?" I asked.

"Sure there was, but it didn't amount to much, since my immediate department chief didn't want me to join. He thought I might become his competitor."

"What happened to him?"

"The Amis threw him out on his ass, just like all the other Party members," he chuckled, "but don't worry too much about him. Like most of them, he's back though he's been busted to clerk. I'm his boss now."

"Must be sweet," I said, "you grinding his balls now."

"Come off it," he said, "he paid his price for shouting *Heil Hitler*! Besides, the Amis saw that the whole works here in Bavaria ground to a halt when they threw all the Nazis out. Now the fellow travelers are all back already, and before long the bigger Nazis will be back too. You mark my words."

Herr Friedrich's prophesy turned out to be correct, although I wouldn't have believed it then. The Cold War with its growing tensions between the United States and the Soviet Union was the single most important factor in stopping prosecution of the majority of Nazi Party members unless they had carried out or abetted mass murder. The reality was that both the Americans and Soviets were wooing the despised Germans again. As early as January of 1946, the Americans had turned over the denazification process to German authorities (limited as their authority was) partly because they found it too difficult to believe that every Party member had been misled. Since reading Eugen Kogon's book *The SS State* (the first objective postwar account depicting the scope of the *SS* Empire and its mind-boggling atrocities) I had waited to hear somebody say, "I am guilty." Nobody seemed able to utter these three simple words without reservation, including me.

One man whom I had held in the very highest esteem next to Hitler had come close. That was Baldur von Schirach, the *Reichsjugendführer*, leader of the Hitler Youth who, in 1940, had been appointed *Gauleiter* and Defense Commissar of Vienna. He was now awaiting his sentence at Nuremberg. During the last chaotic days of fighting in Vienna, it was reported that the Viennese had strung up their Defense Commissar on the Florisdorfer Bridge over the Danube. When the Russians marched into the Austrian capital, Schirach, who had grown a beard, escaped to the small town of Schwaz in the Tyrol and boarded in a farmhouse under the name of Richard Falk. His hosts had no idea who he was, and Schirach, whose mother was American, had the gall to work for an American unit as an occasional interpreter, his English being nearly flawless.

The occupation authorities were stunned when they received a letter from the man they had assumed to be dead: "Of my own free will I surrender to American imprisonment, so as to have the opportunity to vindicate myself before an international court of law. Baldur von Schirach."

Why did Schirach, who easily could have disappeared later to Spain or Argentina as did hundreds of other wanted Nazis, give himself up voluntarily? His wife Henriette, equally startled by the appearance of her presumably dead husband, asked him the same question in his prison cell.

"I have thought over everything very carefully," said Schirach, who was later described by one Tribunal judge as 'good material gone bad.' "I want to speak before a court of law and take the blame myself. Through me, youth learned to believe in Hitler. I taught them to have faith in him; now I must free them from this. When I have had the opportunity to say this before an international court of law, then they can hang me."

According to his wife, who had incurred Hitler's lasting disfavor for having protested the treatment of Jews, Schirach was convinced all accused would be hanged. I am certain he was thinking of his own activities as *Gauleiter* of Vienna when he made that speech to his wife. Although only 60,000 Jews were left in Vienna when he arrived in 1940, he had caused their speedy deportation to the domain of Hans Frank, the Governor General of the vast enclave in Poland known as the *General*

Gouvernment. Frank considered it a holy mission to destroy all Jews in his territory. Although Schirach wept when he listened to the testimony of the extermination, particularly of the infamous Rudolf Hoess, (Camp Commander of Auschwitz between 1940-1943), it is inconceivable that he knew nothing of the genocide.

I had followed Schirach's case with unflagging fascination, for I sensed that he held some answers as to why I had become so entranced with the ideology. After hearing on the radio on June 5, 1945, that the Allies were considering declaring the Hitler Youth a criminal organization and putting 16-year-old leaders on trial, Schirach surrendered. I was almost in tears. Here at last was one German ready to assume responsibility for having lead us into unbridled fanaticism. A little more than a month later, I was arrested by the French, and during my tribulations began to feel a special kinship with my former leader.

Gradually, as my danger diminished, that feeling of loyalty evaporated, and I began to look with dawning objectivity on the whole Nazi experience. When the International Military Tribunal handed down the indictments, Schirach stood accused on Count One: Conspiracy To Commit Aggression, based on his extremely successful indoctrination of Germany's youth. Ironically, he was convicted only on Count Four: Crimes Against Humanity, for his duties as *Gauleiter* of Vienna. The Tribunal remained unmoved by his insulting claim that he had only asked for deportation of the Viennese Jews because he thought it would be "better for the Jews."

I was incensed by the flagrant stupidity of his assertion. Schirach had boasted in a public speech that his deporting of tens of thousands of Jews to the eastern ghetto was a "contribution to European culture." I remembered all too vividly some of Schirach's writing in the monthly issues of our publication *Hitlerjugend*, as well as numerous texts used in membership indoctrination. Most were so repetitious that we leaders found it difficult to keep our followers from taking cat naps. One recurring theme was the exhortation to regard all Jews as the cunning, implacable enemy, deserving of no mercy.

To me, Schirach's self-styled image as the virtuous young idealist who had been led astray was just a smoke screen. I had listened to the real Schirach at a leadership conference in 1942.

Although he had then transferred active leadership to his successor, Artur Axmann, he still held the honorary title of *Reichsjugendführer*. Speaking as a sort of elder statesman (he was all of 35) he exhorted us to military service in a war "caused by international Jewish conspirators."

I began to suspect that the moody Schirach was essentially a weak man, to whom image was all important. I cringed in the face of his denials when it became apparent that he, like other *Gauleiter*, had routinely implemented slave labor in addition to deportation of the Jews. The crucial issue to the Court seemed to be the extent of his knowledge of the extermination. When the prosecution produced a document which showed that Schirach's office was on the circulation list for reports made by the four *Einsatzgruppen* of the *SS*, the murder squads which followed the conquering *Wehrmacht*, liquidating hundreds of thousands of Jews in the east, I knew that Schirach would surely hang. These reports constituted a detailed record of the slaughter, which had taken place *after* Schirach's initial deportation request. During most of the time that the murder reports were accumulating in his office, the deportation trains he had asked for continued to roll. His defense attorneys claimed that Schirach was such an inefficient administrator and so indifferent to office routine, that he had neither read the reports nor knew the official's name who had been filing them.

The French occupation forces apparently did not consider Schirach too newsworthy, for I had seen him on only two newsreels in our local cinema during the course of the trial. He looked like a peevish college boy in his ill-fitting suit. The aura of the splendidly attired, energetic and arrogant youth leader had totally evaporated. His shifty gaze befitted a pocket thief. But there remained a way that he might yet redeem himself in my eyes. On August 31, 1946, the 21 accused were given one final opportunity to have their say, after the prosecution and defense had presented their final arguments. Again, Schirach was considered too insignificant to be shown in a newsreel, except as part of the group of criminals. I eagerly awaited the paper the next day. These were his words:

"At this hour, as I speak to the Military Court of the four victorious Powers for the last time, I wish to state, with a clear conscience to our German youth, that they are completely innocent of the excesses and atrocities of the Hitler regime as proved by this Trial. They know nothing of the innumerable acts of horror that have been committed by Germans. My Lords, please help by your verdict to create for the young generation an atmosphere of mutual respect, an atmosphere that is free of hatred and vengeance. That is my last request, a request from the heart for our German youth."

The words *with a clear conscience* almost struck me physically. None of us who had risen to any rank had a clear conscience. All of us, perhaps subconsciously, had looked the other way, preferring not to know. This was, seemingly, a very different Schirach from the one who on May 26, 1946, stated on the witness stand that he had been guilty of helping to sacrifice our youth. Then, he had ended with this statement:

"Like myself, many millions of young people saw their ideal in National Socialism. Many have fallen for their creed. It is my guilt, which I bear before God, before the German people, and before our nation, that I have trained the youth to believe in a man whom I regarded as above reproach as our leader and as the head of state for many a year; I organized for him a youth that would look up to him as I did. It is my guilt that I have trained youth for a man who became a murderer a million times over."

As it went, this was a confession of personal responsibility as rare as Albert Speer's (the Minister of Armaments and Ammunition), and perhaps just as calculated, because it evaded the most damning admission of having known of the mass extermination of Jews and other "enemies of the Reich." But I did not recognize this fact in May of 1946, and it was one of the reasons I had felt compelled to come to Nuremberg.

Now, on October 1, 1946, the day of the verdicts, I was there. The security around the massive mud-colored Palace of Justice was impressive. I would have given all my meager earthly possessions to be allowed into the courtroom. After the first few weeks of the trial, much of the world's attention had shifted away from Nuremberg. But during the last week of September the international media returned in force, when it was learned that the sentences would be pronounced on the last day of the month. Of the 250 press, radio and newsreel reporters, strictly screened and physically searched before being admitted to the heavily policed building, only five were representatives of the German media. Apparently that reflected the average German's interest in the trial. On a gray, drizzly, cold Tuesday, October 1, the day on which the reading of the sentences would be completed, only a few dozen Germans milled around the square, well away from the protective cordon of the soldiers. Most of the well-dressed people in front of the entrance were foreign newsmen who had not found room inside. If the authorities feared a last-minute suicidal attack of die-hard Nazis to free their leaders, they need not have worried.

While I was leaning against a lamp post, staring at the somber facade of the building, I was twice approached by men who asked if I had anything to barter. Several others were ready to pounce on cigarette butts that the foreigners threw on the street. Despite the early hour, half a dozen prostitutes crooked their fingers invitingly at reporters and soldiers. In occupied Germany, it was business as usual.

The verdict was read in two parts. First, the accused were told on which four counts of the indictment they had been found guilty. The counts were listed in order: 1-Conspiracy To Commit Crimes (alleged in other counts); 2-Crimes Against Peace; 3-War Crimes; 4-Crimes Against Humanity.

A loudspeaker had been mounted near the entrance for the benefit of the press, and I was close enough to understand the metallic-sounding voice of the English-speaking announcer. The Chief Prosecutor for the United States, Justice Robert H. Jackson, had routinely asked the death penalty for each of the 21 accused. I was quite certain the eight judges of the four Powers (the United States, Russia, Britain and France) would concur with him, except for the military men on trial. It was no secret that many Allied generals felt uneasy about their counterparts being on trial for their lives. On trial here were not only the men, but the principle of following directions from superiors. An order by the supreme commander was an order-- in any country. American Admiral Chester Nimitz had stated in a letter to the Tribunal that American submarine warfare had operated under the very same harsh directives as Admiral Karl Doenitz' U-Boats: namely that vessels should disregard drifting survivors when they endangered their own position. This acknowledgment had undoubtedly torpedoed the prosecution's case and saved Doenitz' life.

I thought, however, that Field Marshal Keitel might go to prison. As Chief of the High Command of the *Wehrmacht*,

Keitel had been so obsequious to Hitler that he had earned the sobriquet "The Lackey" among officers of the General Staff. Although he had signed for distribution Hitler's so-called "Commissar Order," stating that Soviet political education officers be shot when captured, I imagined the Tribunal would agree with his defense that he had not originated the order. At first I thought I had misunderstood his verdict. He was found guilty on all four counts of the indictment, just like General Alfred Jodl, Chief of Hitler's Military Operations Staff. Anybody familiar with the chain of command under Hitler should have known that the *Führer* alone gave the orders. Admiral Karl Doenitz, whom Hitler had designated as Chief of State before committing suicide, was found guilty on counts 2 and 3, while Grand Admiral Erich Räder, who had retired as Commander-in-Chief of the Navy in 1943, was found culpable on counts 2, 3 and 4.

But the real sensation of the morning were the three acquittals of high ranking officials. How, after this act could the denazification courts justify depriving a "fellow traveler" (a Party member in charge of a block, comprising as few as 50 families) of his job and his freedom? I would have wagered all I owned that none of the 21 accused would stand the slightest chance of being acquitted. They had, after all, been designated as major war criminals.

The first of the three, Hans Fritzsche, Head of the Radio Division of the Propaganda Ministry, had been the voice of Goebbels, the diabolically effective chief who, like Hitler, *SS Reichsführer* Heinrich Himmler, and Labor Front Chief Dr. Robert Ley, had judged himself by committing suicide. Night after night, often with considerable glee, millions of Germans, myself included, had listened to Fritzsche's resonant baritone, resembling that of Goebbels. In his political commentary he had trumpeted the Party line, derided our enemies with biting sarcasm, and to the last exhorted German youth to die for a cause long lost. He was now free, and I had already served a month at hard labor.

The other lucky two were Franz von Papen, once Hitler's Vice Chancellor, then Minister and Ambassador in Vienna and Turkey, and Dr. Hjalmar Schacht, the brilliant Minister of Economics from 1934 to 1937. While it is true that Schacht began to see the light, had the courage to protest the outrages against the Jews before the war, and was eventually confined to a concentration camp, it is also a fact that his financial genius kept the Nazi regime from going bankrupt. Few did more to help consolidate Hitler's hold over the economy.

Franz von Papen, the horse-faced, spineless Catholic never opposed Hitler in the early days when the Nazis supplied three members of the Cabinet. In his "Marburg Speech," he had shown a flash of defiance by warning against absolute power of the state, but had become frightened by this one act of courage. Not only had he meekly accepted the demise of his own *Zentrum* Party, he had helped Hitler prepare for the annexation of Austria. Was the Tribunal blind?

I spent the long noon recess before the actual sentences were pronounced in a dingy cafe on the once stately *Königsstrasse*, the main street of Nuremberg leading from the *Bahnhofsplatz* to the Pegnitz river and the Imperial Castle beyond. The bomb-cratered avenue bore only a faint resemblance to the bunting-draped, sparkling thoroughfare down which I had marched in 1938.

For five Camel cigarettes, I was served a thick rye sandwich spread with a layer of lard--"under the table," of course. The *Ersatzkaffee* was legitimate, as was the thin beer. The cafe was quite full, mostly with poorly-clad working men and women who had been conscripted by the city employment office to remove the rubble. Most of the men were elderly or very young. The prime of German manhood was either dead or in Allied prisoner of war camps. I heard only a few comments about the trial which was judging the former masters of these people and would set a precedent for future conduct of nations at war. "How do you think it'll go this afternoon?" I asked a man in his fifties, who looked hungrily at my cigarette.

"Who in the hell cares?" he shrugged. "As far as I'm concerned they're all guilty, and that includes the victors. Say, comrade, how about letting me have that Camel butt?" That accurately reflected the opinion of the average German. There was no wide-spread feeling of compassion for any of the accused, although they had taken the heat off many Germans, most of whom believed that a trial such as this would appease the Allied thirst for revenge and let the common man off the hook. The Tribunal would have had an incomparably greater impact on the German psyche if it had included German judges, for their presence would have refuted the claim that it was merely a ritual of the victors' revenge.

Shortly before 3:00 p.m., the Tribunal began its 407th and last session. All photographers and newsreel cameramen had been banned from the room. At the moment when the prisoners were told whether they would live or die, their faces were not to be photographed. That was announced over the loudspeaker, and a brittle tension lay over the crowd. In accordance with his rank as the top surviving Nazi, the first to be sentenced was Hermann Wilhelm Göring, the *Reichsmarschall* and Commander-in-Chief of the *Luftwaffe*, creator of the *Gestapo* and, until he fell in disgrace, the most powerful follower of Hitler and his declared heir. The obese, drug-addicted Göring, famous for his narcissistic life style, had awakened from his lethargy while a prisoner, lost nearly a hundred pounds, and given a most spirited defense. Still it was a foregone conclusion that he was doomed. He had once advised his fellow accused to limit their defense to just three words: "Kiss my ass."

"Defendant Hermann Wilhelm Göring," boomed the loudspeaker, "in accordance with the counts of the indictment on which you were found guilty, the International Military Court sentences you to death by hanging." I read in the paper the next day that Göring had stood motionless while the sentence was read, then taken the headphones from his ears and made a military-style about face.

The next defendant, Rudolf Hess, the befuddled deputy of the *Führer*, had secretly flown to England on May 10, 1941, to offer the British a peace treaty of his own, and to avoid, in his words, "an endless row of German and British graves." Hitler had disowned him as mentally unbalanced, and undoubtedly would have put him before a firing squad or confined him to a mental asylum where he belonged had he returned. Despite the fact that the Tribunal admitted that Hess had deteriorated mentally during the trial and suffered from loss of memory, he was sentenced to life in prison. When I heard that sentence, I did not think any of the following accused would receive less than a life term, with the exception of the military men. Far from having committed war crimes, Hess was the only top Nazi who sacrificed his career to seek some sort of accommodation before the onset of total war in the east. To convict him of conspiracy to plan aggression and crimes against the peace because he had simply known of Hitler's plans, was ludicrous. Hitler treated the fawning Hess, his most enthusiastic cheerleader, little better than an office secretary. He had hardly more say in Hitler's decisions than his mistress Eva Braun, and she had none.

Of the 21 men on trial (Martin Bormann was tried and sentenced to death in absentia), I was most concerned with the fate of Baldur von Schirach. The Hitler Youth, like the *SA* (the storm troopers), the German High Command, and the Reich Cabinet, had been acquitted of being criminal organizations. It was only the Leadership Corps of the Nazi Party and all formations of the *SS*, in particular the *Gestapo* and *SD* (*Sicherheitsdienst*), that had been so convicted. But to me it seemed von Schirach surely had to die. He had been convicted only on Count 4, Crimes against Humanity, primarily for his deeds as *Gauleiter* of Vienna, but his seduction of Germany's youth had, to my way of thinking, killed many more people than had the deportation of 60,000 Jews. The fanaticism he had inculcated lead to the death of millions of German adolescents.

After approximately 40 minutes, the Court arrived at the case of my former supreme leader. By then I had received several severe jolts. Field Marshal Wilhelm Keitel and General Alfred Jodl had been sentenced to death by hanging, a fate they shared with Foreign Minister Joachim von Ribbentrop, another spineless lackey. I did not mourn von Ribbentrop; but it seemed incongruous to put these men on the same level with Ernst Kaltenbrunner (Head of the Security Service of the *SS*), or the Jew-baiter Julius Streicher, or even the ranting Party Philosopher Alfred Rosenberg. Hans Frank, Governor General of occupied Polish territory, surely deserved to die, as he himself admitted after that harrowing day of testimony when Auschwitz Commandant, Franz Rudolf Hoess recited the death of three million people. Hoess, ironically, testified in defense of Kaltenbrunner who had the gall to deny the scope of the mass murder. The Commandant's unblinking report of genocide at its peak efficiency touched the listeners with an icy hand. When I had read the newspaper account months before the end of the trial, I wished for the first time that I had not been born German. We would never erase this stain on Germany's honor, despite our own current suffering.

The last three death sentences were expected. Wilhelm

Frick, Hitler's Minister of the Interior from 1933 on, a colorless figure among the top rank, had ruthlessly subjugated the civil service under the Nazi regime and routinely approved harsh police measures. The Austrian Artur Seyss-Inquart had precipitated the fall of the Austrian government and during the war conducted a reign of terror as Reich Commissioner for the occupied Netherlands. Finally there was the common, pig-eyed Fritz Sauckel, Plenipotentiary for Labor Allocation, who had impressed more than five million foreign slave laborers into the service of the Nazi war machine. Sauckel was one of the few condemned who lost his composure. He could not accept the fact that he was to die merely for having carried out the orders of his superiors.

He had a valid point. His boss Albert Speer, the super-efficient Minister of Ammunitions and War Production, received a surprisingly light sentence of 20 years. He had succeeded by his conduct in court and his confession of personal guilt, in swaying the Tribunal from the death sentence. The fact that he had thwarted Hitler's order to scorch Germany further strengthened his case.

I laughed aloud when I heard the verdict. Speer who, by his organizational genius had certainly prolonged the war, had fooled our conquerors. His assertion that he had not been aware of the extent of the extermination camps was ridiculous. He was a cold intellectual, greatly aware of the power struggle in Hitler's immediate entourage. He also had authority over all camps which furnished slave labor, including Auschwitz. Unlike the members of the Tribunal, I had met Speer at a time when he, by his own postwar admission, knew we had lost the war. He nevertheless had exhorted us to the utmost sacrifice for the Fatherland, just like Baldur von Schirach.

Perhaps fittingly, Schirach received the same sentence as Speer--20 years. My first reaction, of which I later felt ashamed, was one of protest. In any objective comparison of the deeds of General Alfred Jodl (who received the death penalty) and Schirach, the *Reichsführer* of the Hitler Youth was by far the greater culprit. With regard to rendering the most efficient service to Hitler, Speer was the champion. The Jew-baiter Julius Streicher, for whom nobody felt compassion, had incited Germans to hatred of Jews but had never been directly implicated in the crimes of the SS. He died as the odious Nazi symbol of race hatred, but Schirach and Speer should have dangled beside him, for they were as guilty as the 11 who were sent to the gallows.

In less than an hour the sentences had been pronounced. Deeply upset, I wandered through the ruins of Nuremberg on which the dusk of the early evening had begun to descend. I was bothered more by the acquittals than the convictions. They sent a confusing signal to the people of Germany--namely that it was possible to serve evil in a high capacity and yet be exonerated. Millions of low or middle class echelon Nazis in particular would compare themselves to the acquitted and reach the comfortable conclusion that they too were blameless, especially since they had never attained such clout or status. The Tribunal had handed them the moral equivalent of a *Persilschein*, an abso-lution. Those who were later indicted, even the sadistic guards of the "Auschwitz Trial" in Frankfurt, would resentfully cite these acquittals of the "real" culprits, casting themselves as mere helpless recipients of higher orders.

The Nuremberg Trial has often been castigated for imposing *ex post facto* justice: creating the rules after the deeds have been committed. One can even argue that it served as a necessary catharsis for the victors, who needed to put someone in the dock to alleviate their hatred. Despite its shortcomings--it had, after all, violated nearly every tradition of Anglo-American juris-prudence--the Tribunal did accomplish several important objec-tives.

First, it prevented a blood bath by trying the Nazis in a court which allowed them a very able defense. This was a far cry from Josef Stalin's idea that the Allies had briefly favored: a summary execution of 50,000 Nazis including the General Staff. Winston Churchill objected violently to the proposal, and so, eventually, did the United States. Secretary of War Henry Stimson had prevailed against his cabinet colleague, Treasury Secretary Henry Morgenthau Jr., who wanted to see the Germans severely punished. At one point, Morgenthau had even suggested removing members of the Hitler Youth from postwar Germany in order to kill the bad seed. President Truman eventually asked for his resignation.

Nuremberg certainly gave the accused more justice than they would have issued had the roles been reversed. It also established the principle of individual responsibility and personal accountability, refuting the defense that orders must be obeyed under all circumstances. The hope of Nuremberg, though, to establish a world-wide deterrent to aggressive war, evaporated quickly. The Federal Republic of Germany did, however, insert a clause in its constitution which makes aggressive war criminal. To date the West Germans have meticulously observed that clause. As a result of the Tribunal's actions, the United Nations adopted a Declaration of Human Rights, but it has failed to prevent numerous subsequent atrocities, including the mass murder of Cambodians under cover of war. In Cambodia, an estimated 30 percent of the population was annihilated by the Khmer Rouge, while the world stood by.

It was almost dark when I reached my destination in Nuremberg on that somber fall evening. Almost instinctively I had retraced my steps from 1938 and arrived at the *Zeppelinswiese*, the huge stadium in which hundreds of thousands, myself included, had greeted Adolf Hitler with frenetic storms of "*Sieg Heil.*"

Apart from three GIs with their *Fräuleins*, the enormous field lay desolate before me. I sat on the lowest tier of stone benches and looked at the granite pillar from which the German eagle and the swastika had dominated the field. It was gone. American pioneer troops had blown it to bits, like every other symbol of the regime.

It was here, in the thin, cold drizzle that I began to dissociate myself from the ideology I had once revered. If a measure of any German's character is taken by the way he views the Third Reich, my rehabilitation had started. It was a slow, torturous process which would take many years. Despite the acquittals and confusing sentences, the Nuremberg Trial had served justice. More important, no thinking German could henceforth deny the validity of the shameful evidence. The defense of the accused had confirmed that as convincingly as the indictment of the prosecution. While I could question the merits of certain individual sentences and deride the hypocrisy of the Soviet judges whose country had signed a treaty with Hitler, I could not comprehend, much less condone, the mindless slaughter of so many millions merely because they were "inferior."

I wondered if Hans Fritzsche, mouthpiece of the regime, felt even a slight measure of guilt mixed with his relief at having been acquitted. I was sure that Baldur von Schirach, at least for the moment, considered his 20 years an act of mercy. I compared my fate to his and recognized how fortunate I had been. I could claim that because of my youth I had merely been used. While that was certainly true, there was an undeniable nostalgia for the past, the echo of the sound of fanfares heralding the glorious New Age, and the awareness of my own enthusiasm. What route would I have taken had I been an adult when Hitler came to power? And what, in the name of God, had happened to me, here in the land of poets and thinkers?

TOP: Hitler Youth in Berlin *Lustgarten*, 1933

BOTTOM: Cigarette advertising photo mid-1930s shows a Bugle *Schar* of the *Jungvolk* like mine. The men are *SA* Storm Troopers who gave the cymbals as a gift from their unit.

Chapter Three:

BEFORE THE STORM

I consciously heard the voice of Adolf Hitler and the stirring sounds of the Third Reich he was proclaiming when I was less than five years old. My paternal grandfather Jakob Heck, on whose farm I was raised, had mounted an expensive *Blaupunkt* radio on a teak shelf above his favorite chair in the large kitchen. I usually fell asleep there on his lap after the late national news at 10 o'clock. It was the chaotic year of 1932, when the Communists and Nazis battled each other on the streets of Germany with increasing violence, occasionally drawing the Social Democrats into the fray.

"Mark my words, boy," cried my grandfather, fire in his dark French eyes and waving his ever-present pipe, "these damn fool Communists and Social Democrats hate each other so much that they're going to hand the country over to this crazy Austrian." My grandfather, a devout Catholic, had always voted for the Catholic *Zentrum* Party, but that changed after Hitler was appointed Chancellor on January 30, 1933. On that Monday evening, our kitchen was crowded with family and neighbors. Only a few had radios at home, and none had one as powerful as ours. It easily brought in not only Berlin, but most European cities. Years later, listening to the BBC from London became an irresistible and dangerous attraction to my Aunt Maria, who lived in fear that I would catch and report her to the *Gestapo* for spreading enemy propaganda.

Among our neighbors, two already stood nearly at attention when Hitler's raspy, but strangely compelling voice filled the room on that night of undisguised triumph. Few Germans can resist marching music, especially when it is interspersed with the promise of national renaissance and punctuated by the singing of torch-bearing columns. Quite in contrast to their usually dour and pessimistic nature, the hard-bitten faces of these farmers showed a sudden glow.

"Do you really think he can pull it off?" asked *Herr* Kaspar, who was close to losing his three cows and meager vineyard in this period of grave depression. Currently more than six million people were out of work, 25 percent of the labor force.

"Nonsense," yelled my grandfather, filling everybody's glass with *Viez*, the apple wine of my hometown that can be as astringent as vinegar. "He isn't going to perform any miracles. It's mostly show, but it's better than having the damn Communists take over."

Less than two years later, my grandfather and nearly all our neighbors were solidly behind Hitler, and not only because of his astonishing success in creating employment. Equally important, he had restored his people's pride as Rhineland Germans who had been under French occupation since the infamous 1919 Treaty of Versailles. The terms of that document had plunged the country into more than a decade of political turmoil. France, and to a lesser degree the unprotesting British, handed Hitler the first and perhaps most decisive of his bloodless victories, by allowing fewer than 3,000 German troops to re-enter the region, unchallenged by the vastly superior French Army, which sat placidly on its vaunted Maginot Line. That was on March 7, 1936, and the 8,000 people of Wittlich went wild with joy when they saw our troops. That evening, perched on the shoulders of my Uncle Franz, surrounded by what seemed to be all of the population, I briefly glimpsed Adolf Hitler, but more impressive was the unrestrained rapture he evoked in the delirious crowd. For the first time I understood what *Herr* Becker, our elementary school teacher, meant when he said we were now *ein Reich, ein Volk, ein Führer*, one nation, one country, one leader.

All children are defenseless receptacles, waiting to be filled with wisdom or venom by their parents and educators. We who were born into Nazism never had a chance unless our parents were brave enough to resist the tide and transmit their opposition to their children. There were few of those. The majority of Germans lined up solidly behind Hitler, once he had proven he could indeed wreak fundamental changes.

I might have been one of the few, had I been raised by my parents. My father, the oldest son, would have been first heir to the farm, had he been extremely patient. But my grandmother, next in line after her husband, was only 56, and despite her small size (she stood a little over five feet and weighed 98 pounds) carried the punch of a farmhand. Like all sensible German women, she let her husband do the shouting, but she quietly influenced all his major business decisions. Her passions were milk cows and good land, which sometimes blinded her to other opportunities. When my foresighted grandfather wanted to buy half ownership in the only movie theatre within 20 kilometers, she raised so much hell that he abandoned the project. She later told me it had been a bad miscalculation, influenced by the only movie she had ever seen (she had thought it nonsense).

Our farm, situated about 25 miles east of the French border amid the breathtaking beauty of the Mosel valley, had become quite prosperous, mainly because of my grandfather's daring decision to plant tobacco below our vineyards and thus diversify in three directions. Even the horrendous inflation of 1923, when a single dollar could buy 4.2 *billion* marks, never put the farm in danger of foreclosure, although my grandparents had to pay the mortgage in meat and butter.

Hecks had been sitting on this choice property since 1813 when my French forebear, Joseph de Berghe, an impoverished aristocrat and soldier in Napoleon's army, died and left a daughter who married a farmer named Heck. Joseph, like the Roman Centurion Vitellius after whom Wittlich is named, must have been taken by the charms of the then tiny hamlet, for he never returned to Le Bugue in the Dordogne region of Southern France.

When my father was given the choice of waiting for the farm or receiving some help to become established as the owner of a produce store, he didn't hesitate. The year was 1928, my twin brother Rudolf and I had just been born, and our parents were already 35. My father was the typical tough, loud German male, while my mother was soft and gentle to the point of diffidence.

Her father had been known as "crazy Wambach" because he recited poetry at the slightest encouragement. Over six feet tall, he had served in Kaiser Wilhelm II's famed Imperial Guards before World War I, and brought home from Berlin my tiny East Prussian grandmother Anna, whom I never saw angry or despondent. With her considerable dowry, her husband had bought a well-kept hotel and restaurant on the outskirts of

My parents' wedding reception, 1927. Next to the bride is my grandmother, Margaret Heck. Beside the groom, my maternal grandparents.

Penitentiary in Wittlich

Helmut Hagedorn

Wittlich. To this day, the *Felsenburg* is one of the favorite excursion spots of the region, sitting at the crest of a steep slope of vineyards which overlook the river and valley of the Lieser. My grandparents lost it during the misery of the '20s, but were able to keep the orchards below. There they built a small house, and for the rest of their long lives lived quite contentedly as small fruit farmers, neither one affected by their misfortune. On the contrary, they seemed relieved of a burden.

Johann Wambach did have enough business sense to arrange my parents' marriage. He wanted to get rid of a gangly 34-year-old daughter, and my grandmother Heck liked a piece of his orchard that bordered one of our meadows. In the end, though, the marriage was more an escape for two people who worked virtually as farmhands on their parents' property, waiting for them to die. Love and romance, never an essential ingredient of a German marriage, had little to do with the union. But despite the odds against it, it lasted a lifetime. I was an adult before I understood that my mother's tolerance made it work. She was a pious woman, who never would have dared to contradict my father. Perhaps in spite, she was a total failure as a *Hausfrau*, and could neither cook nor keep house properly.

My brother Rudolf and I were six weeks old when my parents established their business in Oberhausen, a large city in the grimy industrial heartland of Germany, the Ruhr. My grandmother, whose six remaining children were all adults, persuaded my parents to leave me behind "temporarily," especially since Rudolf was still frail from a hernia operation. With this move, my grandmother, the undisputed matriarch of the family, separated us for good, for she had not the slightest intention of returning me to my parents. After three years of pleading, my mother gave up because my father never encouraged her. He believed I was much better off on the farm.

I must have been four years old when I first remember meeting my mother. She scooped me up in her arms, broke into uncontrollable sobs and covered my face with kisses. Deeply embarrassed, I tore myself loose and ran toward my grandmother. It must have broken my mother's heart, for to me, my grandmother was my mother. It was a mutually deep and abiding love. The tough and decisive woman adored me, and I was very much aware of my good fortune. While Rudolf grew up in an apartment in the grimiest area of Germany, I was raised on a prosperous farm by a woman who was eager to give me every social and educational opportunity.

My brother did have one marked advantage, however. While my grandparents were indifferent to politics and approved of Hitler and his regime only because of his economic success, my father hated the Nazis with an unrelenting fury, and he transmitted that to my brother with some success. Rudolf eventually joined the Hitler Youth, but not voluntarily as I had done.

Like many disillusioned front line soldiers, my father had briefly joined the Communists after the armistice of 1918, partly because he despised most officers. He soon changed to the Social Democrats, perhaps out of deference to my grandmother who was a rigidly devout Catholic and couldn't stand the "heathen Bolsheviks." When my father and the Social Democrats fought the Nazis in pubs and on the streets, they were a rather forlorn band among a plethora of right wing groups. No sane person could have predicted that just 12 years later they would rule the nation. But the Nazis had long memories. My father was twice interrogated by the *Gestapo* about his early opposition. By then he was no longer a card-carrying Social Democrat, mainly because the party had become too fragmented. But to his credit, and unlike countless other Communists and Social Democrats, the Nazis could never persuade him to join their ranks. As a result, he was classified as "politically unreliable," a dangerous category indeed.

Since we lived 200 miles apart, I wasn't at first aware of my father's violent dislike of the regime. That was fortuitous for him; I eventually became such a fanatic disciple of the *Führer* that I might have turned in my own father if he had goaded me once too often. Luckily, we saw each other no more than twice a year when he returned to the farm to help with the harvest.

By 1936, the glorious year in which our troops regained the Rhineland and Germany hosted the spectacular, successful Olympic Games, I was eight, but already deeply under the spell of the new ideology. It's often assumed that our indoctrination began at ten, when we joined the *Jungvolk*, the junior branch of the Hitler Youth, for children 10 to 14. We did, at that age, become the political soldiers of the Third Reich, but our basic training had begun at six, when we entered elementary school. For me that year was 1933, three months after the aging and near-senile President Paul von Hindenburg reluctantly appointed Hitler the Chancellor, believing that only his NSDAP (*Nationalsozialistische Deutsche Arbeiterpartei*) was strong enough to contain the Communists. Besides, Hitler, as the leader of the party with most members in the *Reichstag*, adamantly refused to accept anything less than the chancellorship and threatened to boycott all parliamentary functions. The disunity of the other parties made his threat effective. The opposition dismantled itself before Hitler did.

Unlike our elders, we five- and six-year-olds knew nothing of the freedom, the turmoil and the death throes of the Weimar Republic. We had never heard the bracing tones of public dissent, let alone opposition. We just went to school. My first teacher was *Herr* Becker, former company commander in World War I, super patriot and strict disciplinarian who, in the first three months, wholeheartedly embraced the new guidelines imposed by the Nazis. The Law Against Overcrowding of German Schools was put in effect on April 7, 1933. In imposing a quota system, it was specifically directed at the Jews.

More than any other political party, the NSDAP recognized that those who control the children own the future. We swallowed our daily dose of nationalistic instruction as naturally as our morning milk. Soon the portrait of Hitler hung harmonically on the same wall with the crucifix, as the saviour who had restored Germany's dignity and pride. Even in working democracies, children are too immature and dependent to question the veracity of what they are taught. That should be the task of aware parents. Most of our elders failed us because they themselves were captivated by the new spirit.

Herr Becker, the good Party member and pious Catholic, (not an unusual combination in the overwhelmingly Catholic Rhineland), was most influential in forming our picture of the world. Even before it became the official government policy to discriminate against the Jews, he had told us they were "different."

This prejudice, shared by millions of Germans, turned often to hatred after the promulgation of the Nuremberg Racial Laws of September 1935. Henceforth, Jews were no longer legal German citizens, but members of an inferior, alien race despite their impressive achievements. *Herr* Becker demonstrated in his weekly "racial science" instruction how and why they were different. We absorbed his demented views as matter-of-factly as if he were teaching arithmetic. "If their noses are shaped like an upside down 6," he declared, "they are usually Jewish, although some of these telltale signs have become hidden by their unfortunate mixing with our pure blood."

When I asked my grandmother what this mixing of blood meant, she looked at me with some consternation. "Well," she said finally, "it's like taking a cow to a strange bull to get a different kind of calf."

"That's good, isn't it?" I asked, aware that we had three different breeds of milk cows. "It is," she said, "but apparently this bunch wants to stick to the same bull."

In the late summer of 1936, after my grandfather and I had been glued to the radio during the Olympic Games, he had fallen asleep outside and contacted pneumonia. Ten days later my Aunt Maria woke me in the middle of the night. "Come and say good-bye to your *Grossvater*," she said, tears rolling down her cheeks. He still clutched his pipe when I saw him for the last time in his huge poster bed. His white beard was clean of all soup stains and his face was deadly pale. A terrible cough shook his body, but suddenly his eyes focused on me and he smiled. My aunt shoved me closer and he fumbled for my hand. "Don't give any more *Schnapps* to the chickens, you little bum," he croaked, "or I'll..." He never finished the sentence.

My grandfather's funeral was memorable, attended by more than 1,200 people. His body had been on display for three days in our living room, which was draped in black velvet. The entire time, his dog Heini lay next to the coffin and one of the cats sat on the open rim. We owned the funeral coach concession and I helped our senior farmhand Hans dress our two Belgian horses in their funeral finery: embroidered blankets which covered them from head to tail. Even their ears were encased in velvet hoods and silver tassels dangled from their massive necks. Their hoofs shone like dark marble.

When the pall bearers in their black silken top hats began to slide the coffin into the lacquered, fringe-topped coach, Frieda, the older of the two horses, turned her head, snorted, reared up on her forelegs and kicked two spokes off the left front wheel. Finally, my Uncle Franz calmed the wild-eyed horse long enough to unhinge her. The coffin had to be unloaded while Hans changed the wheel, and we transferred Frieda's finery to

Berta, our youngest horse. "Frieda has never done anything like that before," remarked the astonished Hans, crossing himself. "I swear to God she knew it was him in that coffin." My grandmother suggested that Frieda had become enraged merely because she was used to seeing my grandfather on the seat of the coach instead of Hans.

From the time I could walk, my grandfather, our dog Heini and I had been inseparable. He even took me to the *Eifeler Hof*, his favorite pub, every evening before dinner, and talked to me as if I were an adult. Unlike my grandmother, my Aunt Maria, and my Uncles Franz and Gustav, who were all quick with their hands, he never hit me, although he often threatened to beat hell out of me with his walking stick. But I quickly learned that nobody, my grandmother included, dared to hit me in his presence. Grandfather taught me to read the newspaper, however falteringly, before I started school. I thought I had lost my protector when he died, but my grandmother soon took his place. Within weeks of the funeral it became apparent that henceforth she alone was in charge.

Our property was large enough to be declared an *Erbhof*, an inheritance farm, which meant it could not be divided by quarreling heirs. On that issue, Adolf Hitler and my grandmother saw eye to eye. Many of Hitler's early supporters were mid-sized farmers who, like my grandmother, shared his reverence for the soil. It was from the soil that *Das Volk*, that mythical, superior race which excluded gypsies, Jews and foreigners, drew its strength. My grandmother didn't view it in such lofty terms. Land to her meant only security, especially since the devastating inflation of the early '20s, which had robbed the family of nearly a quarter million marks. "You can't eat money," she often said, but she lived as frugally as if we had none. She didn't hesitate to spend a small fortune on a good milk cow, but the only personal frivolity she allowed herself was a bar of bitter-sweet chocolate on a Sunday afternoon. Only once did she take a vacation. In the "Holy Year" of 1925 she went on a pilgrimage to Rome and visited Naples, Venice, Genoa and the German Alps on the way home. She never again left Wittlich for longer than a day. Although she recounted with awe the audience in which she had kissed the ring of the Pope, her biggest memory was of the lice in a luxury hotel in Naples. "For that kind of money," she said indignantly, "you shouldn't have to scratch yourself all night." From then on, she rated the Italians just a step above the gypsies and below the French.

With the resilience of the young, my grief over the loss of my grandfather soon abated. Heini's didn't; the dog was found dead on my grandfather's grave that fall. My grandmother shook her head when I put a handful of my grandfather's tobacco on Heini's grave in our garden. From that day on, she never again hit me, no matter how much I provoked her. She didn't stop my Aunt Maria from slapping me, but on occasion she would interfere when my uncles spanked me too enthusiastically. German parents believed in corporal punishment as a necessary educational tool.

Herr Becker was an effective teacher, partly because of the terror he evoked in us. If you did not do your homework, you'd better have padded your leather shorts with newspaper, although *Herr* Becker was wise to that and sometimes caned our open palms. But when a less intelligent pupil tried, he showed him a condescending kind of mercy, citing Goethe, "Against stupidity, even the Gods battle in vain." By 1936, I had become one of *Herr* Becker's favorites, since I learned with ease. But our introduction had been shaky because of my association with Heinz Ermann.

Heinz was the first friend of my childhood. His parents owned a cattle business just up the street from us, and we had taken an immediate liking to each other in kindergarten. *Frau* Ermann was very generous with cookies and I usually followed Heinz home. I was impressed by his Uncle Siegfried's wooden leg, a remembrance of the 1914 Battle of the Sommes, where he had earned the Iron Cross I. Class for conspicuous bravery. Uncle Siegfried taught us how to ride and wasn't above playing marbles with us, something my uncles would never have done. Uncle Siegfried was proud of his service for the Fatherland. But the new Fatherland wasn't proud of him. Just 13 years after he had shown me how to saddle a horse properly, Siegfried and most members of the Ermann family were gassed in Auschwitz for being Jewish "subhumans."

Although the Law Against Overcrowding of German Schools was already in effect, Heinz and I started school together. But within weeks, he and two other Jewish children were ostracized by *Herr* Becker, who made it clear to us that these classmates were "different." He didn't harass them, he never whipped them, he just ignored them. The three sat forlornly on a bench in a corner, which the teacher sneeringly designated as "Palestine."

During a recess when I played with Heinz as we had done in kindergarten, *Herr* Becker pulled me to one side and hissed, "Good German boys don't play with Jews." I was bewildered. Was Heinz no longer a German? When I asked my grandmother, she became angry. "Of course Heinz is a German. I'll talk to *Herr* Becker about this nonsense."

I never knew whether she did, for within a week the issue became moot. The Jewish children were "transferred" to their own school in a room of the synagogue. When I brought up the subject again, my grandmother was embarrassed, something I had never seen before. "Listen, boy," she said, "it has something to do with the Ermanns not being Catholic. We have a new government now that thinks Jews shouldn't be with you Catholic kids. It'll soon pass and you can play with Heinz again."

There was widespread anti-Semitism throughout Germany long before Hitler came to power, although the half million Jews (less than one percent of our population) had become remarkably well assimilated. The exceptions were the *Ostjuden*, the East European Jews, largely impoverished and ostracized by the successful native German Jews. Many prosperous Jews, in fact, advocated closing the borders to them. The 20 percent or so who comprised the *Ostjuden* were, they reasoned, too visible and likely to incite more discrimination. When the Nazis came to power, though, most Jews buried their internal dissension and closed ranks against their now hostile government.

The Jews, primarily liberals who had supported the Weimar Republic, knew they were going to face tough times, but only a demented prophet of doom could have foreseen their terrible fate. For the past 14 years, Hitler had blamed them for every misfortune that had befallen Germany, especially the country's defeat in World War I. This, he claimed, had been triggered by Jew-inspired Leftist radicals on the home front. Many optimists believed he would moderate once he legitimately headed the government. These, after all, were not the Middle Ages. Many influential leaders of the well-organized Jewish community counseled that there was no reason for panic. They were dead wrong. Hitler changed his mind on many issues, but never on the "Jewish Question." His hatred of all Jews remained an abiding, all-consuming obsession to his last breath.

The common man's dislike of Jews ranged from non-existent to violent, but not even rabid Nazis yet advocated their deaths. There was an element of envy which Hitler cleverly exploited, for the Jews were seen as the economically privileged class which had not suffered as much during the '20s. There was some truth in that since nearly half the Jews of Germany who were gainfully employed, had their own businesses. A disproportionately high percentage of physicians and attorneys were Jewish, so when Hitler almost immediately excluded Jews from practicing law, his measure was widely applauded. Even my grandmother agreed that there were too many "blood-sucking" lawyers around, but she included the Gentile ones. Most farmers worth anything were always in one litigation or another over land or livestock.

In Catholic provinces like the Rhineland and Bavaria, religious intolerance was a remnant of centuries of persecution by the church. Some form of dislike was almost respectable, and all Catholic children were taught that the Jews had killed Christ. In my own family, I had overheard remarks which sounded anti-Semitic, although my grandmother remained friends with *Frau* Ermann and lit her Sabbath fire to the day of their deportation.

"*Du dummer Narr*," she once chided my Uncle Franz when he had bought a calf from *Herr* Ermann without haggling. "He is a Jew, and if you don't try to beat him down he considers you dumb." This was a statement of fact, and had nothing to do with intolerance.

Wittlich being the county seat and major trade center within 50 kilometers, had a fairly sizable Jewish population, about 250. Jews came from smaller towns to worship in the stately 1910 synagogue. In the early years, the few open acts of hostility against the Jews were perpetrated by outside Nazis. Most demonstrations were day-long boycotts by brown-shirted storm troopers who displayed signs with warnings like, "Good Germans don't buy from Jews." Some customers like my Aunt Maria paid no attention, but many did, since the troopers asked the customers for their names. In any small town it was much harder to be a Jew; there was no anonymity. When Jews were forced to display the yellow star on their clothing after September 1941, no place afforded them anonymity. By then, the Jews of Wittlich were long gone.

One afternoon Heinz came to our farm, dressed in his best

velvet suit, to say good-bye. "My Uncle Herbert is taking me
with him for a while," he said, but with no enthusiasm. Uncle
Herbert was a rabbi in, I believe, Cologne. "It'll be nice for you
to see a big city," said my grandmother. She gave each of us a big
piece of cake, usually only a Sunday treat. We shook hands
awkwardly. "*Auf Wiedersehen, Frau* Heck," he said, but just
nodded to me. She smoothed his hair and put her arm around
his shoulder, which was quite a display of affection for her. "I
think it'll be better this way, Heinz."

Maybe my grandmother sensed it would be better for both of
us. Our friendship, which never had a chance to mature, could
not have withstood the pressure of disapproval by the state. I
already felt a sense of relief at Heinz' departure. I had never
included Heinz and his family with the Jewish "traitors" who,
with the Bolsheviks, were determined to do us in, but I never
mentioned his name either, particularly when I was asked in
Hitler Youth character interviews if I had ever associated with a
Jew. Moreover, I readily admitted that I considered my father a
misguided former Social Democrat who was too stupid to grasp
our new order. Instinctively I realized that such an admission
would not hurt my career: it was a measure of one's dedication
to prevail against parental hostility.

In 1937, Rudolf and I celebrated our First Holy Communion, a three-day festival on which my grandmother spent
more money than her daughter's wedding. I remembered Heinz
then, only because he sent me a card of congratulation. It was
the first summer that Rudi and I had spent together, and the
instruction leading up to the First Communion took three
months. We were the only twins that year and my grandmother
insisted we should be together for this momentous event, so
Rudi came from Oberhausen where he lived with my parents.
As usual, nobody asked my mother. Rudi and I were difficult to
tell apart, particularly in our summer attire--leather shorts and a
shirt. To ease the identity problem, my grandmother had Rudi's
hair cut a little shorter which worked until I took the scissors to
mine! We were highly competitive, and a bit too much for one
family.

At the end of that summer, I visited Oberhausen for the first
time with my Aunt Luise. So impressed was I by the huge city,
the fire-belching steel plants, the clanging street cars and the
chance to go to the movies, that I tolerated my mother's

frequent kisses. Even my father was pleased when I admired his
three-story-high steam shovel.

Disaster struck on the third evening when my mother served
my favorite beverage, a cup of cocoa. I made a face and my
father looked up from his dinner. "What's the matter?" he
asked. "Doesn't our young gentleman like his cocoa?" His
sarcasm made me reckless. "On the farm, we wouldn't serve this
kind of milk to the pigs," I said, and found myself sitting on the
floor. My father had knocked me off my chair with a swift
backhand. What I would have tolerated from my uncles, I
couldn't take from my father. Stunned, I got up from the floor.
"I'm going home tomorrow morning," I announced. My mother
began to wail, "It's all right, child. I'll make you another cup."

"Like hell you will," yelled my father. "I'll be damned if I'll
cater to a nine-year-old punk." Wildly, he shook his fist at me.
"You have all the makings of an arrogant Nazi." He went to
work at six o'clock the next morning, and we boarded the eight
o'clock express for Koblenz. My aunt was so angry she kicked
me when I asked her to buy me a bottle of lemonade. "Drink
water, you spoiled *Schwein*," she hissed, "you just ruined my
summer vacation. Now it's back to the grind, thanks to you."

Far from being angry, my grandmother chuckled with glee
when my aunt told her why we had returned so soon. "I just
knew he couldn't stand that dump for two full weeks," she said,
"and he's right about their milk; it isn't fit for our pigs." That
encounter set the tone of my relationship with my father until
the end of the war, for the next year I did the unforgivable in his
eyes: I voluntarily joined the *Jungvolk*. When he first saw me in
uniform on one of his brief visits to the farm, he couldn't
contain himself. "They're going to bury you in that monkey suit,
Du verdammter Idiot," he shouted, but I looked coldly through
him and walked away. I had just returned from the most soul-
shaking event of my life and was beyond his petty venom.

When I was sworn into the *Jungvolk* on April 20, 1938,
Hitler's 49th birthday, I had no idea I would attend the
Nuremberg Party Congress, the annual *Reichsparteitag*--high
mass of Nazism--that fall. Far from being forced, my peers and I
could hardly wait to join the Hitler Youth. We craved action,
which was offered in abundance. There was the monotonous
drill, but that could be endured for the opportunity to hike,
camp, enact war games in the field, and play a variety of sports.

All these activities were designed to make us fit according to our motto: swift as greyhounds, tough as leather and hard as the steel of Krupp. In that, the Hitler Youth succeeded. In _The Rise and Fall of the Third Reich_, author William L. Shirer noted that Germany was filled with superbly fit children, always marching and singing. Our prewar activities resembled those of the Boy Scouts, but with much more emphasis on discipline and political indoctrination. The paraphernalia, the parades, the flags and the symbols, the soul-stirring music and the pomp and mysticism were very close in feeling to religious rituals.

When I raised three fingers of my right hand to the sky in the oath to the _Führer_, my left gripping the flag of my unit, my spine tingled in the conviction that I now belonged to something both majestic and threatened by bitter enemies. It was _Deutschland_.

> _"I promise in the Hitler Youth to do my_
> _duty at all times in love and faithfulness_
> _to help the Führer - so help me God"._

As the final act of the induction ceremony, we were handed the dagger with the Swastika inlaid in the handle and the inscription "Blood and Honor" on its blade. On that cool, windy April afternoon, I accepted the two basic tenets of the Nazi creed: belief in the innate superiority of the Germanic-Nordic race, and the conviction that total submission to Germany and to the _Führer_ was our first duty.

My attendance that year at the Nuremberg Party Congress hinged on a promise to my grandmother that I would enter the _Cusanus Gymnasium_ to study for the priesthood. Normally delegates were carefully selected and limited to the older members, but the district had been ordered to include even 10-year-olds that year, if they could afford the 25 marks for the trip. Although that was a week's wages for the average worker, it was a bargain since it included transportation, all meals and a bunk in the immense tent city Camp Langwasser. Nuremberg, the medieval showcase of Germany, was the ideal location for the congress with its super nationalistic appeal. Austria had been annexed that year, with the enthusiastic approval of most Austrians, and the theme of the congress was "Greater Germany."

On Saturday, September 10, the "Day of the Hitler Youth," I stood in the first row of the immense stadium, facing the twin grandstands, where huge Swastikas were held in the grip of granite eagles. The tension ran high among us 80,000 lined up in rows as long as the entire stadium, each 12 boys or girls deep.

The *Reichsführer* of the Hitler Youth, Baldur von Schirach, whose mother was an American, made a short, flowery and forgettable speech, and then introduced Hitler. We greeted him with a thunderous triple "*Sieg Heil*," and it took all of our discipline to end it there, as we had been instructed. My knees were shaking, and when the *Führer* beamed down on us, his eyes caught mine--I was absolutely sure of that, as was every other one of my comrades. Then he began to speak quietly, almost conversationally, man to man. Soon, he increased both tempo and intensity, but occasionally returned to the slower pace, piquing us for the next crescendo. It was a sure-fire method which frequently mesmerized the non-believers and even his bitter foes. We never had a chance. I'm certain none of us took our eyes off him. We simply became an instrument in the hands of the supreme master.

Much later, in one of my postwar history classes, I had a teacher who had joined the Nazi Party in 1928, and was thus indicted as an "Old Fighter." When I asked him why he, as an educated adult, had fallen for the siren song, he smiled wistfully, "Hitler appealed to the atavistic instinct in us by not being afraid to shout out loud what we only silently admitted to ourselves-- that we Germans were indeed the superior race."

That echoed exactly my feelings at the closing of Hitler's speech. His right fist punctuated the air in a staccato of short, powerful jabs as he roared out a promise and an irresistible enticement of power already proven to the world. "You, my youth," he shouted, with his eyes seemingly fixed only on me, "are our nation's most precious guarantee for a great future, and you are destined to be the leaders of a glorious new world order under the supremacy of National Socialism." From that moment on, I belonged to Adolf Hitler body and soul.

The remainder of our week in Nuremberg, despite its intense high, was anticlimactic, except for the last evening when the *Reichsjugendführer* Baldur von Schirach visited our camp. With a hand shake, he presented us with the commemorative medal of the congress. Hundreds of us then ringed the flames of a huge bonfire and sang our anthem, the most effective party song ever composed. Schirach, who considered himself the poet of the regime, had written its words:

"Forward, forward call the bright fanfares...
we march for Hitler through night and suffering with
the banner for freedom and bread..."
It's last line, repeated for emphasis, carried a message which
turned out to be prophetic for many of us:
"Our banner means more to us than death."
Death was just an abstract concept to us youngsters on this,
the last *Parteitag* of the Thousand Year Reich. Germany was a
country of sun-flecked, unlimited promise, unless one were a
Jew, a gypsy, a Jehovah's Witness (who refused to bear arms), a
homosexual, or a political opponent. If Hitler had died that
year, he would have been celebrated as one of the greatest
statesmen of German history, despite his persecution of the
Jews. No contemporary world leader approached Hitler's ability
to evoke the adulation of his people. I watched women faint
hysterically when he smiled at them.

My grandmother shook her head at such silliness, but even
she was taken by the new spirit. "He got the damn gypsies off
the streets and put them to work," she admitted. Wittlich
received a tremendous economic boost that fall when the
garrison was opened. By then I had, for some mysterious reason
unrelated to my musical ability, been assigned to the drum and
bugle platoon. In a most impressive display, soldiers of the 105th
Infantry Regiment goose-stepped past their commanding general with such razor-sharp precision that the townspeople
spontaneously broke into applause. Next, our unit was inspected
by the top liaison officer for youth affairs in the *Wehrmacht*. We
respectfully glanced at "Blue Max," the blue cross of the *Order
pour le Mèrite*, Germany's highest World War I decoration, that
hung around the colonel's neck. His name meant nothing to us,
but just five years later the world would know him as one of our
top military strategists, Field Marshal Erwin Rommel, the
"Desert Fox." Although he later came to despise Hitler and was
eventually forced to commit suicide, the prewar Rommel was a
dedicated Nazi. He admired Hitler for creating the superb
Wehrmacht by discarding the Versailles Treaty. The hated
Treaty had limited our country's military strength to the 100,000
men of the *Reichswehr*, and allowed no war planes, battle ships
or submarines. It even restricted the size of our merchant fleet.

Shortly after the opening of the garrison, its troops were
suddenly put on alert. The large, well-equipped Czech army was

mobilized and the British fleet was sent to its war stations. It was the height of the Munich crisis, the result of Hitler's plan to bring the 3,000,000 ethnic Germans of the Sudetenland back into the Reich. Negotiations had been going on in secret, and an appeal had been sent to Mussolini to mediate. These negotiations helped to convince Hitler that his suspicions were correct regarding Anglo-French vacillation. British Prime Minister Neville Chamberlain, who believed that Hitler, despite his bluster, was a statesman who could be trusted to keep his word, dominated policy on the English-French side. On September 29, he and French Premier Daladier accepted the proposals put forth by Mussolini but actually drafted by Hitler. Czechoslovakia was abandoned by its allies in the shameful appeasement agreement of Munich. Hitler had triumphed again. Rather than having secured "peace for our time," Chamberlain had merely postponed war. Just six months later, in March 1939, Germany completed the destruction of Czechoslovakia, when internal political troubles between the Ruthenian and Slovak governments gave Hitler his chance. Under the pretext of protecting the German minority, he summoned President Hacha to Berlin and forced him to capitulate. German troops moved in and Hitler proclaimed the establishment of the Protectorate of Bohemia and Moravia. Without bloodshed, he had eliminated a Czech army nearly as powerful as the *Wehrmacht*. From then on, he considered himself invincible. That delusion cost an estimated 50 million lives.

The Munich agreement caused a palpable sigh of relief throughout Europe. The Wittlich garrison returned to normal; my grandmother bought a second team of horses and hired a third farmhand. The government had begun construction of the *Westwall* (known to our enemies as the Siegfried Line) and with it came an unprecedented boom along the French-German border. Wittlich lay in the third and last line of fortifications. The regime sold the construction of the *Westwall* to the people by insisting that it was purely a measure of defense against France's formidable Maginot Line, erected during the '20s as a bulwark against a then impotent Germany. Some Frenchmen, as well as millions of Germans believed that explanation. They saw the two systems as a mutual deterrent. Britain, which had made its own naval agreement with Hitler in 1935, voiced no objections, for many Britons valued Hitler as Europe's foremost crusader against Communism.

On the afternoon of November 9, 1938, I watched open-mouthed as small troops of *SA* (brown-shirted storm troopers) and *SS* men jumped off trucks in our market place and fanned out in several directions. Their purpose, it seemed, was to smash the windows of every Jewish business in town. The infamous *Kristallnacht*, the night of the broken glass, was underway as punishment against all German Jews for the murder of Ernst vom Rath, a minor diplomat in our Paris embassy. A young Polish Jew named Herschel Grynszpan, distraught over the treatment of his parents who had been deported from Germany into a Polish no-man's land, had sought revenge and insured the coming pogrom. The virulently anti-Semitic Polish government kept thousands of deported Jews out in an open field adjacent to the German-Polish border in East Prussia, reluctant to readmit them.

My neighbor Helmut and I were on our way home from school, walking past the synagogue when a group of men led by Paul Wolff, a local carpenter and fervent member of the *SS*, marched in front of us singing. Suddenly they broke into a run and stormed the entrance of the building. Seconds later, the intricate lead crystal window above the door crashed into the street, and pieces of furniture came flying through doors and windows. A shouting *SA* man climbed to the roof, waving the rolls of the Torah. "Wipe your asses with it, Jews," he screamed, while he hurled them like bands of confetti on *Karnival*.

At that, some of the townspeople thronging the street turned shame-facedly away. But most stayed, as if riveted to the ground, some even grinning maliciously. The brutality of it was stunning, but I also experienced an unmistakable feeling of excitement. Helmut picked up a rock and with eyes shining, fired it toward one of the windows. Just as I bent down, my Uncle Franz booted me in the rear, grabbed both of us by our necks and shook us like rag dolls.

"Get the hell home, you two *Schweinhunde*", he yelled. "What do you think this is, a *verdammter Zirkus?*" As we ran toward the entrance to our farm, two burly troopers dragged my old friend Heinz's Uncle Siegfried, to whom I hadn't spoken in years, toward an open truck. When he raised his voice in protest, one of the troopers, unmistakably a farmhand, smashed his fist into Siegfried's nose, causing a jet of blood to erupt. They then picked him up like a bale of hay and heaved him on the truck with his wooden leg. *Herr* Marks, who owned the butcher shop down the street, was one of the half dozen Jewish men already on the truck. Still wearing his white apron, he leaned forward and wiped the blood off Uncle Siegfried's face. At that moment I felt deeply sorry for all of them, Jews or no Jews. The *SA* men were laughing at *Frau* Marks who stood in front of her smashed plate glass window, both hands raised in bewildered despair. "Why are you people doing this to us?" she wailed at the circle of silent faces in the windows, her life-long neighbors. "What have we ever done to you?"

After *Kristallnacht*, no German old enough to walk could ever plead ignorance of the persecution of the Jews, and no Jew could harbor any delusion that Hitler wanted Germany anything but *judenrein*, clean of Jews. By the following year, more than half of the 500,000 German Jews had emigrated. Most of the remainder, many elderly, could not get visas. Nobody, including the United States, wanted Jews.

And then, the war began.

Jungvolk drummers in the Stadium in Berlin

Chapter Four:

TODAY GERMANY, TOMORROW THE WORLD

On the morning of September 1, 1939, I was awakened by the fanfare blast on the radio from the kitchen below my bedroom. Fanfares always announced a *Sondermeldung*, a special bulletin. Suddenly I realized that the radio had never been on at 6:30 in the morning since my grandfather died. I jumped out of bed, but by the time I got downstairs the *Deutschlandsender*, the national radio station, had returned to march music.

"What was that all about?" I asked Aunt Maria who was clearing off the table, since everybody but me had already started work.

"We are at war," she said tonelessly, "our troops went into Poland this morning." I let out a whoop, and she wheeled on me.

"What's wrong with you, *verdammter Idiot*? Don't you realize that hundreds of young men are dying at this very hour? This isn't one of your dumb Hitler Youth exercises." She had tears in her eyes. In recent months she had become very friendly with a lieutenant of the 105th Infantry who was a veterinary in civilian life. Unlike her younger sister Luise, she was reticent and quite disciplined, her cool, grey eyes dominating her somewhat sharp features. She was as trim as a marathon runner and her hair was always fixed neatly in a tidy bun, even when she was milking the cows at dawn. Luise, whose black unruly hair framed her high cheekbones and dark, luminous eyes, was much more outgoing. Within three months of the opening of the garrison, she was married to a 22-year-old corporal of the regimental band. Viktor, a brilliant pianist, darkly handsome, and in great demand at parties, had come home with my Uncle Franz one

Saturday night. He hated the army and couldn't wait for the end of his compulsory two-year service. He managed to get out of the *Wehrmacht* for exactly three days, but was immediately recalled when we invaded Poland. Like Friedrich, Aunt Maria's veterinary, he had been transferred to the Polish border with the 105th Infantry, and was almost surely now in the offensive.

I envied them, but my aunt's reaction was typical of most Germans that day, whether they had loved ones in the fighting or not. Far from the exuberance which had greeted the outbreak of World War I, the attack on Poland cast fear and apprehension into the hearts of our people. World War I with its terrible bloodletting was still fresh in the memories of most families. My Uncle Joseph had been shot through the head by a French sniper three days before the armistice of 1918, the last soldier of Wittlich to lose his life in that war. The current attack against Poland had been provoked, we were told, by a Polish raid against the German radio station of Gleiwitz. (The "raiders" had, in reality, been *SS* men disguised as Poles.)

Ironically Hitler succeeded with the operation against Poland (code-named *Fall Weiss*), because his one-time bitter foe had given his assent. When Stalin and Hitler had concluded the Soviet-German Non-Aggression Pact at the Kremlin on August 24, 1939, Poland's fate had been sealed. Communists the world over were stunned by its cynicism. The full hypocrisy became apparent only after we had vanquished Poland less than three weeks later, the antiquated Polish army being no match for the *Wehrmacht*. For the first time in military history, massive air power was smoothly coordinated with ground forces, particularly fast-moving tanks, and the term *Blitzkrieg* was born.

When the Poles surrendered, Germany's initial dread quickly evaporated, despite the fact that Hitler's incredible string of bloodless victories had ended. He had proven that his *Wehrmacht* was invincible. The big winner, though, was Stalin. According to a secret clause in the pact, nearly half of Poland-- its eastern part--fell to the Russians, although Germany had done all the fighting. In return, the Soviets began supplying us with vast quantities of grain and oil. Despite the success of our "Four Year Plans" which, under the stewardship of Hermann Göring, Commander-in-Chief of the *Luftwaffe*, had started to prepare the country economically for war as early as 1936, we were still not autarkic, especially in our need for gasoline.

The British and French declarations of war against Germany on September 3, 1939, stunned Hitler. Since the appeasement of Munich, he had convinced himself that the British would never go to war against us over the fate of Poland. The Poles, after all, were Slavs, and thus racially not equal to Germans or Britons. Without the British, Hitler was certain, the lethargic French surely wouldn't move.

And so the period of the "phony war" began, the final pause before the storm. Millions of Germans, my Uncle Franz included, believed the storm would never break. "The French could have beaten hell out of us when we were fighting the Poles," he argued. "They just sat on their asses on the Maginot Line while we had only a handful of divisions along the entire *Westwall*. Why in hell would they attack us now, when we face them full strength again?"

My grandmother merely snorted, "If it's all over, why does this whole valley look like an armed camp?"

"Just propaganda," replied my uncle disdainfully. He had recently become a member of the police commission, which seemed to make him an authority on everything. "What would Hitler do with France anyway? What he always wanted was land in the east, *Lebensraum*, and he sure as hell has a chunk of that now, hasn't he?"

The craving for land was something my grandmother understood better than my uncle. "Hitler won't rest until he has gotten back Alsace-Lorraine," she predicted, land which the French had stolen from us in 1918. "My God, Mother," he cried, "he gave the French a formal agreement renouncing all territorial claims. Doesn't that mean anything to you?" She fixed him with a pitiful glance. "No wonder any fool can beat you in a cattle deal. He said the very same thing about Poland just six months ago. All he wanted then was Danzig, remember?"

I was 11 years old, and not the least concerned with their argument. I knew that whatever the *Führer* decided would be right for Germany. Part of this unquestioning acceptance was due to our indoctrination in the Hitler Youth and in our schools; but part of it was my conviction that I was smarter than my elders. I had kept my promise to my grandmother and easily passed the entrance exams to the *Cusanus Gymnasium*, more of a combination prep school and college than a high school. Only about seven percent of *Volksschule* pupils went on to high school. The others finished eight years in elementary school, and then went into three years of apprenticeship.

It was a good system because it selected the more academic students for higher education and provided those trade-oriented with solid training in their fields. Much of Germany's generally high craftsmanship is due to this educational structure, although today a much higher percentage go on to universities. Hitler's insistence that higher education should be available to all qualified children never quite overcame the class system. Advanced study was still largely the province of middle and upper class families.

Herr Studienrat Fetten, my first Latin teacher whom we called the "cuckoo," told us in 1939 what to expect. "Most of you blithering incompetents don't belong here," he sneered, "and at least 50 percent of you won't be around for graduation." He didn't know how right he was, if for a different reason. More than half of my classmates would be dead before they reached 18.

Herr Fetten, like most of my other teachers, never discussed politics. Our system of government allowed no such thing as a political debate; we knew ours was the best in the world. From 1936 on, the Hitler Youth, the sole legal youth movement, in conjunction with the ministry of education, oversaw the ideological aspects of all education. Teachers, more than any other group of professionals, were urged to join the Nazi Party, and beginning in 1937, they all belonged to the National Socialist Teachers League, an auxiliary of the Party. Over 40 percent were full-fledged Party members, in contrast to about nine percent of the general population.

Still, only one of my *Gymnasium* teachers was a fanatic Nazi. Dr. Siemeister, who taught physics and mathematics, two subjects which did not appeal to me, always ended one of his instruction periods with some form of propaganda. Later he urged us to join the armed forces as early as possible, especially the *Waffen SS*. He helped me make up my mind to volunteer for the *Luftwaffe* as an officer cadet. The *SS* required its future officers to formally renounce their religion, and for that, my grandmother surely would have disowned me.

In December of 1939, the Reich Youth Service Law which regulated all youth labor laws, made membership in the Hitler Youth compulsory for every German child between 10 and 18.

That included Aryan children only, of course, and excluded children with even one Jewish grandparent. They were classified as *Mischlinge* of the second degree. The only racially acceptable German children who were exempt from the Hitler Youth were those chronically ill, severely handicapped or retarded. That carried its own danger, for from 1937 on, severely retarded adults and children, even infants, were killed in euthanasia centers which the regime had quietly established, located usually in mental institutions, such as Hadamar. Here the *nutzlose Esser* (useless eaters) were put to death by injection or gas. This practice continued on a mass scale until 1940, when courageous Catholic prelates including Archbishop Rudolf Bornewasser of our diocese staged one of the rare effective protests. The procedure had, however, proven an effective testing ground for a method of killing that would soon exterminate millions in near total secrecy, with factory-like efficiency.

During my first four years in the *Jungvolk*, I was an altar boy, and frequently served early Sunday mass in full uniform, complete with dagger under my garments. Nobody found this peculiar, since our weekly parades were often held on Sunday mornings. Few parents complained publicly about the Hitler Youth, although my grandmother often grumbled that our twice-weekly *Appelle* (roll calls), usually on Wednesday and Saturday afternoons, kept me from doing my chores on the farm. Many parents appreciated the supervision and discipline the regime exerted over their children. By today's standards, there was almost no juvenile delinquency. We even had our own patrol force, the *Streifendienst*, which would, for example, haul any youngster under 14 out of the local movie house at 9:00 p.m., the curfew hour before the war. The patrol also kept watch on uncaring parents. A repeat offense could cost them a monetary fine. In severe cases of neglect or abuse, they could be taken from their children and thrown in jail or even in a concentration camp. A parent opposing the Hitler Youth risked death.

Expulsion from the Hitler Youth was a harsh punishment. It stamped the offender as "politically unreliable" and ended any meaningful career. During the war, such action was tantamount to a death sentence, because the culprit was usually sent to a penal battalion on the Russian Front. Of all the branches in the Nazi Party, the Hitler Youth was by far the largest, and by far

Air raid drill for *Pimpfe* of the *Jungvolk*, 1939

Pennant of our *Gebiet*

Triangle worn on upper left arm

the most naively fanatic. Its power increased disproportionately as Germany headed toward the abyss. Soon, even our parents became afraid of us. Never in the history of the world was such power wielded by mere teenagers.

The quality of the units varied widely and depended largely on the zeal of its leaders, who became younger and younger as the war took its toll. All Hitler Youth leaders shared a disdain for the average Party member, but especially for the *Goldfasanen*, the "golden pheasants," the usual overweight, loudmouthed leaders who tramped around in their black boots and silken brown uniforms (hence their nickname) and exhorted everybody to do his duty.

As the tide of war turned against us, education (never an item of the highest priority on Hitler's list) began to suffer grievously. Beginning in the summer of 1944, all boys over 15 could be called up for emergency duty. Entire school classes were shipped to the front to dig ditches, man antiaircraft guns as *Flakhelfer* and, finally, to fight the enemy in close combat.

The portents were there in 1940. After that year, the *Bannführer*, district leader of the Hitler Youth (comparable in rank to a brigadier general in the army) could, at any time, override all school authorities. The authority of the Hitler Youth reached into the smallest hamlet because Germany was divided into 223 Hitler Youth districts called *Banne*.

A *Bann* might have from 3,000 to 7,000 members, depending on whether it were rural or urban. Five *Banne* comprised an *Oberbann*, which was eventually eliminated as being too cumbersome. Above that was the *Gebiet*, as large as half a province with at least a quarter of a million members, corresponding to the *Gau* of the Nazi Party. There were six *Obergebiete*, but they were largely administrative entities. Like the tentacles of an octopus, the supreme headquarters of the Hitler Youth in Berlin reached into the smallest one-room school.

Hitler knew we were essential for the future of his movement, and he instilled in us the immensely flattering conviction that we were his most trusted vassals. He was most relaxed when surrounded by us, and there never was a Nazi spectacle after 1933 in which formations of the Hitler Youth were not featured prominently. Ours was the only one of the Party branches with the right to address Hitler in the familiar *Du*, although I knew of no instance of that outside of a poem or paean to the *Führer*.

The winter of 1939-40, the first of the now becalmed war, was one of the coldest in memory. I spent much of my free time skating the solidly frozen river Lieser which bordered the meadow behind our farm. At band practice, our fanfares stuck to our lips. The snow rose so high that all *Appelle* were suspended, but we still had to make the rounds as auxiliary air raid defense wardens. We were only 25 miles from France as the bullet flies, and well aware that a French cannon mounted on a railroad flat car could hurl a projectile into the middle of our market place. Strict blackout was enforced, and we sometimes abused our authority by hurling a rock through a window which showed a sliver of light.

With the first sign of spring thaw in March, Wittlich was flooded with so many troops that each house was allotted two soldiers. Any hope of peace was shattered when, on April 9, 1940, two German divisions invaded Denmark and took Copenhagen within 12 hours. On the same day, German naval units began landing troops on the shores of Norway, beating the Royal Navy literally by hours. That was just four days after Prime Minister Chamberlain's unfortunate remark that "*Herr* Hitler has missed the bus." Two days later he resigned, and Winston Churchill became his successor on the fateful day of May 10.

That morning at 4 a.m., all of Wittlich awakened to the thunderous roar of *Panzer* engines. I rushed to the market place in the wan light and gawked at a seemingly endless row of trucks and *Panzers* rolling west. One of Monsignor Thomas' young chaplains was blessing the soldiers with holy water, but he soon lost heart when the men ignored him to reach eagerly for the bottles of fine Riesling wine the people handed them. "Damn fool priest," muttered my Uncle Gustav, "doesn't he know they'd sooner be drunk than blessed?"

Within the hour, our troops swarmed across the borders of France, Luxembourg, Belgium and Holland. The French had expected to break our initial thrust at the Maginot Line, but General Gerd von Rundstedt's *Panzers* drove north instead, through the difficult terrain of the Ardennes which, they assumed, was impassable for tanks. It was a daring plan, conceived by General von Manstein and approved by Hitler, and it worked brilliantly. By-passing the Maginot Line and rolling through Luxembourg into neutral Belgium and Holland--

clearly a breach of international law--threw the French totally off guard. On the first day of war, the Dutch opened their dikes, flooding vast areas of land and highways to hinder German motorized units. But for the first time in modern warfare, large units of paratroopers were used. By jumping deep behind the Dutch lines, thus overcoming the obstacle of the flooded dikes, they sowed confusion and paralyzed the resistance, creating confusion and panic and implying all was lost when actually the Dutch front was still largely intact. The most spectacular feat on this first day was the glider landings on Belgium's vaunted Fort Eben Emael, which guarded the crossings to the Albert Canal. The fort fell the next day. The Dutch army, threatened on its flank, capitulated five days later. On May 28, King Leopold of Belgium surrendered his army, still very much intact, without consulting his allies. The premature action of King Leopold dangerously exposed the flank of the British Expeditionary Force, which had counted on the cover of the Belgian Army. It now faced the *Wehrmacht's* superior *Panzer* units by itself, making the retreat toward Dunkirk a prudent move.

In postwar literature, the evacuation of Dunkirk stands for heroism, which it was, and even for victory, which it wasn't. While rescuers, some of them civilians in pleasure boats, succeeded in evacuating 338,226 men, of which 112,000 were French, Dunkirk was a major defeat. It again proved to skeptics that the *Wehrmacht* was the most formidable fighting machine yet mobilized.

To a 12-year-old, the continual radio news of the enemy's frantic and successful attempts to slip through the noose smacked of chaos. I didn't know then that Hitler had ordered the *Panzers* to hold short of the beach for several crucial days. Some historians claim that this delay resulted from a disagreement over the next phase of the campaign. Others say Hitler wanted to spare the British total humiliation, to make them receptive to peace overtures. After Dunkirk, the surrender of France was only a matter of time. The armistice was signed on June 22 in the same Compiegne railroad carriage in which we Germans had been forced to accept the defeat of 1918. This setting was a great morale booster for the German people, and climaxed an emotional highlight that had occurred a week earlier when Paris fell.

The country was in a triumphant mood, earlier trepidations

forgotten. No German soldier of World War I had come close to the French capital. "You've got to hand it to Hitler," said my grandmother. "He's finally paid them back for occupying us." Her hounding me to do my chores was also abating, because each summer from 1940 on, every boy and most girls over 15, had to perform *Landdienst*, land service. We were assigned a boy and girl to help with the harvest and in the kitchen. This was patriotic duty for the Fatherland, for which they received a few marks pocket money. The boy worked under the supervision of my uncles, but the girls usually didn't last long with my Aunt Maria, who was a stickler for cleanliness. "I'm worn out just keeping an eye on them," she complained to my grandmother. "Put them to work herding the cows."

Shortly after the fall of France, Wittlich received the first tangible fruit of victory: a contingent of French prisoners of war. They were quartered in the synagogue, which was fenced in with barbed wire, and ordered to perform land service for the townspeople. From the throng of prisoners, my grandmother unerringly picked a short, wiry man, although my Uncle Franz leaned toward a taller Frenchman. "No," she hissed at my uncle, "this one is faster on his feet." For a moment I thought she'd pry open his mouth and check his teeth, as she did with animals she bought, but they merely smiled at each other, and thus began an association which would outlast the *Third Reich*.

For the first few months, I had to collect George Dupont, a former Parisian baker, at the Synagogue gate each morning and return him at night. On the first day I wore my *Jungvolk* summer uniform--black shorts, brown shirt with swastika arm band, kepi, black kerchief gathered through the leather ring, shoulder strap and belt with my dagger. When I signed for him, I greeted him with my arm outstretched. "*Heil Hitler!*"

He grinned crookedly at me. "*Bonjour, 'err 'itler.*" I stared coldly at him for this obvious disrespect, but I secretly admired his courage. I wasn't sure if he had to reply with the mandatory German greeting, since he was merely a prisoner. Maybe it was even an insult for him to use the *Führer*'s name. I made a mental note to check that out with my *Fähnleinführer*, the leader of a military style unit of 160, called *Fähnlein*, meaning "little flag." In the senior Hitler Youth, such a unit was a *Gefolgschaft*.

Soon, George became invaluable to us, for my younger Uncle Gustav, a barber by trade who still lived and worked on the farm, was inducted into the *Wehrmacht*. Gustav was 26, healthy as an ox, and he had already done his compulsory *Arbeitsdienst*, the labor service required of most German males prior to conscription. He was superbly fit, and came close to glory in 1936 when he earned the German Sports Medal in gold and barely missed making the Olympic team as a 10,000-meter runner.

Gustav was a rarity among the men of Wittlich; he neither drank nor smoked. That was considered almost effeminate in the Rhineland, where men were expected to get roaring drunk on occasion. Gustav did that only once, when his girl friend ditched him for some smooth-talking sergeant of the 105th Infantry. That night he came staggering into our yard, waving a half empty bottle of *Schnapps*, yelling that he was going to drink himself to death. "*Du dummer Idiot*," said my grandmother imperturbably, and turned the icy blast of the garden hose on him. My Uncle Franz and I howled with laughter.

After basic training, Gustav was assigned to a carrier pigeon platoon just three miles west of Wittlich. For the next three years the only action he saw was an occasional field trip to the English Channel to release pigeons. It was an *Etappenschwein's* dream.

The other happy family matter of 1940 was Aunt Maria's engagement to *Oberleutnant* Dr. Friedrich Wingen, her veterinary. I was glad that she decided not to get married immediately. Despite her daily lecture on my countless failings as a young gentleman, she was as much a part of my life as my grandmother.

In the fall of 1940, tragedy struck our family. It was near the time of the Battle of Britain, during which our *Luftwaffe* was fought to its first standstill. The setback was partly the result of *Reichsmarschall* Hermann Göring's decision to bomb London instead of finishing off the perilously weakened fighter bases of the Royal Air Force. That fall, while harvesting grapes, my eldest Uncle Konrad was killed when he fell off his wagon. Nobody saw the accident; it happened on a steep incline when he was hauling a load of grapes out of a vineyard.

Konrad, the most gentle of the three Heck brothers, rented an apartment on our farm, but was otherwise his own boss. He, like my father, had chosen his own, deeply private, political independence. Konrad had married Gretchen, a vivacious girl from Adenau in the Eifel mountains, site of the *Nürburgring*, Germany's premier racing track. Their daughter Gisela was born seven years to the day after my brother and I, and I had spent a dream vacation with her family in 1937. Uncle Konrad's death at 40 hung like a shroud over our farm, but soon a second cruel blow fell. His infant son Gustav contracted a throat infection which quickly penetrated his lungs. Perhaps the doctor misdiagnosed his early condition, but all measures to save him failed. We buried him in the family plot, while the earth was still fresh from his father's funeral.

By now, the situation of the Jews had become intolerable. After *Kristallnacht*, 13 additional restrictions had followed the racial laws of 1935. Jews, for instance, were no longer allowed to have *any* business or personal contact with Aryans. Most of their shops had been closed or taken over by Christians, usually at a fraction of the true value. The few I saw on the street hurried along without lifting their heads. Their sanctuary had been desecrated into a prisoner-of-war camp.

I read in the *SS* paper *Das Schwarze Korps*, which was displayed on our post office wall, that they were still trying to pollute our pure blood by seducing young, preferably blonde girls, but I no longer saw them as a great danger. Most Jews had been forced to emigrate. Our English teacher, Dr. Paul Harheil, had reinforced my feeling one day when he gave me a low grade on a composition. "Compared to the danger you run in failing in English, Heck," he said bitingly, "the Jewish threat to you is minimal."

But the condition of the Jews took on a more personal note one cold November evening when my grandmother called me into the milk kitchen next to the stable. "Come in here," she demanded, "and say *Auf Wiedersehen* to *Frau* Ermann." If *Frau* Ermann were as embarrassed as I, she didn't show it. I hadn't talked to her for years outside of a quick nod when I saw her on the street and I hadn't seen Heinz since he left with his uncle for Cologne more than five years earlier. His last card had been for my Communion in 1937.

"We'll be gone in four days, Margaret," she said to my grandmother, and started to sob. "God only knows where exactly, but it looks like Poland. Can you figure out this madness? All we are allowed to take is money and a hundred pounds of luggage per person. I'm so grateful to you, Margaret, for storing some of our things."

And then she glanced at me, obviously regretting her conversation, and put her hand over her mouth. "Get out," my grandmother hissed at me, "and you didn't hear a damn thing, you understand?" I nodded, relieved I didn't have to look at *Frau* Ermann any longer. I had known that my grandmother still lit *Frau* Ermann's Sabbath fire, despite Uncle Franz's mild protestations, but storing Jewish property needed the permission of the authorities.

Later that evening she made it a point to tell my Uncle Franz in my presence that she had put three boxes of the Ermann's valuables in our lower wine cellar.

"My God, Mother," he paled, "don't you realize you could end up in a *KZ* for that?"

"Nonsense," she said sharply. "Let me worry about that. I can produce a bill of sale if I have to. What do you suppose is going to happen to the stuff if the Party bigwigs get a hold of it? This is a private matter between *Frau* Ermann and me, nobody else. Is that understood?" She talked to him but looked at me. We both nodded.

Early one morning that week, as I came home from serving the six o'clock mass, the remaining 80 Jews of Wittlich, all dragging heavy suitcases, were marching to the station, guarded by a single *SA* man. They were among the first German Jews to be deported, perhaps because of our proximity to France. The wearing of yellow stars was not yet mandatory, and they boarded third class railroad cars as if they were passengers with tickets. A few windows opened here and there, but nobody came out to say good-bye to them. Jews had become lepers.

Most townspeople did not doubt that the regime would deport them to Poland, into the enclave known as the *General Gouvernment*. Our conquest of Poland had solved the Nazis' problem of where to ship the Jews. When I told my grandmother that eventually they all would atone for their crimes by working the land for us, she shrieked in a rage, triggered by her own feelings of shame, "How would you like to work as a slave on a lousy farm in godforsaken, lice-ridden Poland, *Du dummer Idiot*?"

That was our concept of the "Final Solution." Not even the most fanatic Hitler Youth leader believed that the term indeed meant annihilation. So desperate for labor were we that we asked children to do the work of men and eventually employed over five million slave laborers. Why would we kill people who were able to work for us? We in the Hitler Youth whole-heartedly approved of Jewish slave labor, although nobody asked our opinion. Despite their newly-found postwar consciences, at the time, most citizens of Wittlich felt the same. A measure of guilt must be borne by nearly all Germans, for they neither disputed nor opposed the deportation of their neighbors. But the incredible, incomprehensible order to destroy an entire race was always kept secret from the German populace, under threat of execution to those in the know.

The decision to exterminate had been made at a small top-secret conference in Wannsee, a suburb of Berlin. The year was 1942, and the *SS* had captured millions of Polish, Russian and Eastern Jews. With the exception of *SS* General Reinhard Heydrich, Himmler's deputy, none of the men present at Wannsee were well-known. Most were mere bureaucrats, among them an obscure *SS* lieutenant colonel by the name of Adolf Eichmann who recorded the agenda of the meeting. Not one written order exists which decreed death to all captured Jews, but there is no doubt after Göring's testimony at the Nuremberg Tribunal that the verbal order came directly from Adolf Hitler and was transmitted to Heydrich.

The enormity of the order served as its best protection. I remember somebody commenting early in 1943, when the massive Allied raids on our cities began, that the Jews weren't all that unfortunate now. "Nobody bombs the hell out of them on a Polish farm." The notion of Auschwitz as a farm (a name I never heard until after our defeat), seems grotesque to me now. In 1940, it would have been perfectly believable.

In retrospect, the years from 1940 to the spring of 1942 were quite uneventful for me. There was brief excitement after the Japanese attack on Pearl Harbor, followed by our declaration of war on the United States, but the country's attention was focused on Russia. Our seemingly invincible Russian Campaign of June 22, 1941, had ground to a halt before the very gates of Moscow because of the ferocious early winter. Even our supremely confident Josef Goebbels, Minister of Propaganda and Volk Enlightenment (next to Hitler, the most spellbinding orator of the regime as well as a Rhinelander from a deeply Catholic family), admitted the timetable had gone awry. Post-

ABOVE: Hitler at his Berghof retreat with pre-war Hitler Youth.

RIGHT: Hitler greets *Pimpf* at his *Junkers* aircraft.

ponement of the attack had caused its downfall; it had been
planned originally for April. Our intrepid Axis partners the
Italians had, however, decided to invade Greece, and had to be
bailed out by the *Wehrmacht*. Their rescue very likely cost
Germany the conquest of Moscow.

In March 1942, I had nearly finished my four years of service
in the *Jungvolk*. It wasn't much to brag about. Occasionally I had
drilled a few of my comrades in the *Fanfarenzug*, but I had risen
no higher than *Hordenführer*, literally leader of a horde of 10
boys. I enjoyed the challenge of the *Gymnasium* more than the
Jungvolk, which often was boring. Our band practices continued
but the *Jungvolk* emphasis had shifted to more serious matters.
We collected materials for the war economy such as brass and
iron, we delivered call-up notices, and occasionally collected for
the *Winterhilfe*, the "winter help," by jingling swastika-painted
cans at churchgoers. Our favorite task was small-caliber rifle
shooting, which was often the last item of training in our day-
long sports festivals.

At 14, we left the *Jungvolk* and were sworn into the senior
branch, the *Hitlerjugend*, usually on April 20, Hitler's birthday.
The majority of the *Jungvolk* joined the *Allgemeine*, the general
Hitler Youth, but there were more desirable options. One could
apply to the *Motor Hitlerjugend*, which put a special emphasis on
motor mechanics and driving, or the *Flieger Hitlerjugend* which
sent its members to glider training camps. In northern Germany, the *Marine Hitlerjugend* was very popular with naval
aspirants, since it taught boating and navigation. The tiniest
branch was the equestrian *Hitlerjugend*, usually a part of the
rural general Hitler Youth. The most prestigious was the *Flieger
Hitlerjugend*. At any one time only 55,000 of the more than five
million Hitler Youth members belonged to it. It was for boys
only, and it was the elite.

Two of the more remarkable features of the Hitler Youth
were that its leaders were chosen from its ranks, and that it did
not discriminate on the basis of class. One of my first unit
leaders was the son of day laborers, a boy with whom I normally
would have had no social contact. The Flying Hitler Youth,
however, was always eager to attract boys with a higher
education as well as superb physical fitness, since the *Luftwaffe*
considered these boys its future pool of manpower.

When I was asked to join the 160 or so members of the

Flieger Gefolgschaft 12, I almost refused the honor because I wasn't fond of heights. Dr. Harheil, our English teacher, helped me make the decision. "Don't be dumb, Heck," he counseled. "The sensation of height only affects you on the ground." Then he grew more serious. "Listen, Heck. We're in for a long war. You boys are going to be handed your emergency graduation certificates at 17. With your Hitler Youth training, it only takes a few weeks to turn you into an infantry officer, but it takes at least a year to become a combat-ready pilot." When I told my grandmother of my decision and how I had arrived at it with Dr. Harheil's advice, she snorted, "By the time they get around to you kids, it'll be all over and you'll be in the seminary studying for the priesthood." Dr. Harheil's prediction, as it turned out, was optimistic. We were handed our certificates at 16.

My grandmother was pleased that at least I was out of reach of the *SS*, which recruited us zealously. "Only over my dead body will you join these black heathens," she had earlier informed me. But just a few weeks later, at the start of our Easter vacation in 1942, I was ordered to report for glider training at Camp Wengerohr, a former *Luftwaffe* base just four miles south of Wittlich. My grandmother exploded. "My God," she yelled, as if it were my fault, "you're only 14. You are not going to kill yourself in some damn plywood contraption. I'm going to see the *Bannführer* himself."

The *Bannführer* was leader of the *Bann 244 Wittlich*, a district with more than 6,000 Hitler Youth members which encompassed the town and 50 villages. Undoubtedly he would have pointed out to my grandmother that she was hindering the war effort, a charge so serious it could have brought in the *Gestapo*. But for once, my Uncle Franz was able to change her mind.

Like all Germans, I was fully aware of the unlimited power of the *Gestapo*, which surpassed that of any branch of government including the judiciary and the armed forces. But unlike most adults, I did not fear the *Gestapo* any more than the regular police. I had no intention of doing anything that might land me in a *KZ*, a concentration camp. We saw the *Gestapo* chief or his wife every day, for they bought their milk from us. *SS* Captain Guntermann, a sandy-haired, thin man about 40, was never in uniform when he picked up the milk on his way home. When it was cool he wore a gray leather coat and felt hat, the preferred civilian clothing of the *Gestapo*. My grandmother was impressed with his knowledge of agriculture, and they usually chatted a few minutes when she clipped his ration coupon. Unlike some of our other customers, neither he nor his wife ever asked for more than the coupon allowed. When he left, he lifted his arm in the prescribed German salute, but usually said: "*Gute Nacht, Frau* Heck."

Because the *Gestapo* approved all measures governing prisoners of war, my grandmother's acquaintance with its assistant chief surely helped us. She was one of the first farmers to obtain permission to keep George, our French prisoner, permanently on the farm. That required the payment of a large bond, which would be forfeited should George be rash enough to escape. There wasn't the slightest chance of that. George knew his parents in Paris would be in jeopardy, and that he might be shot since he had signed a document giving his word not to escape. Furthermore, compared to citizens of his occupied country and also to most Germans, George had an abundance of good food. Within a couple of years he spoke our dialect as fluently as a native, wore some of my uncle's clothing, and had acquired a girl friend, although surreptitiously. My grandmother, who valued his hard work after both of my uncles were inducted, paid him a wage--contrary to regulations for prisoners of war. It did not compensate for the loss of his freedom, but millions of German prisoners, especially those in Russia, would have thought he lived in paradise.

Far from hiding the existence of concentration camps, the Nazi regime used them as its most effective terror weapon to contain so-called "people's parasites," a very flexible description which included anyone from a political opponent to a housewife caught listening to enemy propaganda. The first camp was Dachau, established in 1933 to incarcerate Social Democrats, Communists and other political enemies. Soon, habitual criminals, Jehovah's Witnesses (if they refused to bear arms), and homosexuals were added. Only much later, especially after the *Kristallnacht* of 1938, were large numbers of Jewish males sent to the camps merely because they were Jewish. Gypsies and their families were often seized for being habitual (if petty) criminals who "plagued" the land as pocket thieves and fortune tellers.

In addition to Dachau, places such as Buchenwald, Oranien

burg, Ravensbrück, Flossenburg and Neuengamme became feared names in our language. These were only some of the largest camps; there were hundreds more. The terror of being in such "protective custody" was due largely to the uncertainty-- there was no appeal process and no fixed sentence. An inmate might be released after days, weeks, months, kept for years, or quickly executed. Anyone who talked after his release was shot.

I accepted the camps merely as another feature of our system, especially since the Hitler Youth urged us to be as vigilant against domestic and foreign enemies as the *Gestapo*. It was our duty to report suspicious actions against the regime to our leaders, who in turn would notify the *Gestapo*.

Walter Hess, a minor Hitler Youth leader, acquired a certain amount of fame and a promotion for reporting his own father directly to the *Gestapo*. It appeared *Herr* Hess, once a Communist, had called the *Führer* a blood-crazed maniac and scolded his son for his allegiance. *Herr* Hess was arrested the same night and sent to Dachau, where he died of sudden "heart failure," at a healthy age 40.

I usually paid no attention to jokes about the regime which were made by people on our farm. Hermann Göring, the *Luftwaffe* chief, was often the butt of jokes regarding his well-known vanity. While he was the only top leader who occasionally poked fun at himself, he was as ruthless as *SS Reichsführer* Heinrich Himmler, and nobody joked about him.

Hitler employed cutting sarcasm in many of his speeches, but he never laughed at himself. Propaganda Minister Josef Goebbels displayed flashes of self-irony, such as when he said "the most peculiar body is the 'whip of true genius'"--a clear reference to his own diminutive body (5 foot 3 inches) and his misshapen clubfoot--rare features in a regime that revered physical prowess and perfection. This was a humor which Berliners typically appreciate. Despite his cynicism and size, Goebbels was a fearless fighter who not only converted tens of thousands of Communists to Nazism as *Gauleiter* of "Red" Berlin prior to 1933, but remained loyal to Hitler, sacrificing even the lives of his family. His speech exhorting the Reich to total war remains unsurpassed, even by Hitler's oratory. It is particularly remarkable considering that by the time he made it he knew we were no longer winning. But nobody ever would have taken Goebbels for a buffoon as they did the well-functioning alcoholic Dr. Robert Ley, head of the German Labor Front and of the Party Organization Office.

We, in the Hitler Youth, did a lot of griping, especially when we were ordered to crawl through patches of mud on our bellies, but we never complained when on duty. The comparative ease with which mere children controlled other children and later adults, was the result of our uppermost dogma: unquestioning obedience to any order.

Instinctively, I knew the difference between a joke and open hostility against the regime. Raised in an atmosphere of supercharged nationalism, I was sensitive to insults against Germany. Once when an elderly day laborer who often worked for us in the summer, greeted a passing unit of Hitler Youth and its flag bearer with a grinning "*Drei Liter*", which sounds exactly like "*Heil Hitler*" but means three quarts, I warned him against insulting the *Führer*. He blanched, abjectly apologized, and pleaded with me not to report him.

The only two people who could have criticized Germany with impunity were my grandmother and George, our prisoner. He told me as early as 1942, when we were the masters of most of central Europe, that the end would soon come. With a cutting motion against his throat, he grinned at me, "Very soon, *Deutschland kaputt*." I merely laughed at him; he was venting his rage as our slave. Within the confines of the family, my grandmother always spoke her mind. Like most German women, she considered politics the foolish business of men, just like their proclivity to get drunk. As I began to rise in the Hitler Youth, she avoided criticizing our leaders in my presence.

I started to fly at age 14. On my second day in Camp Wengerohr, I was strapped down on the wooden seat of the basic glider SG 38, which was nothing more than an open laminated plywood beam with wings. After a reassuring tap on my helmet, *Sturmführer* Meister of the National Socialist Flying Corps lifted his arm. Twenty of my comrades grabbed a thick rubber rope and catapulted me into the air like the stone in a giant sling shot. The grass rushed at me, I pulled back the stick and was airborne! After an incomparably exciting trip the cumbersome machine bumped to a stop and the wing tipped to its side. The flight had taken no longer than a minute, but I was hooked. At that moment, I permanently abandoned the priesthood. Only once, much later, did I experience a greater feeling of sudden and total exhilaration. I was writing lazy circles high in a pale-blue summer sky in a top performance sailplane, while the world swirled silently below me like the scene in a vast kaleidoscope. After a few moments of unsurpassed ecstasy, I felt I could leave the earth and soar into the universe. I had become one with the wind.

These three weeks in my first flight course gave my life a firm direction. Despite my 14 years, I not only knew what to do with my future, but I was willing to work hard for it. I didn't mention it to my grandmother, of course, but I was determined to join the *Luftwaffe* as a cadet and future pilot as soon as I was old enough. Since I had to serve the duration of the war anyway, there was no need to tell her now that I would become a career officer instead of a priest. If I got killed, she'd be spared that disappointment.

During the summer, I was ordered back to Camp Wengerohr, exempt from compulsory land service because flight training took priority. In addition, I was permitted to get in an extra flight or two by bicycling down to the base every Sunday, something only a few of us truly obsessed flyers did. We usually spent the full day on kitchen duty. In addition, I spent three evenings a week in our barracks hut listening to theoretical instruction, learning the Morse code, the rudiments of navigation, or enemy aircraft recognition. Occasionally we wrestled with a piece of wood or metal in the superbly equipped workshop, the domain of *Sturmführer* Weber, a former mechanic who preferred apprentices to *Gymnasium* students. "You're nothing but a smug, overeducated *Arschloch*, Heck," he once sneered at me when I mistreated a bolt. But by the end of that summer, I had equalled his own "B" rating as a glider pilot with 60 flights. His rank was comparable to a lieutenant, while I was still a mere *Hitlerjunge*, a private.

Children of war become adults very quickly. To this day, if I had to single out the two best years of my life despite the eventual bitter awakening, I would choose late 1942 to early 1944. That period, 1942 in particular, was the most promising time to be a young German. Our country stood at the pinnacle of its power. From the tip of Norway to the shores of Africa, from the British Channel to the Caucasus, extended the largest German empire the world had ever known. Only a glorious death on the battlefield stood between me and final victory.

My transformation from average member of the Hitler
Youth to fanatic adherent of the Master Race began with my
promotions in the *Flieger Hitlerjugend*. All of the early promotions were the result of my flying. The Hitler Youth was always
on the lookout for leadership quality, and my dedication beyond
the call of duty did not go unnoticed. Ironically, I had no
intention of making the Hitler Youth my career. My dream was
to become a fighter ace in the *Luftwaffe*. I collected post cards
with the photos of such heroes as Colonel Werner Moelders, a
leading ace with a score of 150 "kills," who had invented the
"Four Finger" formation of attack, later adopted by the Royal
Air Force. Moelders died in an accident in 1941 on the way to
the funeral of General Ernst Udet, the Inspector General of the
Luftwaffe. Udet, a World War I ace and famous stunt pilot, had
become disillusioned with Hitler and despondent over the
tactical state of the *Luftwaffe*, and intentionally dove his test
aircraft into the ground. His suicide was disguised as an
accident.

During my second training course at Wengerohr, General
Adolf Galland, Commander of the Fighter Arm and Moelders'
successor, walked in on us as we were eating lunch. We gave him
a spontaneous ovation and crowded around him. Galland, too,
was a household name as an ace, and always defended his pilots
fearlessly. He later dared to argue with Göring and Hitler about
the conduct of the air war, which he thought should be one of
offense after the Allied air forces dominated the skies over
Germany. He was later dismissed for his audacity, but returned
to command an elite jet squadron of *Messerschmitt* 262s in the
final days of the war. Galland was shot down but survived, and
spent six postwar years as an adviser to the Argentinian air
force. He was briefly considered a candidate as chief of the
postwar West German air force. That made some NATO allies
nervous, although Galland (who was, like me, of French
Huguenot descent) had never been a Nazi.

That noon in the mess hall at Wengerohr, Galland, who bore
a marked resemblance to Clark Gable, waved his ever-present
cigar jauntily at us. Still in his flight gear, the Knight's Cross with
Swords dangling from his neck, he said smilingly and without the
bombast typical of many Party leaders, "Boys, please hurry and
give us a hand. The Fatherland needs you badly and our old
bones are getting tired." After that he could have asked anything

of us.

We were so conditioned to believe in the *Endsieg*, the final victory, that no setback could have shaken my confidence that Germany would eventually be victorious. The alternative, the endless night of Bolshevik-Jewish slavery, was too horrible to contemplate. Still, I could not dismiss the loss of our entire 6th Army at Stalingrad without some trepidation, especially since it followed so closely on the heels of the successful Allied landings in North Africa, November 8, 1942.

Stalingrad, the most savage battle of the war, ended on February 2, 1943, when Field Marshal von Paulus surrendered his 90,000 troops that remained out of nearly 300,000. The capitulation sent Hitler into a rage, although his stubborn insistence to fight to the last man had caused the disaster. Days before the surrender, he ordered the *Deutschlandsender* to play Chopin's Funeral March, thus unofficially writing off the men. Eventually only 5,000 would return home, the last of them in 1955.

Although the war began to get grim for most of Germany from that point on, I remained curiously buoyant. I had just finished a small weapons course in the barracks of the 105th Infantry as part of the intensified pre-military training of the Hitler Youth. I was promoted to *Scharführer*, which put me in charge of 50 boys. George threw me a mock salute when I attached the one star to my shoulder boards and the green braid from the shoulder to a button on my *Luftwaffe*-blue winter blouse. I now also had the option of wearing a white shirt and black tie.

Flight training during the Easter vacation of 1943 was a disappointment. I had been ordered to a small glider base in the Eifel mountains near their highest point, the *Hohe Acht*. There I had expected to fly a real high performance sailplane, the *Möve* (sea gull), in my pursuit of my third classification, the "C" rating. On the third day the weather turned foul and it began to hail and snow. No thermal updrafts necessary for sailing are created at such cold temperatures, so apart from getting instruction in a single engine tow plane (the sturdy two-seater *Bücker-Jungmann*) we accomplished little. I returned home with just five more flights in my logbook, still 25 short of the "C".

Since we had met at Wengerohr, I had been in unofficial competition with my best flying friend Hans Jordan. "Rabbit" as we called him for his almost white, girlishly long eyelashes, was such a rare natural pilot that he was almost certain to make the national aerobatic team; but before that, he had to get the "C." "Listen, Alfie, you misbegotten *Schweinhund*," he had remarked the year before when we parted at the railway station of Wengerohr, "I'll beat you to the goddamn "C" despite your cheating with extra flights on weekends." As the two youngest pilots so close to the "C," many of our comrades began placing bets on us. I was relieved when I found out that his training on another base had also been a disaster because of the weather. I looked forward to the summer with Rabbit, for we had immediately become close friends.

With the full deployment of the American 8th Air Force in Britain early in 1943, the raids on our cities began in a deadly one-two punch. The Royal Air Force bombed us at night and the Americans in daytime which was, for them, much more dangerous. One of the first casualties was the beautiful Rhine city of Cologne, the target of the first 1000-bomber attack. My mother and brother soon spent night after night either in their fortified basement or in the impenetrable, huge public air raid bunker down the street. Oberhausen is located in the heart of the industrial Ruhr, traditionally Germany's weapons forgery. That circle of cities, which included Essen and the enormous Krupp factories as well as dozens of coal mines and steel mills, became the priority target of the enemy.

After a particularly heavy raid on June 11, 1943, my brother and his entire school were evacuated to the Tatra mountains of Czechoslovakia in the compulsory program of the *KLV, Kinder Land Verschickung* (child evacuation to the land). Normal schooling in the Ruhr had become all but impossible. Soon, other large German cities followed suit, usually with the blessing of the parents who were given no choice anyway, since the Party and Hitler Youth gave the orders.

Most smaller cities and towns remained untouched until the last months of the war, when Germany began to resemble an unfinished construction site. The worst raid of that year--next to Dresden in February of 1945 as the costliest--levelled much of Hamburg. In July, the Royal Air Force attacked in four consecutive nights and U.S. 8th Air Force joined in on two days. For the first time, large numbers of incendiary bombs created a fire storm and 50,000 people died. After that, Dr. Goebbels had an easy time convincing most Germans that the enemy wasn't merely content to eradicate National Socialism, but was bent on destruction of the German people. As with our terror raids on London in 1940-1941, the bombings achieved the opposite of their objective, which was to demoralize the population. Combined with a major tactical blunder--the demand for "unconditional surrender" proclaimed by President Roosevelt after the Conference of Casablanca--the raids cost millions of lives by prolonging the war.

Still I lived in a fool's paradise that year, partly because I had not yet experienced any danger, and partly because I was always busy. On one occasion, I was commanded to attend a three-day Hitler Youth leadership conference at the *Gebiet* (provincial) headquarters in Koblenz. At the close, we were addressed by Artur Axmann, who had succeeded Baldur von Schirach as Reich Youth Leader when Schirach was appointed the governor of Vienna in May of 1940. We were impressed by Axmann's dedication, because he had lost an arm fighting in Russia in 1941. He was 30 when he, like many wounded veterans, returned to the Hitler Youth. Unlike Schirach, he was rather laconic. He did not belittle the danger to Germany. "I ask of you to give your all, and the Fatherland will surely prevail," he said quietly. We believed him, for he had proven himself. It's revealing that he was never charged with war crimes, although he sent tens of thousands of boys into battle and death. He himself was one of the last defenders of Hitler's bunker.

Although I had been one of the youngest attending and lowest in rank, I was elated after meeting Axmann. To celebrate, I decided to see a movie before taking the last train home. (In Wittlich, you watched what happened to be playing in our only theatre.) On my way to the station, the sirens began to wail a full alarm. Within minutes, ghostly fingers of searchlights were probing the sky and 88mm Flak cannons began to boom. As I watched open-mouthed, a young woman caught my arm. "What are you waiting for?" she yelled, "they'll be dropping their load in a second."

My heart began to hammer, and I raced along with her toward the huge station bunker. Hundreds of people were milling around in its narrow, dank corridors, but we found a couple of spaces on a bench. Then, for the first time in my life, I heard the eerie whistle of descending bombs and the ear-splitting detonation, magnified by the concrete shell of the bunker. I squeezed the girl's hand. She returned the pressure and smiled reassuringly. "Not even an aerial mine can punch a hole into this bunker. That's why I come here, *Liebchen*."

Her unexpected familiarity was pleasant under the circumstances, especially since she was very good looking. Her long dark hair curled down to her shoulders, framing her narrow, swarthy face with its slightly aquiline nose. "Listen," I said, a little hoarsely, astonished at the implausibility of finding romance in an air raid bunker, "would you like to go some place after this for a glass of wine?"

"Sure, *Liebchen*," she smiled, "that can be arranged, but are you old enough? You don't look 16 to me."

"I'm close," I said indignantly, "and I have unrestricted travel orders."

Just then the all clear sounded and we surged out into the sweet, cool night air with the crowd. She hooked her arm in mine and squeezed it. "Listen, *Liebchen*, for a slight contribution to my rent, we can go directly to my place. It's near the station and I'll supply the wine." It only dawned on me then that I was being picked up by a prostitute, which didn't dim my ardor in the least. Prostitution was legal, and it was a new experience for me. I was assuming she did not belong to the BDM (*Bund Deutscher Mädel*) since their members did not usually wear make up. When I questioned her, she doubled up with laughter. "*Verdammt, Liebchen*, you do catch on fast, don't you? I couldn't have joined your Hitler Youth if I had wanted to--I'm a gypsy."

I felt as if I had been drenched with a bucket of ice water, and I pulled my arm out of hers. "Look here," I said awkwardly. "Some other time. I can't miss the last train to Wittlich. Here's five marks for a good bottle of wine."

She looked at me with suddenly cold eyes and snapped up the bill. "Suit yourself, *Herr* General," she said, "but you'll never know what you missed. I really did like you until a second ago." She left me standing dumbfounded on the street.

One of my five or six close friends in school was Fred Stein, always in demand because he played the accordion with professional expertise. We spent quite a bit of our free time chasing the apprentices at his mother's expensive dress shop. When I confessed to Fred that I had passed up a night with a gypsy because she was racially inferior, he slapped his forehead.

"*Verdammte Scheisse,* Alf, you are really beginning to worry me. Never, but never, let ideology get in the way of lust. They are totally different concepts, no matter what Himmler claims. You weren't going to marry the damn whore, were you?" He must have passed on the story to our buddies, because subsequently Wolfgang Knopp tapped me on the shoulder in class. If anything, he was even more sarcastic. When we were off duty and out of uniform, especially in the *Gymnasium,* I had not the slightest power over my comrades. That iron rule was never broken.

In the summer of 1943, Rabbit and I were assigned together at Wengerohr for our "C" course. In the first two weeks there was no problem and it appeared certain we would get our rating. Only eight test flights remained when disaster struck.

I was approaching the field at low altitude after executing a mandatory figure "8" when a shift in wind increased my speed. I had already consigned myself to blowing the landing by over-shooting the marker on the grass, when I glimpsed a green flag being circled at me. We had no radio communication, but this was the signal to make another turn. "That *Arschloch* Meister must be nuts," I mumbled to myself. "I'm not going to ram myself into the ground at this speed at no more than 30 meters above the field."

Disastrously for me, it had not been the rather easy-going instructor who had waved the flag, but our feared *Kommandant* himself. A *Sturmbannführer* in the National Socialist Flying Corps, and former *Luftwaffe* major, Winkler was a bitter man. He had been shot down during the Battle of Britain in 1940 and become unfit for combat flying because of a paralyzed arm, just short of earning the coveted Knight's Cross for having downed 25 enemy aircraft.

Rabbit and I had come under his scrutiny briefly during our first course when he had caught us taking a nap in the noon sun. Despite his exalted rank, the diminutive Winkler, who wore simple coveralls like ours, had "ground our balls" by chasing us across the field on his motorbike until we dropped. The commandant was a fanatic Nazi, proud to have joined the Party in the '20s, and he had a special mistrust of us Catholics, since we (according to his interpretation) showed at least some fealty to the Pope. Once he had instantly dismissed a boy who had attended a sunrise mass on Easter, and that meant he was broken to the infantry.

When Winkler was through shouting at me, no flight crew on the field had any doubt that my career as a promising sailplane pilot was over. In the commandant's view, I had done the unforgivable: disobeyed a direct order. On the front, that would have been a capital offense. For the next three days, while I was banished to the kitchen scrubbing pots and pans for 16-hour stretches, I seriously thought of ways to commit suicide. It was fortunate that we wore no arms in camp. The best I could expect, as Winkler had promised me, was service as a *Landser*, a foot soldier in a Russian trench. The dream of becoming an officer and fighter ace had vanished. Besides my personal humiliation, I had also disgraced my own unit, *Flieger Gefolgschaft 12*. Suddenly I had become a leper. Only Rabbit comforted me when I dragged myself to my bunk and fell on it exhausted.

"Look here, Alfie, *Du Arschloch*," he said, disguising his tenderness with our most common obscenity. "I just know you'll fly again some day." He advised me against seeing my *Gefolgschaftsführer*, who was also on flight duty. "It's just going to make it awkward," he counseled. "See what kind of charges the commandant proposes to the Hitler Youth first."

On the second to last day of the course, a miracle happened, likely because of the instructor's intervention, and because the commandant was under considerable pressure to turn out finished glider pilots. Winkler accepted my claim that I had only disobeyed the order to circle because of my judgment as a pilot. But he gave me only two tries for the two tests--absolutely no chance for error. Rabbit and I both had sweat on our brows when I was being strapped into the glider for my tests. But the sweat turned to tears of joy a short time later when he loosened my parachute harness and helped me out of the cockpit. "I just won five marks betting on your ass, Alfie, my lovely *Schweinhund*." We both earned the "C" that day.

The year 1944 was proclaimed by the Hitler Youth as "The Year of the War Volunteer." But as the year wore on, that definition became a joke. We were *ordered* to volunteer. The first grim news for our family came when my Uncle Gustav was reported missing in action after a sudden, massive push by the Russians in the Leningrad sector. Gustav had lost his cushy pigeon billet late in 1943, but had remained fortunate in the beginning. The commander of the artillery brigade to which he had been transferred made him his personal chauffeur and barber while the unit was stationed in Warsaw. But Gustav and the entire headquarters staff were captured in their very first battle...At least that's what my grandmother believed. I was convinced he was dead. In the savage fighting on the Soviet Front, neither side took many prisoners. Capture to me seemed worse than death.

During the Easter vacation of 1944, I attended a weapons training camp run by *Wehrmacht* officers. These *Wehrertüchtigungslager*--literally "defense-strengthening camps"--taught the handling of the standard infantry weapons from *Karabiner* 98 to the rapid-firing MG 42, as well as various pistols, grenades and bazookas. Other than field exercises in camouflage, there was little drill. Although I had been accepted formally as a future *Fähnrich*, an officer cadet for the *Luftwaffe*, I was beginning to realize that this was no guarantee of actually being chosen as a pilot. Most soldiers of the *Luftwaffe* didn't fly. Just when my spirits began to ebb, I was ordered back to Camp Wengerohr unexpectedly for an advanced sailplane course. My hopes soared...And thus began the last, most pleasant, interlude of the war for me.

During May 1944, the enemy air force directed the bulk of its fighter activity toward targets in France, and the massive bombing raids on our major cities lessened. Unknown to us in Wengerohr, the Allies were in the last stages of preparation before their invasion of France. Occasionally a few *Messerschmitt* 109s or *Focke Wulf* 190s landed on our base for refueling, and the pilots often threw dice to see who would get a full tank to pursue a straggling American B 17. Twice, Flying Fortresses were shot down within sight of our field, which did not require the skills of an ace, since the lumbering machines were alone and already damaged from antiaircraft fire. "I feel like a damn vulture," said a lieutenant who wore the Knight's Cross, when we congratulated him for shooting down a bomber in flames. "No doubt some Ami P 51s will soon be on my tail six to one for downing this poor bastard."

Rabbit and I were part of a four-man team aiming for the aeronaut's certificate in sailplane flying. Our big goal was a possible chance to compete in the national glider championships at the *Rhön*, Germany's most venerated glider base. On a hot

summer day during the long respite granted by the enemy, I
sailed on the currents of a strong thermal updraft to our
permitted height of 6,000 feet. For three-and-a-half hours I
played with the wind, occasionally brushing a cumulus cloud in
silent, ever-widening circles. There was no thought of war or
conquest, no other desire but to continue soaring. For a crazy
split second, I felt I could leave the cockpit and rise toward the
sun like Icarus. Despite the high stakes, this last flight course
was a prolonged holiday. *Sturmbannführer* Winkler, our neme-
sis, was in central Germany, setting up a new base. His
temporary successor, *Sturmführer* Meister, was a dedicated
instructor and left disciplinary matters to non-commissioned
officers. He liked Rabbit and me. The year before, Rabbit had
become our first minor casualty when two American P 51s
roared in from the west without warning, likely on a detour from
their bomber escort duties, and shot down our tow plane
moments after it had released Rabbit's aircraft. Its pilot,
Sergeant Baum, had deliberately turned toward the enemy
planes to divert attention from Rabbit, who dove toward the
field in panic and broke his arm when he jumped out of the
cockpit. Baum's death weighed heavily on Rabbit for some time,
and made him an even more committed pilot, if that were
possible.

On the last day of May, Rabbit and I completed our final test
by executing a loop and landing our machines smack on the
center of the landing cross within 10 minutes of each other. That
evening, a beaming Meister handed us the white wing on a blue
background, framed by tiny oak leaves, the *Luftfahrerschein*.
Three weeks younger than Rabbit, I was, for the next four
months, Germany's youngest recipient of the aeronaut's certificate in sailplane flying. I was 16.

"I'll see you either at the *Rhön* this fall, Rabbit, you lousy
excuse for a pilot," I reminded him at our parting. "Or better yet,
in a fighter squadron."

"I sure hope so, Alfie," he said, uncharacteristically subdued,
"but I think you and I have seen our best days. The fun is over."

Nazi party *Gauleiter* Gustav Simon of Trier visits civilian excavating tank ditches near Trier, October 13, 1944.

Volkssturm receives bazookas in Wittlich, December 23, 1944.

Chapter Five:

TOWARD THE ABYSS

Historians generally agree that the single most decisive day of World War II was June 6, 1944, when the Allies landed on the beaches of Normandy. By now our empire had shrunk drastically and Italy, our closest Axis partner, had signed an armistice with the enemy and turned against us. Nevertheless, a failed invasion of _Festung Europa_ would have been a most severe psychological blow to the Supreme Allied Command. It would have been impossible to mount another attack of such immensity in any reasonable time. Allied intelligence had done a superb job of misleading our High Command as to the exact location of the landings, which we knew all too well were imminent.

Ironically, both Hitler and Field Marshal Rommel had initially considered the Normandy coast, but had been persuaded that the Pas de Calais area, being the shortest distance to England, was more likely. Still, had Rommel received his three additional battle-tested armored divisions in time for deployment along the Normandy coast, it is conceivable the invasion might have failed. To make matters worse, Rommel had been assured that the inclement weather over the British Channel would make a landing impossible for at least two weeks. When the greatest armada in military history was sighted by our coastal defense, the Field Marshal was in bed, back home in Bavaria. It was his wife's birthday, and he had planned to continue the next day to nearby Eagle's Nest, Hitler's retreat at Berchtesgaden, where he would demand an immediate transfer of _Panzer_ units to the _Atlantik Wall_. He had done a remarkable job of shoring up its defenses in recent months, but he was critically short of hardened front-line troops.

Nobody at Field Marshal Gerd von Rundstedt's headquarters in Paris took the confused early reports too seriously--
at first. In recent months, dozens of alarms had been sounded
which turned out to be minor diversions. General Dollmann of
the German 7th Army had even ordered a stand-down. Some of
his commanders were at a map exercise in Rennes, far from
their units, and (like Rommel) in bed when the invasion began.
It was nearly dawn when von Rundstedt's Western Command
realized that a gigantic fleet was approaching the beaches.
Frantically they implored General Alfred Jodl at Hitler's
headquarters to apprise the *Führer* of the situation and ask him
to unleash the 12th *Waffen SS Panzer* division *Hitlerjugend*, as
well as the *Panzer* division *Lehr*, vital reserves which could be
released only by Hitler himself. Incredibly, Jodl flatly refused to
awaken him. Von Rundstedt, as the Supreme Commander
West, could have demanded to be put through to the *Führer* at
any hour, but that went against the grain of the old aristocrat,
who openly called his commander-in-chief that "Bohemian
corporal."

Field Marshal Rommel was the only other man who would
have acted immediately. When he was finally reached it was
nine in the morning, and the Allies were not only solidly
entrenched on several beaches, but had begun to fan into the
countryside at some locations. Rommel, severely shaken by his
stupidity, raced to the front. That afternoon, the *Panzers* finally
began to roll, but it was too late. The Allied air forces
dominated the front so totally that the armored units were badly
mauled, long before they could be deployed effectively during
daylight. And thus Rommel's prophetic observation made to his
aide Major Lange during an inspection tour, at last came true.
"My dear Lange," the Field Marshal had said, "the first 24 hours
of the invasion will decide the fate of Germany." Unlike his
superior, von Rundstedt, he believed the invasion had to be
stopped at the beach, not inland. On July 17, Rommel himself
was severely wounded, either by a strafing Royal Air Force
Spitfire or a Mosquito bomber. Just a month earlier he and von
Rundstedt had met Hitler in a bunker at Soissons and asked for
permission to withdraw to a shorter, more effective line of
defense. Hitler had flown into a rage and accused the army of
cowardice. On July 6, the High Command announced that Field
Marshal Kluge had replaced von Rundstedt, who had bluntly

told General Jodl: "Quit, you damned fools." Strangely, Hitler sent him a polite note of dismissal instead of having him shot, and toward the end, the aging Field Marshal would again be recalled to duty.

At the time, of course, I had not the slightest idea of these high-level command intrigues and decisions. Little did I realize that the events of D-Day would change not only my career but my whole life. When I returned from my latest flight training course, I expected to remain in the *Gymnasium* only a few more weeks before the *Luftwaffe* would claim me. Rolf Geisen, Heinz Kranz, and Hermann Weiermann, some of my fellow soccer players, had been inducted as *Flakhelfer* with their class, which was senior to mine by one year. Some of their teachers even accompanied them as they manned antiaircraft positions within Germany, but with nearly continuous day and night air raids, effective teaching soon stopped.

These boys, technically still in the Hitler Youth, were inducted into the armed forces one by one. I expected my own *Cusanus Gymnasium* class would be next, and hoped that the *Luftwaffe* would draft me directly as a future pilot, since I had long been an officer cadet. I reasoned that my outstanding record as a sailplane pilot would make that a certainty.

In retrospect, it's astonishing how calmly we took the news of the invasion. Just like Hitler, millions of Germans did not grasp the reality for the first two or three days. They assumed it was similar to the landing attempt on Dieppe by the 2nd Canadian Division on August 19, 1942. That had been very costly for the enemy, with casualties exceeding 3,500. For a few days, I believed Dr. Goebbels' strident assertion that this, too, had been a major Allied blunder. It would, he insisted, finally give us the chance to get at the elusive enemy and throw him speedily back into the sea.

I was elated to watch the V1 flying bombs, the first of the so-called *Vergeltungswaffen* (weapons of revenge) streak toward England on June 13. There was a launching site in the forest north of us, and I often followed the trajectory from our yard with a pair of binoculars. The earlier "buzz bombs" had such a tricky steering mechanism that at least two out of ten crashed in Germany. "Our Holy Mother Mary help us," pleaded my grandmother mockingly, "these things are digging more holes around Wittlich than in London." That was an exaggeration, but the

bombs were quickly dubbed the "farmer's horror." Hanna
Reitsch, Germany's top woman pilot, had been decorated with
the Iron Cross II. Class by Hitler himself for flying one. The
V1's only victims in Wittlich would be the forester, his wife and
their dog, on New Years Eve 1944. I could not have imagined in
June that their deaths would be merely part of an endless
obituary for Wittlich.

Early in July, when not even a fanatic could overlook the
disturbing progress of General Eisenhower's "Operation Over-
lord," the leader of the Hitler Youth *Bann Wittlich* assembled
several hundred of us in the *aula* (auditorium) of the *Gymnasium*. *Gebietsführer* Karbach, the leader of our *Gebiet Moselland
12* with its more than half million members, gave a short speech.
Rather off-handedly he mentioned that the Allied advance,
however temporary, would require some counter measures
involving extensive participation by the Hitler Youth. With that,
he threw us a snappy "*Heil Hitler, Kameraden*," and left with his
entourage.

"I'll keep an eye on you from my *Messerschmitt* 109," I
grinned at my buddy Wolfgang Knopp, who merely snorted in
disgust. A few minutes later *Bannführer* Horst Wendt, a veteran
of about 35 who had returned from the Russian Front with his
right hand missing, dismissed all but 50 of us leaders. I was
astonished when he motioned me to the stage. I was a mere
Oberscharführer, in charge of 50 of my peers, and I assumed that
the man in command of 6,000 Hitler Youth barely knew my
name. He pulled a map out of his aide's case, spread it on the
table and pointed to a village on the border of Luxembourg and
Germany. "That's where you are going tomorrow with your
Flieger Gefolgschaft 12," he said as casually as if he had
scheduled a Sunday parade. "Your unit is the easiest to get on
the road since most of the boys are students here, right?" I
nodded, dumbfounded, and he grinned. "By the way, this is *your*
unit. I have just promoted you to *Gefolgschaftsführer*."

I was stunned by the fact that I had followed Fritz Laux and
Manfred Hert, both excellent flyers and respected leaders, in
assuming command of the 180 members of the unquestionably
elite unit of our *Bann 244*. That afternoon I met the *Bannführer*
at Hitler Youth headquarters for final instructions. Wendt
threw an approving glance at the thick green-white braid and
the three stars affixed to the shoulder boards of my *Luftwaffe-*

blue blouse.

"Manfred proposed you as his successor," he said, "he just received his orders to the *Luftwaffe* in time. You're stuck with me for the foreseeable future and exempt from induction, so don't even mention that you want to become a goddamn fighter ace, right?"

When I left Wendt's office, I had become a professional, salaried Hitler Youth leader on full duty. In peacetime, nearly all members of the Hitler Youth short of the higher ranks or those employed in its vast administration, were unpaid part-timers. Rarely did a boy become a leader of a *Gefolgschaft* before reaching 17, since he would normally leave the Hitler Youth at 18 for labor service and two years duty in the armed forces. Also at 18, one was urged to join the Nazi Party, although that was not compulsory like the Hitler Youth. The girls followed a similar pattern to age 18, but the regime and its leader were male-oriented, in the German tradition. Hitler preferred women in the kitchen, not in the Party. Not one became a widely-known leader.

I feared my grandmother might explode at this newest development, but on the contrary, she seemed relieved that I wasn't going into combat flight training. One look at the sky filled with enemy aircraft was enough to weigh one's chances. By late 1944, the life expectancy of a green *Luftwaffe* pilot was all of 33 days. She felt that our main duty would be excavating antitank barriers on the *Westwall*, which had been cannibalized to shore up the *Atlantik Wall*, now almost entirely in Allied hands.

She did throw a disapproving glance at the Walther 7.65 mm pistol on my belt, however. "I hope you kids don't get so close to the front you'll have to use this thing," she remarked. I didn't tell her that the pistol, with its inlaid swastika, had been the *Bannführer's* parting gift, with the admonition to use it on myself should I foul up my assignment. I quickly learned that nearly unlimited power has its own price: accountability.

Unless there was a penetrating overcast with only a few hundred feet ceiling, it had become too dangerous to travel the rails and roads of Germany and Nazi-occupied Europe, especially France, during the day. We left Wittlich late at night, attached to a *Wehrmacht* train. The distance to Remisch, a Luxembourg town on the Mosel in the triangle where Germany,

France and Luxembourg meet, is only about 40 miles. As we traversed Trier, Germany's oldest city, I barely glimpsed the outline of the 2,000-year-old Roman Porta Nigra against the black sky. We stopped numerous times as freight cars were shunted to sidings, and it was dawn before we arrived, hitched to an elegant Pullman car. Nobody was waiting for us. The ebullience of the departure had evaporated when I ordered the unit to line up on the platform. I began to pace up and down impatiently while rows of boys urinated on the tracks. During the long night, the two toilets had become filled and the small station was still closed. I had about decided to march into the sleeping town, when an officer clad in the black tunic of a *Panzer* regiment rode up on a horse.

"Sorry for the delay," he said rather jauntily, "but we hadn't expected you until about eight. I suppose the Royal Air Force took the night off." That's how I met *Oberleutnant* Hans Leiwitz, who held the German Cross in gold as well as the Iron Cross I. Class, a genuine hero who had lost his right arm in Russia while busting Soviet tanks. Despite the shaky start, we soon became good friends. That likely saved his life, because he was the first man I admired who told me that we were both serving a mass murderer by the name of Adolf Hitler.

My unit was the vanguard of tens of thousands of Hitler Youth workers that would soon be employed excavating ditches and erecting antitank barriers along the *Westwall*, the entire western border of Germany. Not only were we the first contingent in our sector; we manned three 2cm antiaircraft cannons of the *Flakvierling* model 38 which had quadruple barrels. Although not as effective as our 88 mm cannon--the terror of enemy bombers and tanks--each cannon could fire 900 rounds per minute and was deadly against low-flying aircraft. The bridge across the Mosel at Remisch spanning Germany and Luxembourg was a vital supply line to our front. I had strict orders not to draw undue enemy attention to it, but only to open fire at aircraft which were about to attack it. American bomber formations were beyond the cannon's ceiling of 6,500 feet. They usually approached Germany at about 30,000 feet, painting the whole sky with innocent-looking condensation trails which, on a clear day, pinpointed the location of each bomber as if it were an insect pinned to a board. Despite the destruction they wreaked on our cities, I admired the courage of the American bomber crews. Until early 1944, they occasionally suffered severe losses because their fighter aircraft cover with their lower fuel capacity could not reach their targets. At those times, massive attacks were often suspended for weeks, giving us the needed breathing spell to resume our war production. But after D-Day, most of Germany was within range of U.S. fighter planes based in France.

During my entire stay at the *Westwall*, I barely glanced at bomber formations, but American P51s and British Spitfires appeared without warning, out of nowhere, like bloodhounds sniffing out prey. During the first few weeks, they were of little danger to us, since we worked close to the cover of trees. *Oberleutnant* Leiwitz was our construction coordinator, and although he had no direct command over my unit, he set the work targets. In the beginning, we had only picks and shovels and Leiwitz put us to work digging infantry slit trenches in front of the bunker line facing occupied France, near the village of Perl. As there was yet no particular urgency, I rotated my unit so that each member had an opportunity to be trained on the gun position.

My biggest problem was to ensure discipline. Unlike a Hitler Youth camp, my unit was dispersed over several locations in the tiny village of Dirndorf on the German side of the Mosel. We had been trained to accept direct orders with unconditional obedience, but 180 boys in a strange village can create a lot of mischief. Some were my classmates and close friends, such as Wolfgang Knopp whom I had met in elementary school, and Hans-Peter Petri, called "Oma" because he had screamed for his grandmother when *Herr* Becker thrashed him. Others like Roman Follmann had been fellow glider pilots. I relied on them to help me keep control by promoting them to leadership positions, but I was well aware that I alone would be held responsible by Hitler Youth regional headquarters.

Once, when I was speculating why the *Bannführer* had picked me out of four possible candidates, Wolfgang, who never withheld his opinion when we were alone, gave me his interpretation. "It's not because you're such a goddamn hot sailplane pilot; Wendt just realized you're more like him--a ruthless, ambitious bastard. You don't give a damn for anybody but your dog, your horse, your grandmother, and just maybe, a couple of your long-suffering buddies. Besides, you're as devious as a goddamn Jesuit."

"I ought to make you do 500 push-ups until you drop on your big mouth, *Du Schweinhund*," I retorted. "You're lucky we're off duty."

"Why don't you have me shot, *Arschloch*," he grinned, "just like you almost did that poor Luxembourger? Most of the villagers hate your guts. I'll bet you don't know they call you *Herr Himmler*."

On our very first day, I had ordered the closing of the small local school because it was located close to our gun positions. Furthermore, it was an ideal place to house nearly half of my unit in one space. The elderly principal, who obviously knew nothing of the workings of the Hitler Youth, had shaken his finger at me and told me my actions were illegal. I was so astonished to hear such nonsense from a civilian, a conquered Luxembourger, that I ordered two of my *Scharführer* to throw him bodily out the door and shoot him if he came back. That immediately put the village, which had a number of Luxembourgers as well as French, on notice that the Hitler Youth was now in charge.

After the war, it likely would have cost me my life had the man returned, for I would have had him executed if he had persisted in his protest. But we were, as the *Bannführer* had emphasized in his final instructions to me, not in Germany but in a war zone where disobedience was instantly punishable by death. Despite my 16 years, I was the senior Hitler Youth leader and solely in charge of the entire village.

Shortly, we were settled into our quarters, evenly divided between the small Carmelite cloister near the river and the village school. A few days later, on July 20, 1944, Colonel Klaus von Stauffenberg placed a bomb under the map room table at Hitler's Wolf's Lair headquarters in East Prussia. The *Führer*, his voice harsh with bitterness for the infamy committed by "a few traitorous officers," addressed the nation at one o'clock the following morning, and attributed his miraculous escape to providence. He alone could save Germany from the fury of her enemies. Millions of Germans shared his belief, even as their cities were being turned to rubble. There was widespread, often genuinely spontaneous condemnation of the plotters, with church services and demonstrations of thanksgiving held all over the country. I went to early mass in the morning, something I hadn't done since leaving home, and lit a candle for the *Führer*.

Germany sustained more casualties from July 1944 until our surrender on May 8, 1945, than in all the previous war years combined. The immediate armistice advocated by the conspirators against the *Führer* would have averted unspeakable misery and saved the lives of many millions. From a more personal perspective, Wittlich would not have been destroyed and *Oberleutnant* Hans Leiwitz might still be alive. In retrospect, I have often wished I had lit that candle for him instead.

When it became apparent that the conspiracy, far from being limited to a few disgruntled senior officers was in fact, widespread, Hitler wreaked a terrible vengeance. Klaus von Stauffenberg and three other plotters were lucky. They were shot that night in the courtyard of the General Staff headquarters in the Bendler Strasse. Their shooting spared them from being strangled with piano wire on meat hooks, after being tried by the sadistic Roland Freisler, President of the *Volksgerichthof*, the people's court. Among the most notable victims were General Ludwig Beck, former Chief of Staff of the *Wehrmacht*, several active generals and field marshals, and the former mayor of Leipzig, Carl Gördeler, who was in line to become Chancellor once Hitler was removed.

Despite their noble intentions to save Germany from total disaster, the conspirators were poorly organized, indecisive, and fell apart upon hearing that Hitler had survived the bomb blast. He had lived because an officer had unknowingly moved the briefcase with the bomb behind one of the sturdy oaken table supports. In addition, the windows of the conference barrack were open, which diminished the impact of the explosion. Four men were killed, many more wounded, but Hitler escaped with minor injuries, and displayed his shredded trousers with some glee to the visiting Mussolini the same afternoon. Henceforth, the *Gestapo* became merciless, and began to settle scores with those who had not the remotest connection to the plot. At least 5,000 people were eventually executed during these last nine months of the regime. It became deadly to voice any criticism. To show its loyalty to the *Führer*, the *Wehrmacht* was required to salute in the Party fashion with arm outstretched, as we had always done in the Hitler Youth and in the *SS*.

The war was over when we learned that Field Marshal Erwin Rommel had not died of battle wounds, but had been forced to commit suicide for his sympathy with the conspiracy. Although he would not condone the murder of Hitler, it can be argued that if Rommel had supported the removal of Hitler by any means, it might have strengthened the resolve of wavering generals, some of whom shamefully tried to distance themselves after the failure of the plot. Rommel had privately urged Hitler to seek an armistice, as had Field Marshal Gerd von Rundstedt, who detested Hitler and yet turned suspected officers over to the *Gestapo* by allowing them to be cashiered from the *Wehrmacht*. (In order for *Wehrmacht* officers above the rank of Major to be tried by a "civilian" court such as the *Volksgerichthof*, they first had to be drummed out of the officer corps. Rundstedt allowed this to happen and signed their orders of discharge.)

Few officers showed the resolve, honor and integrity of Colonel von Stauffenberg, which was a major reason for the conspirators' failure. Rommel commanded such admiration that his appeal to stop fighting, even under terms of unconditional surrender, would have been heeded by most soldiers on the Western Front, had there been some assurance the Soviets would be denied entry to Berlin. With Hitler out of the way, Germany would have had plenty of first-rate generals who could have pulled the armies back toward the Fatherland and offered a very costly defense if an offer of armistice were refused. It is more likely, though, that Hitler's death would have ended the war within a few weeks. The Third Reich lived and died with that one man.

I had no mercy with the plotters. They were heinous criminals trying to stab us in the back, just like the traitors of 1918. I learned only after the war that my own father had been detained overnight by the *Gestapo* early in September and questioned about his connections to prominent former Social Democrats. The rounding up of "politically unreliable" persons was so routine that it frightened my mother more than my father, who had severed all connection to his former party long ago. To his credit, he never claimed after the war, as did so many Germans, that he had been persecuted or tortured by the *Gestapo* on the basis of one arrest. He also disdained to tell the *Gestapo* that he had fathered me, a leader of the Hitler Youth. If the *Gestapo* had found him involved in the slightest anti-Nazi activity, my status as loyal adherent to the regime wouldn't have saved him. Despite our opposing views of Nazism, I did not want to see my father come to harm; but if he had plotted against Hitler I would have stopped him. Would I have sent my own father to a concentration camp and likely death? It's conceivable, although I like to think I would have given him one warning before calling the *Gestapo*.

Oberleutnant Hans Leiwitz was unmoved by Hitler's narrow escape. "I'm surprised it didn't happen sooner," he quipped. "Not everybody appreciates his military genius." He grinned and wiggled the stump of his arm as if it were a puppet. "Has it ever occurred to you that you might have lived on quite happily even if the *Führer* had been killed?" It was hard to imagine.

By early September of 1944, first hundreds and then thousands of Hitler Youth were deployed in construction units all along the *Westwall*. Soon, every house had to take at least ten boys. The primary task in our sector, which encompassed four villages, was to excavate an antitank barrier, closing off the flat, open land between the Mosel river and the softly rising foothills of the Vosges Mountains.

The fall of Paris on August 25 had brought Germany's danger vividly into focus. Suddenly the unimaginable had become reality: the very soil of the Fatherland was threatened. The invaders' armies stood a scant 300 kilometers to the west, about 45 minutes flying time.

Our sector headquarters was in the large village of Perl, within shouting distance of the French border. After the initial confusion of allocating dozens of units (usually the size of a *Gefolgschaft*, between 160-180 members) to their section of the immense ditch, the tedious, back-breaking work began. We lived in constant dread of Allied fighter attacks. At 40 to 1, the *Luftwaffe* was hopelessly outnumbered, and the training of our pilots had become so short that most were no match for the skilled enemy fliers who roamed our skies at will.

Despite the heavy overcast and foul weather which were our best defense against enemy strafings, the inevitable did happen. Two British Spitfires broke through the low ceiling one cold afternoon, drawn by the movement of three *Wehrmacht* trucks on the poplar-lined road. The fighters raked them with cannon and machine gun fire and the fuel-laden vehicles burst into balls of flame. Two of our Hitler Youth units stationed in Perl were marching single file to their quarters under cover of the trees.

They were caught in the attack, and two boys died instantly in a hail of machine gun fire. A dozen more were badly burned in the exploding debris. A stray bullet in the thigh struck the senior Hitler Youth commander of the entire sector. He had been preceding the column on his motor bike and never heard the diving enemy aircraft because the noisy trucks were passing him at that moment. He lost control of the heavy bike, slammed into a tree and broke his right arm.

The Spitfires, likely low on fuel, made only one pass and roared west across our ditch on whose bottom we lay with our faces pressed into the mud. When I reached our commander minutes later, a medic was applying a tourniquet above the gaping wound. The ricocheting bullet had torn off a chunk of flesh and severed the thigh bone. I thought *Unterbannführer* Lammers was unconscious, but when I leaned over him he opened his eyes, spat out a tooth and grinned, "You're now in charge, Heck."

I was one of 18 *Gefolgschaftsführer* in our sector, with less seniority than most. Nevertheless, Hitler Youth headquarters in Trier confirmed Lammers' final order the next morning. By now it wasn't uncommon for a 16-year-old to head an *Unterbann* (four to six units numbering up to 800 members), but ours was a priority sector. I now commanded nearly 3,000.

Lammers made me his successor because I was in the right place at the right time. He was severely wounded and barely conscious when I came upon him. Like any good leader, his duty was to ensure an unbroken chain of command. If his second-in-command had been present, he would have chosen him. I was more shocked than elated when his order was approved. My promotion had more to do with the fact that my unit was the only one equipped with antiaircraft guns than with my ability as a leader, although in terms of service mine had been the first unit in our sector.

Within a week, I transferred the sector headquarters from Perl to my village. We took over the first floor of the parish and installed a command center with direct phone lines to unit leaders and to regional headquarters in Trier. There was no need for a large staff. Like my predecessor, I put the burden of performance on each of the 18 unit leaders. It was up to them not only to reach their weekly construction goals, but to ensure discipline, order and rotation of manpower directly to their home districts. I functioned mainly as a top liaison. Twice weekly we met to agree on the work schedule. *Oberleutnant* Hans Leiwitz, as senior construction coordinator, had his hands full setting a pace that was fair to 18 different leaders. But once a consensus was reached, only enemy interference was accepted as an excuse for falling behind. I spent most of the daylight hours in the side car of the BMW, visiting each unit at the construction site and at their quarters in the four villages. I was under no illusion that I could inspire nearly 3,000 boys to work harder. Many who worked in the ditch had no idea who I was. We were so pressed for time that I could ill afford to set aside half a day for a mass rally to introduce myself. The two main incentives for working hard were the nearness of the enemy and the rotation system. Even the densest boy understood that we were in a deadly race for time. As it was, the Americans had granted us a surprisingly long reprieve, but the distant thunder of their artillery reminded us day and night that time was running out.

Short of getting hurt on the job or wounded by enemy fire, there was no honorable way of escaping the dirty, brutal work, except by completing at first 90, later at least 60 working days. The length depended on the home district of each unit and on its efficiency in rotating the workers. All I demanded from each unit leader was a reasonably full work force at all times. In my own unit, I settled for 60 days rotation. Any member who fulfilled that quota without missing a day was sent home decorated with the War Service Cross Second Class, a genuine hero of the *Westwall*.

Despite the ingrained habit of following orders unconditionally, there was a lot of griping. Had it not been for the certainty of going home after 60 days, there would have been more desertions despite the severe punishment. Each unit leader was held accountable for any desertion, and each did his best to implore his boys not to risk the fate of traitors. The *mildest* punishment given a 15-year-old deserter who had witnessed the death of a comrade in a strafing run of enemy planes, was immediate arrest, expulsion from the Hitler Youth and transferral to a concentration camp. If he were extremely lucky, he would be sent to service in a penal battalion on the Russian Front, doing such suicidal chores as clearing mine fields. Occasionally a crying boy was found hiding in the basement of his quarters. Since he had not completed his desertion by leaving the *Westwall*, he was commonly sent to a punishment unit, assigned the dirtiest labor at no pay. Generally he was reinstated after he had served a month.

I only knew of one *Scharführer* in charge of 40 boys who disappeared from his unit during the night. Several weeks later, he was arrested in his uncle's house in Germany, and the uncle was sentenced to two years in prison for hiding a deserter. His 16-year-old nephew was brought back to the *Westwall* and shot in front of the unit he had deserted. He was sobbing so uncontrollably and shaking his head wildly from side to side after he was tied to the stake, that the *SS* Field Police firing squad could not take proper aim. A sergeant stepped up and loosed a submachine gun burst into the boy's chest.

"He hung there like a butchered rabbit," related a unit leader who had been ordered to attend. "Christ, I felt sorry for him, deserter or no deserter. And just as sorry for the boys who where puking their guts out watching the carnage. Why punish them?"

"It's a deterrent, not a punishment," I said lamely, remembering my reaction when one of my squad leaders had been stopped by *SS* Field Police on his way to Germany. He, too, had panicked after the strafing run on our units in which Lammers had been wounded. I had ripped his insignia off and reached for my pistol in a sudden rage to avenge the shame he had inflicted on my unit and my reputation. "I ought to shoot you *Schweinhund*," I had yelled. "There are no cowardly deserters in my unit."

"Let's not get carried away, *Unterbannführer*," said the hard-eyed *SS* sergeant. "We'll do the shooting. Since he hardly made it out of the village, I assume you won't object if we ship him to the Russian Front to redeem himself, will you?" Neither the sergeant nor I determined the deserter's fate, although technically I could have shot him had we been engaged in battle.

On September 25, 1944, Adolf Hitler had created the *Volkssturm*, the people's militia, consisting of all males between 15 and 60 able to carry a weapon. Its task was to assist the active forces of the *Wehrmacht* and (in Hitler's words) "wage a merciless fight wherever the enemy steps on German soil." In total disregard of reality, Hitler had been inspired by the Prussian King Frederick William III who, in "An Appeal To My

People" had rallied his nation against Napoleon in 1813.

Since the assassination attempt of July 20, Hitler had harbored a paranoid distrust of the *Wehrmacht* High Command, and entrusted *SS Reichsführer* Heinrich Himmler to create and lead the *Volkssturm*, assisted primarily by leaders of the Party and the Hitler Youth. Himmler, as the chief of the replacement army, had neither the experience nor the ability of a field commander, but his very name inspired fear. Although most military theater commanders secretly regarded the *Volkssturm* as a useless waste of poorly trained and ill-equipped adolescents and old men, they didn't protest this final insanity. Tragically, tens of thousands of Hitler Youth fanatics, especially on the eastern front, believed their sacrifice might still turn the tide for Germany.

Although I had been informed of the creation of the *Volkssturm*, it had little impact on my task at the *Westwall*. We were serving in a war zone, while the *Volkssturm* was envisioned as a home-based force, to be employed only in a last-ditch fight for its own territory. In October 1944, I still considered it highly unlikely that the Allies would breach the fortifications of the *Westwall* and invade German soil.

But because of our proximity to the enemy, and despite the fact that our major task was construction, we were put under military law. I received a directive from Himmler that "dereliction of duty in the face of the enemy is subject to the most severe penalty." Any German knew that meant death. Dereliction of duty was never clearly defined; it covered everything from desertion to mere negligence of leadership. I made sure copies of Himmler's directive were distributed to all units, and I impressed upon my leaders the absolute necessity of stopping desertions, by graphically describing the penalty. With every day in the war zone, I became harder and colder, caring little about anybody or anything. My sudden murderous impulse to shoot a panicky boy was I reasoned, partly a reaction to my own fear. The timely completion of the tank barrier consumed all of my energies--until I met Fabianne.

For several days I had been bothered by a nagging toothache. Neither dozens of aspirin tablets nor my grandmother's time-honored remedy of bathing the tooth in potent *Schnapps* had much effect. When I awoke in the middle of the night, hung over from the *Schnapps*, and with a cheek so badly swollen that it lifted my upper lip, I could hardly wait for morning to get to a dentist.

We only had one Hitler Youth dentist for the entire sector, an underqualified butcher stationed at our field hospital in Perl. It was quicker for me to cross the bridge into Remisch.

I wrote myself a pass, since Remisch was off limits to all members of the Hitler Youth without special permission. Despite the harsh retaliation, lone German soldiers frequently were ambushed in occupied territory. There was only one antiaircraft battery of the *Luftwaffe* stationed in Remisch at that time, but there was a *Kommandantur* located in the city hall, which exercised control over the population and served as an information station for German units passing through. A sleepy corporal gave me the address of a dentist nearby. "I'd advise you to leave your BMW parked right here," he said, "no sense in letting a Resistance maniac get a hold of it."

"Resistance?" I asked incredulously, "here in Remisch?" It seemed farfetched.

"That's right," he nodded. "Even the Luxembourgers are getting braver since they can hear the Ami guns in the distance. A captain lost his *Kübelwagen* the other night at a whorehouse. What a change since D-Day," he sighed. "Then you could pass out in an alley in full armament and nobody would lay a hand on you. Now I wouldn't get drunk any place except our quarters. Even some of the whores are getting snippy."

It was still a few minutes before seven when I rang the bell at the dentist's house. Nobody was on the street. After several minutes and some repeated ringing, a woman yelled at me in the Luxembourg dialect, similar to the low German of my hometown.

"You got a hell of a nerve getting us up in the middle of the night. Can't you read the sign? We open at nine, not a minute before. Go away!" I slammed my fist against the door and it swung open. When the elderly woman in a pink dressing gown saw me, her mouth fell open and her eyes widened at the sight of my uniform. It was likely she had never seen a brown greatcoat of the Hitler Youth with its Swastika arm band. Her eyes flickered to the pistol on my belt. I assume she thought I was the *Gestapo*.

"*Heil Hitler*," I saluted. "I'm sorry to get you out of bed, but this is an emergency. As you can see, my face is badly swollen."

Her features sagged in relief.

"Come into the waiting room. My husband will be with you in a few minutes." She motioned me into the cold, sparsely furnished waiting room and drew her gown tightly around her neck. "You realize, *mein Herr*, that there'll be an extra charge for the emergency?" She had recovered quickly from her fear.

"Just get the doctor," I moaned, "money is no object."

When the dentist shuffled in a few minutes later, I stared in dismay. Perhaps I would have been better off with our dental student in Perl; this man was approaching senility. He merely grunted when I greeted him with "*Heil Hitler!*" but he did raise his arm crookedly. As soon as I sat in his chair, however, a transformation took place. The eyes behind his thick bifocals sharpened and his movements became firm.

"Let's see what we have here," he said, and began to whistle the overture to the *Fledermaus*. Obviously, he liked his work.

"This is a mess," he chuckled, "your molar is badly infected, beyond the point of saving. You waited too long. I suppose you tried *Schnapps*?" I nodded and he grinned.

"Do you want one now? It's decision time. I assume you don't want to do the sensible thing and let the infection subside before I extract your tooth." I shook my head, unable to speak. "Fine with me, but it'll hurt like hell. I only have a limited supply of Novocaine." He peered at me. "You Germans don't allot us much. I never use any for mere drilling."

Moving his hand out of my mouth, I pleaded, "Give me a good shot of Novocaine and pull the goddamn tooth. I'll replenish your supply and pay whatever you ask within reason. Let's say 50 Marks and a package of cigarettes?"

"You won't feel a thing, *mein Herr*." He smiled and reached for his needle, then wandered around the chair while the anesthetic took hold, smoking one of my Turkish cigarettes. I began to get dizzy and I wondered if he had given me a fatal injection.

"By the way," I mumbled with leaden lips, "the *Kommandatur* sent me to you. They know I'm here."

"That's nice," he said. "Thank them for the referral. I treat a lot of Germans. Even had a general once." My panic passed and I felt ridiculous. As a prominent citizen, the dentist would likely be on a list of possible hostages. Even if he were sympathetic to the Resistance, surely he would not kill me in his office, or anywhere else for that matter.

Despite his age, the dentist was quite strong. He put his knee on my thigh, applied the pliers to my tooth, and with one sustained pull extracted it. When I had finished spitting blood, he showed me the tooth, but now his hand was shaking as if he had expended all his strength. I felt a surge of gratitude. "I'm very much obliged to you, *Herr Doktor*. Now I can get on with the war." When I said this, his facial muscles set.

"No need for you to come back. Please pay my wife on your way out." He just left me sitting there and walked out of the room.

My whole face was numb when I stepped onto the street. Feeling light-headed, I decided to walk around before getting back on my motor bike. Remisch seemed almost cosmopolitan after our small village. The streets were clean and the shops looked neat, but as in Germany, there was almost nothing for sale anymore. Here the windows were bare except for papier-machè reproductions of food items. The fake sausage looked nauseating.

On a sudden impulse, I stepped into the large, medieval-looking Catholic Church. Morning Mass was over and the last parishioners trickled out, all elderly women with dark kerchiefs on their heads. Most ignored me, but some gave me a startled glance. Surely their church had never harbored a uniformed leader of the Hitler Youth.

Several stubby candles burned in front of the side altar with the statue of the Virgin Mary, my favorite saint. Except for our brief march through Remisch on our arrival, it was my first time outside Germany, but the church exuded the same atmosphere as that of my hometown. The Latin inscriptions evoked memories of the hundreds of hours I had served as an altar boy before the same cloyingly sweet look of the Holy Mother. I felt sheltered, as if I were nine years old again, and I lit a candle for my grandmother and myself, not really believing anymore in its efficacy, but neither discarding it altogether. As I knelt in the first pew, I didn't pray for anything more specific than for my grandmother's and my well-being, and for the successful completion of my task on the *Westwall*. At the moment, it was difficult to see beyond that. One lived each day separately now.

There was a rustle of garments and I looked back. An old woman, somberly dressed in a black skirt that touched her shoes, rose from the third pew behind me. As she passed, she gave me a piercing look of such undisguised malevolence that I shivered. She stepped forward to the bank of candles, cleared her throat noisily two or three times and sent a sizzling blob of spit on my candle, instantly extinguishing it.

As I gaped at her, she glared at me triumphantly, totally unafraid of my uniform and the power it represented, gathered in her skirts and walked calmly past me out the door. I was stunned by the naked display of hatred in her eyes. I could not bear to touch the spit-soiled candle, but I lit a whole row above it, as if to counter the power of her witchcraft. Looking up at the Virgin Mary, I wondered whose side she would take. For the first time it occurred to me that our enemies prayed to the same God, for *our* defeat. As I left the church, I pondered the action of the old woman. It was clear that she hated me for being German, for without my uniform I would have been indistinguishable from a Luxembourger. Did she represent the feelings of most Luxembourgers toward us? It seemed likely, measured by the reception I had received at the dentist. This was enemy territory.

I was jarred from my thoughts by the shrieks of a young woman clutching a tiny Dachshund puppy to her chest while fending off a full-sized German shepherd who was prancing around her. His playful barks became ferocious, for he was getting excited by her flailing arm. Rearing up on his hind legs, he lunged for the puppy. I ran toward her, pulling my pistol and rapping him lightly on the nose with its barrel as he turned toward me.

"Take off, *Schweinhund*," I shouted. The dog let out a yell, more of surprise than anger, and bounded off. I had been raised with shepherds and understood them perfectly. This was no mad dog, merely a playful animal enjoying his fun, but the girl was limp with terror and sank against my chest.

"Oh, thank you, *mein Herr*," she sobbed, "if you hadn't come along, this brute would have eaten my poor Yvonne." I took the sleek little animal out of her shaking arm, barely surpressing a laugh. A swift kick and a sharp command from her would have done the same as my heroics, but it was nice to be looked upon as a savior, particularly after the experience with the old woman in the church. Cradling the dog in my arms, I soothed it with light strokes, giving the girl a chance to regain her composure.

And then I looked at her, and my pulse instantly increased 20 beats.

I was used to the well-scrubbed, healthy maidens of the Hitler Youth. The Luxembourg girl had an exquisite, disturbingly exotic beauty, totally unlike the standards prescribed for our Master Race. I guessed her to be about 18, but there was no trace of adolescence in her face. This was a woman of magnetic sensuality.

I was acutely aware of my swollen face and pointed to it clumsily. "I had an infected tooth pulled, *Fräulein*...?" She held out her hand and smiled.

"I'm Fabianne Mercurier. Sorry I became so emotional, but I was truly frightened by that dog." She spoke flawless High-German, like many educated Luxembourgers, but with an intriguing French cadence. After I had introduced myself she thanked me again, but there was now a difference. She reached for the dog, and I sensed that she wanted to get away quickly.

"Just in case that dog should come back," I said, desperate that she might leave, "may I walk with you?" She blushed, and looked quickly around as if people were watching.

"I was on my way to the river promenade with Yvonne, and it's always deserted at this hour. Would you like to come?"

"Oh, yes," I lisped with such an intensity that she laughed. A few minutes later we crossed the highway running parallel to the Mosel river which flowed forbiddingly cold and gray past us. On the other side was Germany and the war, suddenly an eternity away. The temperature was barely above freezing and the whole promenade lay deserted. While Yvonne ran through the brownish meadow, exploring her world of scents, Fabianne and I sat down on a bench. She was now quite at ease, but I felt both elated and shy. I didn't know what to say and kept touching my face. Suddenly, she removed her glove and reached up to my cheek.

"It hurts badly, doesn't it, *Herr* Heck?" Her touch made my heart race.

"Just a little," I stammered, "the anesthetic is wearing off." When she removed her hand from my face, I reached for it and pressed it. She returned the touch, but then quickly retracted her hand.

"I shouldn't be sitting here with you," she said quietly. "And I shouldn't be seen with you. You're a German."

"What difference does that make?" I asked. "Are you going to spit on my candle too?" She looked at me uncomprehendingly, and in a sudden rush I recounted my visit to the church. When I was finished, she stared at me and then reached for both my hands.

"What insanity this war has bred. I'm just like the old woman. I would have spit on you too if you hadn't saved Yvonne."

"That's ridiculous," I said, suddenly incensed. "What the hell have I ever done to you Luxembourgers?"

"Did we provoke Germany?" she countered. "Your big nation crushed my tiny one, and you expect friendship?"

"Aren't you proud to be part of Greater Germany?" I asked. "We even speak the same language."

"Proud?" she laughed. "Most of us hate it." That very moment was a revelation for both of us. I had no idea of the depth of anti-German feeling in our small border possession, and Fabianne recognized that my ignorance was not the arrogance of the conqueror but the naivite of the fanatic believer. I rose from the bench, downcast but determined to preserve my dignity. Bowing stiffly I said, "_Auf Wiedersehen, Fräulein_ Mercurier. I'm sorry you feel this way." As I began to walk away, Yvonne came bounding up to me, barking happily. When I scooped up the little dog, Fabianne laughed softly behind me.

"Come back, _Herr_ Heck. I won't spit on your candle."

For the next two hours I sat transfixed by her nearness, talking little and listening. Fabianne was the daughter of a Luxembourg railroad official, but her mother was French. Her uncle owned a pharmacy in Remisch, and her father had decided she and her mother should wait out the war in a small town which was less likely to be destroyed than their home in the city of Luxembourg.

I had guessed her age correctly. Fabianne had just passed her eighteenth birthday and was 13 months older than I. She was already in her first year at the University of Luxembourg, studying education. Her goal was to teach French at a _Lyceum_, the equivalent to our _Gymnasium_. There would be an interruption in her education, though, for our military authorities had just turned the university into a barrack for our troops. As long as we avoided politics, we had a lot in common.

"I suppose there's no point in asking about your future plans," she smiled.

"On the contrary," I said. "I was accepted at 15 as an officer cadet of the *Luftwaffe*, and I can't wait to get into a fighter plane instead of digging a huge hole in the countryside. I'm going to become a career officer."

"For life?"

"Yes, but only if I can keep flying. My grandmother, of course, still thinks I'll become a Catholic priest."

"Are you serious?" She looked at the four stars on my epaulets. "Aren't you a Hitler Youth officer?"

"Sure," I said, "but that's only temporary. We believe in God, too, you know."

After a brief pause, I blurted out, "I would very much like to see you again," and at this she blushed.

"So would I, but I don't think it's wise. This is a small town and people just wouldn't understand. I don't want to be called names."

"Such as?"

"Such as German lover," she said calmly. I felt the blood shooting into my face.

"How dare they? I'd have them arrested for insulting Germany."

"You really believe that would change their minds, Alfons?" She reached for my hand.

"I have never felt more attracted to anyone in my whole life, Fabianne," I said, emboldened by her use of my first name. "I must see you again, no matter what. I could pick you up on my motor bike at the bridge and nobody would see you. We could meet at night. Please, don't walk away."

"I must be insane," she whispered, "but listen. I usually go to a movie on Sunday night. The theater is near the bridge. Can you be at the bridge tower on our side at 7 o'clock?"

"I'll be there, Fabianne," I said, and added only half jokingly, "unless I'm dead." I pulled her toward me and our lips touched briefly, sending a current through me, but she pushed me gently away.

"I should have been at the pharmacy an hour ago. Please let me walk back by myself. You understand, don't you?" As I watched her crossing the highway toward the town, I felt an almost physical pain at our parting. Never in all the times I had said farewell to my family, even my grandmother, had I been affected like that. Was this love? As if guessing my thoughts, she turned and blew me a kiss. For the first time, I forgot my impatience to return to flying. I had, at best, no longer than four weeks to finish the project. Why hadn't I met Fabianne months ago when we arrived? But this was a childish, self-pitying question, almost traitorous in the face of the danger that confronted the Fatherland. For an instant I resented the girl from Luxembourg and the claim she had on my emotions at this critical period when time was running out for Germany.

Dr. Goebbels exhorts Hitler Youth to all-out war effort at Berlin reception. On left with swastika armband is *Reichsjugend-führer* Artur Axmann, the successor to Baldur von Schirach

Chapter Six:

A TIME TO SHOUT
AND A TIME TO WEEP

More than four decades later, the last five weeks of 1944 remain cleanly chiselled in my memory. It was a time of soaring hope and vast despair, a time to shout and a time to weep, dictated by events over which I had as little control as the pull of gravity.

It began auspiciously on one of the last gray days of an unseasonably cold November. Late that evening, I received a telephone message from our headquarters in Trier to attend a conference the next morning. I had received similar messages in the past, but this time an _SS_ officer, not a Hitler Youth commander, relayed the message on six hours notice. He refused to give the location.

"You'll be picked up at the parish," he said, adding somewhat mysteriously, "shine your boots. I think you'll like this excursion." It was still dark when I stepped into a camouflage-painted Mercedes, driven by a taciturn _Untersturmführer_, a young second lieutenant of the _Waffen SS_. I couldn't get a thing out of him. The weather was atrocious--rain mixed with snow under a ceiling of low, scurrying clouds. The narrow, paved highway was lined with tall firs, making it nearly invisible from the air. We were headed east, back into Germany, but I had only a general idea of our location. We had crossed the Saar river ten kilometers north of Saarburg, judging by a road sign. There was a fair volume of traffic toward us, mostly _Wehrmacht_ supply vehicles taking advantage of the perfect protection afforded by the weather.

After we had driven at moderate speed for two hours, being

stopped only once for a thorough check of our travel documents by motorized field police, the road began to rise into semi-mountainous country. By now, I calculated, we must be in the foothills of the Hunsrück range which extends to the Rhine. It was full daylight and snowing lightly when we were stopped by the crew of an armored personnel carrier blocking half the gravel road which we had entered. After another inspection, we were allowed to pass and came face to face with a *Panzerzug*, an armored train parked in the center of a dense forest siding. I gaped at the softly humming oversized diesel locomotive hitched to three long cars followed by an 88mm antiaircraft gun mounted on a flatbed. Despite the weather, which made any kind of enemy aircraft detection impossible, a full crew manned the long-barreled cannon.

I had never seen so much dull steel. Armor plate covered the wheels almost to the tracks, and the windows of the cars were protected with rectangular insets of steel, at least an inch thick. Every foot of the train was painted camouflage green, mixed with earthen and black blotches, perfectly matching the pre-dominant colors of the countryside.

After yet another check by an *SS* major who carefully compared the photo on my pass to my face, I was relieved of my pistol and patted down expertly as if I were a criminal. Only then was I allowed to pass the cordon of *SS* soldiers, all armed with submachine guns, some accompanied by watch dogs. As I did so, I couldn't resist reaching for one of the beautifully-groomed shepherds sitting next to its handler. The dog was instantly on its feet, snarling warningly.

"Go ahead," said the soldier. "Try your luck. Old Fritz could use another breakfast." The major gave me a disapproving look as I stepped through the door into the center car. The contrast from the dull steel on the outside to the imposing interior was striking. Down the center and bolted to the floor ran a heavy oak table which matched the paneling on the walls. Oaken benches topped with leather flanked its length on both sides, easily offering enough sitting room for the 50 or so people present. The ceiling was an intricate mahogany mosaic depicting the German eagle clawing a Swastika in the soft glow of three chandeliers. Silver ice buckets with bottles of mineral water dotted the table next to clusters of crystal goblets and ash trays. A thick blue carpet absorbed the sound of the boots and muffled the voices. A huge painting of a steely-eyed Frederick the Great, framed in a wreath of golden leaves, hung on the south wall.

This opulently appointed train was obviously the rolling command quarters of somebody very important, perhaps even that of *Reichsmarschall* Hermann Göring. The flamboyant chief of the *Luftwaffe* was by far the most narcissistic of our leaders. Strangely, most Germans were amused by the unabashed ostentation and public joviality which disguised the unparalleled ruthlessness of the man who had founded the *Gestapo*. Göring, who plundered the art treasures of Europe with unabashed zeal, was a pirate on a grand scale. But it was easier to relate to a high-living fat man than to the ascetic Hitler whose only gourmet tendency was a craving for pastries. The *Führer* existed on spartan vegetarian meals and neither drank nor smoked. Not even Eva Braun dared to light up in his presence. Hitler was offended by women who reeked of cigarettes, undoubtedly the reason that tobacco ration cards were issued to German males at age 16 but to no woman under 25. Even then, women received only half the allotment of males. But by late 1944, Göring's star was sinking as rapidly as that of his outgunned *Luftwaffe*. Soon Hitler would remove him as his successor and in the final days of his life, order him arrested on suspicion of high treason for establishing peace feelers to the enemy without his permission.

A sharp "*Achtung!*" brought us to heel-clicking attention. Oddly, the man who entered the conference car was, in his personal demeanor, the opposite of Göring, despite his immense power which had, by then, exceeded that of the *Reichsmarschall*. Albert Speer with his fine-boned face and pleasant dark eyes shadowed by bushy brows was the antithesis of a boorish Party *Gauleiter*, despite his brown uniform. As our Minister of Armaments and Ammunition and head of the vast construction agency *Organization Todt*, Speer was in charge of all civilian war efforts.

Postwar Allied claims that Speer, in his proficiency, pro-longed the war by nine months are hard to prove. But there is no doubt that he was one of the few top Nazi intellectuals and an organizational genius. Despite the incessant Allied bombing of our factories and refineries, Speer had so effectively decentralized our war industry that it was difficult to obliterate industrial sectors from the air. Germany actually produced more tanks and airplanes in September of 1944 than at the height of its power in 1940. Speer achieved this by employing five million foreign laborers, most brought to Germany against their will, who worked under appalling conditions with little more freedom than slaves.

Most of the men in the room wore the brown tunic of Speer's organization, which was in charge of the *Westwall* construction. Looking around, I recognized several of the inspectors from their weekly evaluation of our sector. They must have been satisfied, for *Reichsleiter* Speer turned to us six Hitler Youth leaders with a broad smile. "I salute the splendid efforts of the Hitler Youth," he said jovially. "Despite the nasty weather conditions, we are about to reach our goal in nearly all sectors. This shows what genuine dedication by young Germans can achieve." The audience of *Todt* officials and high military officers included a *Wehrmacht* general, a brigadier of the *Waffen SS* and several colonels. They applauded us politely and then Speer dropped his bombshell.

"*Meine Herren,*" he said as calmly as if he were discussing the weather, "we are about to be defeated." There was dead silence and I stared at the Hitler Youth comrade next to me, who sucked in his breath in a low whistle. Spreading enemy propaganda was called *Wehrzersetzung*, undermining the will to fight to final victory. It was high treason which would land even a grandmother in a concentration camp. If I, as a Hitler Youth leader had ever expressed to my staff, let alone my units, my fear that Germany might lose, nothing could have saved me from the firing squad. Yet here was the second most powerful man in Germany, the *Führer's* favorite architect and perhaps only remaining personal friend, telling us that all was lost. The tension was palpable, but Speer merely grinned, satisfied with our reaction, and continued as if he had not finished his treasonous sentence.

"Our hope, *meine Herren*, is to stop the enemy exactly where you are now performing your labor, at the *Westwall*." A sigh of relief escaped me. I was a little annoyed at Speer's theatrics, but he had certainly made his point. Thus far, only our medieval border city of Aachen had fallen into enemy hands after ferocious fighting which had left it in ruins but had given the enemy a foretaste of what to expect. Nevertheless, the *Westwall* was the only substantial line of fortifications barring the way into the Fatherland. Should the enemy succeed in breaching it on a wide front, nothing could stop him from reaching the Rhine, our river of fate and our last natural barrier.

In the following 15 minutes, Speer summarized the defense situation along the Western Front. Our sector was especially vulnerable because it lay in the direct path of the U.S. Third and Seventh Armies, and time was running out.

"We must give our badly outnumbered troops the protection of a refurbished *Westwall*," Speer concluded, "and victory will be ours." By his own postwar admission, Speer knew that Germany was doomed at the very time he was exhorting us to do our utmost for a lost cause. Although he could have said little else and still survived, by his very sincerity he condemned hundreds of my comrades to needless deaths, for we believed his implications that victory was yet possible.

As our armaments czar, Albert Speer had access to every facet of the vast Nazi machinery, although he had no say over purely military operations. And though Speer had nothing to do with the administration of concentration or extermination camps, Auschwitz was the largest of all slave labor camps, and he was nominally in charge of all slave labor. It's ridiculous to believe that the best informed of all Nazi leaders next to Hitler did not know what tens of thousands of lesser officials and German citizens knew: namely that the *SS* had been embarked on the course of genocide since 1942. During the 1963 Auschwitz Trial in Frankfurt, testimony showed that about 2,400 German *SS* guards of the "Death Head" units had served in the extermination camp. Add another 6,000 for the other camps in Poland--not including the hundreds of concentration camps inside Germany--and the number approaches 9,000. The four *Einsatzgruppen* which followed the *Wehrmacht* in the east numbered close to 3,000, and had been sworn to secrecy under penalty of death. There were railroad officials, industrialists and casual witnesses like Hans Leiwitz--indeed, many thousands of far lower rank than Speer--who were able to deduce from what they observed. Most disturbingly, in his 1943 *Posen* speech, Himmler had informed several dozen *Wehrmacht* generals as well as Speer (who later claimed to have left before the speech began) about the genocide.

Speer was a modern Faust, a man who sold his soul to the

devil in return for power. While I'm certain he did experience true remorse, I'm equally sure no one would have heard his confession of moral guilt had we won the war. That much we share, which deprives me of the right to condemn him. In my eyes, Speer started on his road to redemption when he risked his life by telling Hitler he had blocked his order to scorch Germany. In January of 1945, Hitler had ordered Speer to demolish everything which might help the invaders, not only bridges and factories but public buildings, railroad stations, even waterworks. To his credit, Speer did not pass on these orders, and told Hitler to his face that he had blocked the order, at least regarding non-military facilities, for he felt such devastation would doom the German people. Hitler responded that the people were no longer worthy of survival, but he spared Speer's life.

Albert Speer finished his remarks to us with an order to extend our work week to 60 hours, so we could finish the major part of the construction by December 10. My contingent was the only Hitler Youth unit which manned antiaircraft guns, and one of the few so close to the front. I often worried about the proximity of the Americans and was just as eager as Albert Speer to get our formations home.

We Hitler Youth leaders were still adolescent enough to be flattered by the appearance of one of our top officials, especially one with the status of Speer. But the man who now followed him into the conference car unannounced literally made my knees shake. I had seen him on four previous occasions, but never in an intimate setting face to face. The man was Adolf Hitler.

The *Führer* wore his usual wartime attire: field gray tunic over black trousers with a white shirt and tie, no belt, no hat. The Iron Cross I. Class on his breast pocket was his only decoration; he had earned it in World War I as a corporal and wore it on all his uniforms. A straight-winged *Wehrmacht* eagle embroidered on his left upper arm and the Golden Party badge on his tie lent some color. The Nazi regime used paraphernalia-- striking decorations and splendid uniforms--to effectively convey importance and power, as well as to intimidate. Although I was not afraid of the *Gestapo*, the *SS* Death Head insignia gave me an ominous, eerie feeling. Hitler's very plainness was calculated. It signalled both personal modesty and the power of the leader who doesn't need fancy uniforms to proclaim his supremacy. Hitler's image of omnipotence vanished, however, in civilian clothes, and very rarely did he wear them in public.

The unexpectedness of his appearance was awesome, for we had no time to prepare as we did in a mass rally of the Hitler Youth. Paradoxically, a feeling of pity seized me. He stood there in the first few seconds, silently lifting his bent right arm in salute, and we greeted him with a thunderous *"Heil, mein Führer!"* He almost flinched, seemed frail and decades older than when I had last seen him two years previously. Although he was only 55, he looked like a man in his 70s. The war and the assassination attempt four months ago had taken their toll. He favored his right leg and strained to listen, but when he began to speak, the power quickly returned to his strangely hoarse and compelling voice.

He told us briefly that very soon the tide of war would turn in our favor. For a moment, I thought I glimpsed a quick, cynical smile on the thin lips of *Reichsleiter* Speer, but it soon turned to beaming approval. Hitler's power of persuasion was magical. "We shall launch an all-out offensive which will not only deny our enemies the holy soil of Germany, but will throw them back into the sea," asserted the *Führer*. "Then we will take care of the savage Bolsheviks in short shrift." Considering the constant reverses since D-Day and the enemy at our doorstep, it seemed like a tall order, but I had no doubt we would succeed. The alternative was unthinkable.

During the last two weeks, aided by the weather, whole divisions had stealthily moved into the bunkers of the *Westwall* and the nights were vibrant with the roar of *Panzer* engines. South of our village, a dozen King Tiger tanks squatted under their camouflage nets. I received reports from my neighboring section commanders that every barn was filled with troops and their equipment. The *Führer's* words now confirmed my hopes that these units were deployed not merely for defense but to launch another *Blitzkrieg*.

Months of gnawing fear culminated in surging elation when we filed past Hitler on our way out. Not only was I meeting the man who held our destiny in his hands, the only man capable of averting catastrophy in this 12th hour, but he greeted me with fatherly kindness as I came to attention before him. "My boy," he said warmly, employing the intimate *Du* as he extended his hand and studied the insignia which identified my Hitler Youth

region, "I know I can depend on you to do your duty to the end.
You Rhinelanders know what it's like to be under the heel of
the enemy."

"*Jawohl, mein Führer,*" I whispered, hoarse with emotion. I
returned the slight pressure of his moist hand and stared into
his surprisingly light-blue eyes. As if in a time suspension, I was
aware of every feature in his pale face. His cheeks were
blotched from the exertion of his speech and there was a razor
nick in the corner of his upper lip. To the fraction of an inch, he
was as tall as I, five feet eight inches. Next to him stood an *SS*
colonel, a member of his personal guard regiment with the
silver-stitched cuff title *Leibstandarte Adolf Hitler*. The colonel, a
hero with the Knights Cross around his neck, handed him a
velvet case with the War Service Cross I. Class with Swords.
Hitler didn't pin it on my chest, but passed it to me with a
slightly trembling hand.

"*Danke, mein Führer,*" I saluted, repressing a tear of emotion,
and he lifted his hand. I was dismissed. At the door, I turned to
take in the room one last time. Hitler's face was set as the
military officers walked passed him. He didn't hold out his hand
to them, but merely stood stiffly with his arm raised in a crooked
stance. Since the attempt on his life, he deeply mistrusted most
high-ranking officers. Too many generals had been implicated.
In that conference car, only the *SS* officers of his staff wore
pistols, which seemed like an insult to us Hitler Youth who
adored him.

I was in a deep reverie much of the way home, barely
noticing the road. At that momentous hour, I could not have
imagined that one day I would come to despise Adolf Hitler as
the grave digger of my country. The *SS* officer, openly envious
because he had not met the *Führer*, soon gave up pumping me
for details about the meeting. "Top secret," I said, paying him
back for his brusque refusal to disclose our destination when he
had picked me up.

Oberleutnant Hans Leiwitz seemed amused by my glowing
recital of the morning's events. "Amazing what a five-mark
medal will do for a good German, isn't it? Actually, you could
have given it to yourself. You have a boxful in your office."
When he saw the look on my face, he patted me on the
shoulder. "I'm sorry, Alf. That was mean of me. You earned the
decoration honestly." And then he grinned in his disarming way.

"I guess I'm jealous that our great leader didn't give me mine."

Hans was the only one I had told about Fabianne, knowing that unlike my other comrades, he wouldn't denigrate my feelings with ribald comments. "I'm very glad for you, my boy. Perhaps it's going to soften your edges a little. There's hope for you yet, falling for a non-German." Then he grew serious. "Go and see her as often as you can. Time is running out very quickly. Grab it while you have the chance and forget about the goddamn ditch. I'll even do some of your bookwork and cover your ass if headquarters calls. Live, my boy."

Despite the incessant pressures on my time, thoughts of Fabianne punctuated all my waking hours. Our second meeting had begun awkwardly, when she confessed in the darkness near the bridge that she didn't dare to walk into the cinema with me. "I understand," I said, nearly trembling with gratitude because she had come at all. "Let's find a small cafe." She shook her head.

"I'd sooner not. Everybody knows me. I suppose you don't have any civilian clothes?"

"Sure," I said, "how about a pair of leather shorts and a warm-up jacket? Just what I need at 30 degrees. On the other hand, I could call in my unit and clear the Luxembourgers out of the theatre at gun point." As soon as I said it, I wished I hadn't. We were at knife's edge, and then she laughed.

"I'm beginning to see how dangerous it is to collaborate with the enemy."

"Please forgive me. It was a stupid remark, but I'm proud of my uniform. Can you understand that, Fabianne?"

"Not really," she said, "but I came anyway, didn't I? And now what?" I pointed to my motor bike parked within the vision of the *SS* guard on the bridge.

"Have you ever ridden in the sidecar of a BMW? We could cross the bridge back into Germany, ride to Perl and sit in a cafe there. I know one that even serves something resembling cake."

"Cake?" Her eyes were round with surprise. "They still serve cake in Perl? Let's go!" We ran toward the bike like children let out of school early, her small hand in mine. The sergeant in charge of the bridge patrol didn't even glance at her identification. He looked at me with obvious envy and whistled softly at Fabianne. "I don't suppose you have a sister over there, *Fräulein*?" She smiled and shook her head. He saluted me

mechanically, but his eyes were fixed on her. I gunned the
engine and we roared into the night, the camouflaged headlight
cutting a thin white ribbon on the asphalt. Fabianne was shaking
with laughter, pointing to the shaft of my submachine gun
clearly sticking out of the sidecar next to her.

"He never asked me if I belonged to the Resistance," she
yelled. That was the moment when I began to love her. In the
total blackout, the few villages flew by like dark clumps along
the narrow road. When we stepped through the blackout
curtain, the lights of the small, dimly lit cafe reflected warmly on
the round marble tables set along both walls. It was a week
night, and only two tables were occupied by a half dozen Hitler
Youth leaders who rose out of their seats when they saw me.

"*Heil Kameraden,*" I said. "At ease." As we walked past them
to a corner table, they fell quiet, just staring at Fabianne with
undisguised awe. Far from being embarrassed, she looked
curiously around as we were seated.

"So this is the famous Hitler Youth," she smiled, very much
aware of the sensation she was causing. This slim-legged,
stunning girl wearing a blue knitted dress was neither a farm
maiden nor a member of the Hitler Youth, but a sensuous
creature from another world, where young women were allowed
to wear lipstick and paint their finger nails.

"You are even more beautiful in the evening, Fabianne," I
whispered, enjoying the envious admiration of my peers.

"Thank you, Ali," she replied without false modesty. When I
told her that nobody had ever called me Ali, she laughed.

"That's simple. I see you as Ali Baba, *Ali Baba and the Forty
Thieves,*" she explained. "You know that tale?"

"Sure, but what's the connection? You think I've fallen in
with robbers?"

"Perhaps you have, but your chivalry has remained intact.
You saved Yvonne, remember?" Her conversation was so unlike
anything I had known, both in the quality of her language and
the uniqueness of her thoughts, that I suffered a pang of
insecurity. Like all Hitler Youth leaders, I regarded girls as
slightly inferior to boys, both physically and intellectually. A rare
exception merely confirmed that. Both the Nazi regime and the
churches strongly stressed the long German tradition of benevo-
lent male domination. Even my grandmother, the undisputed
matriarch of our family, had never publicly defied my grand-

father, although everyone knew she was the final arbiter.

The owner of the cafe was a German woman of ample girth. She treated me deferentially because of my rank, since I could have barred all members of the Hitler Youth from any establishment which served liquor. I did, however, enforce a 10 p.m. curfew and allow the consumption of only beer and wine. Our *Streifendienst*, the Hitler Youth Police, patrolled all pubs and cafes hourly and allowed only leaders to drink on weekdays. Enforcement of curfew presented few problems. Our 12-hour days were so demanding that most boys ate and fell on their straw bags in bone-weary exhaustion. But on Saturdays the pubs were so jammed that dozens of boys had to drink their beer on the sidewalks.

Fabianne's eyes grew round when the fat lady set half of a hot, deep-dish apple pie in front of us and reluctantly took my ration coupons. "We got a little extra flour allotment this week, and these are my own apples, *Herr Unterbannführer*," she said in a falsetto voice, measuring Fabianne who was wiping her mouth.

"My God," she whispered, "I haven't seen a piece of cake like this in a year."

"Help yourself, *Fräulein*," urged the owner. "I'll wrap you a piece to take home. Would you like a cup of cocoa with it? It's the *Herr Unterbannführer's* favorite beverage." Fabianne nodded and dug into the pie, not waiting for me. Basic foodstuffs were getting scarcer all over Germany, and only farmers or black marketeers could get ingredients to bake a cake such as we had been served.

"Is it that bad in Luxembourg, Fabi?" I asked, my heart going out to her. Strangely, my feeling of pity nullified my awe of her. I was quite confident now that I could kiss her.

"If the war lasts much longer," she said between mouthfuls, "people will be killing for food." She suddenly halted and blushed in embarrassment. "I hope you don't get the wrong idea about me."

"What do you mean?" I asked.

"That I'm meeting you just for food." She stared intently at me.

"We were going to the cinema, remember? I don't suppose they serve food in your cinemas, do they? Besides, I had no idea we were going to get hot deep-dish apple pie tonight." Fabianne reached for my hand and pressed her mouth quickly on it.

"Thank you. Please, let's go soon, Ali. I want to be all alone with you." As soon as we left the cafe, we clung to each other in the cold, moonlit night on the deserted village street. I bundled her into the side car, wrapping a blanket around her. As I did, she put her arms around my neck and I knelt on the cobblestones, covering her face with kisses and then touching her lips.

From that night on we met twice a week, on Tuesday and Saturday nights. Those were the evenings when the program in the cinema changed and Fabianne could leave her uncle's home without arousing suspicion. As in Germany, going to the movies was about the only public entertainment left in a small town. Males went to pubs, but unescorted women didn't have that option if they valued their reputations.

As much as I longed to see her, the demands on my time during that last frantic effort to conclude construction seldom allowed me more than six hours of sleep. Daily reports on the 18 units often required my decisions. Around midnight during the first week of December, I was hauled out of bed in a panic. A call had come through that the quarters of of an outlying post along the French border had been shelled. From what I could determine there had been no casualties, merely wounds from broken glass. The shelling had stopped quickly but there had been an ominous rumble of tank engines. They could be ours, moving into position, but they might just as easily be an American spearhead. I ran across the street and got *Oberleutnant* Leiwitz out of his bed. As the construction coordinator, the movement of Hitler Youth units wasn't his responsibility, but he waved aside my apology.

"Get your bike and let's go," he said, already slipping into his tunic. Twenty minutes later we roared up to the church of the hamlet. Only one house had been hit, and most of the hundred members of the unit had followed the general order for this exposed village: to run for shelter in the heavily fortified church basement. The seasoned *Panzer* officer's appearance immediately soothed the worried faces of the boys looking up at us from the basement in the yellow light of kerosene lamps. There had been a few more shells since the first call, and one had set fire to a barn. The unit leader had formed a water brigade and the last flames were dying just as we arrived. Despite the risk, his had been the correct decision. A burning structure was a beacon to the enemy. After a brief discussion, I made my decision.

"Get your unit together and move out now before daylight. Leave a squad of 15 behind to finish whatever you can." The relief in the unit leader's face was palpable, and Leiwitz turned to him.

"You did a good job, boy. Don't worry about the equipment. Stack it beside the church. I'll get a vehicle out tomorrow night."

An hour or so later as we stood beside the bike, with one of the wounded boys sitting in the side car, the unit filed by us on its way to our village, a distance of 16 kilometers. They were singing.

"We should have done that in Stalingrad in '42," said Leiwitz; "march back singing while we still had the chance."

"That's easy for you to say, Hans. I was the one who gave this retreat order."

"I'll hand you your last cigarette when they tie you to the stake," he said, and then put his hand lightly on my shoulder.

"Don't worry. It was the only correct decision. Besides, you can always blame it on me as your advisor."

"Fine," I said, "that way we can give each other our last cigarettes." I had little concern about my order. This had not been a panicky rout, but an orderly withdrawal of manpower from a project that was essentially finished. Still, it was reassuring to have the officer's backing should there be an inquiry.

"I owe you one, Hans," I said. "You didn't have to come out here with me."

"Forget it," he waved me off. "I was getting too soft, buried under my down quilt. Besides, what are friends for?" Just a few days later, that remark may have saved his life.

I sensed that *Oberleutnant* Leiwitz did not share my degree of loyalty to Adolf Hitler, despite the fact that he had also joined the Hitler Youth voluntarily in the '30s. I had run across several front line soldiers with a similar, cynical appraisal of authority. It seemed like a form of battle fatigue. Despite the loss of his arm, Leiwitz was never depressed. He would have been insulted by pity.

About six kilometers southeast of our village, hidden in the dense forest, was a launching site of our vaunted V 2, the world's first ballistic missile. Like its predecessor, the V 1, it was the creation of Wernher von Braun and his fellow scientists at Peenemünde on the shores of the Baltic Sea. The V 2 could hurl a one-ton warhead against Britain or the Allied bases on the continent at supersonic speeds which made it virtually impossible to shoot down. It was a formidable weapon, despite its problems with hitting small targets such as factories or airfields. It was primarily an instrument of *Vergeltung* or revenge as its initial implied--tit for tat against the merciless Allied bombing of our cities. Its success in breaking the morale of the British people was as ineffective as the destruction of German cities had been in breaking ours. These Allied actions confirmed Dr. Goebbels' assertion that the enemy had marked all of us, Nazis or no Nazis, for extinction.

If we had beat the Americans to atomic weaponry, Germany would have won the war. Hitler would have launched swarms of V 2's equipped with nuclear warheads against all our enemies, even at the risk of killing half their populations. It is perhaps the supreme irony that Hitler may have invited his own demise by chasing gifted Jewish scientists such as Albert Einstein out of Germany as racial "inferiors." Would there have been Jewish Nazis if Hitler had designated only gypsies, for instance, as racially tainted? Very likely, for there were tens of thousands of conservative, nationalistic Jews who longed for a strong leader as much as other Germans.

Initially we were elated to watch the fiery tails of the V 2 missiles as they climbed steeply into the sky that early September of 1944. But soon the daily launchings became not only routine, but a source of anxiety, for they attracted enemy aircraft by the score. The launching site itself had not yet been bombed, since it was difficult to locate in the dense woods. No missile was ever sent aloft when Allied planes could have spotted its fire plume, but spies along the French border must have radioed the general location to the Resistance within the first week of launching. Merely bombing countless square miles of forest was a waste of men and material, however, for only massive direct hits by aerial mines or heavy bombs could put a fortified site out of action. For any civilian to enter the woods was suicidal. Even if he survived the ring of concealed mines, he still had to evade sharpshooters positioned in tree tops.

One of my units was working along the western rim, excavating an infantry trench, when two boys chased an errant bull calf into the underbrush. There was a dull boom, followed by shrieks of pain. The calf, guided by its lucky star, galloped wild-eyed back to the meadow, but one youth lay in a pool of blood, his right leg blown off. For that, I busted the unit commander down to squad leader. Eager for some fresh steak, he had allowed the hunt to continue beyond the skull and cross bones signs marked *Achtung Minen*! After that, there was no trespassing.

One early afternoon a V 2 lost power directly after takeoff and exploded in a potato field west of the forest. I was headed back from Perl on my motor bike when the shock wave hit me in the face like a warm blast of wind, although I was at least three kilometers away. My fear that the projectile had landed in the middle of our unit abated as I got closer. The plume of the earth-shaking concussion rose well to the south of our nearest project. As I approached, half a dozen farmers stared in awe at the 15-foot deep crater. One elderly bearded man sat pale-faced on the ground. He had been closest to the site of the impact, plowing his field with a team of horses.

"I was more than a kilometer away," he mumbled, "...was thrown two wagon lengths." He had been fortunate. One of his horses was still running in circles, occasionally stopping to shake its head. Very likely it had lost part of its hearing. A shard of metal had cleanly sheared off the head of its mate. I didn't want to go near it. I was no longer touched by the sight of human corpses, but I didn't want to look into the glazed eyes of a dead horse.

Minutes later a *Luftwaffe* truck came roaring up, followed by a green Mercedes in which were seated two *Luftwaffe* officers and two members of the *Gestapo*, the latter clad in their usual leather coats and felt hats. While the officers descended into the crater, the *Gestapo* men deployed most of the dozen soldiers around the huge hole and then turned to us with undisguised hostility.

"How in the hell did you get here so fast?" demanded the taller one. "Are you all from the village?" The farmers nodded.

"Did anybody pick up anything?" asked the *Gestapo* man. Shortly he came over to me and made an attempt to smile when he saluted. "*Heil Hitler, Unterbannführer.* Did you see anybody collecting souvenirs?" It seemed like a stupid question. What would anybody want with a bomb fragment? I shook my head.

"I'll get back to you in a couple of minutes," he said. "Let me get rid of these clods first." He and his partner asked each farmer for his identity card and took down their names. Such was the reputation of the *Gestapo* that none of the farmers asked to see their interrogators' authorizations, but the man who had lost his horse asked if the *Luftwaffe* were going to pay for it.

"Frankly, I don't give a shit about your horse. We all have to make sacrifices. Put in a claim for it with your Party chief. Besides, you can always eat it, can't you?" He was still grinning when he turned back to me, and instantly I disliked him. It was obvious he didn't like animals and had no idea of the bond between a farmer and his horses.

"I need to know your name and your location, *Unterbannführer*," he said curtly.

"Fine," I said politely. "I need to know yours. I have no idea who you are. The enemy listens in, remember?"

"Goddamn it, *Unterbannführer*, let's not play games," he said, but he produced the oval, silver disk with the eagle and the Swastika on one side and the inscription *Geheime Staatspolizei* on the other. His number was stencilled on it. He looked at my Hitler Youth pass and handed it back.

"Stationed where?"

"The parish at Dirndorf is my headquarters. I'm the sector commander." That interested him.

"Really? Don't you work with *Oberleutnant* Leiwitz? He's your construction coordinator isn't he?" I was astounded.

"Have you met him?"

"Not yet," he smiled. "What do you think of him?"

"He's a genuine hero; my boys worship him."

"That's nice," he said. "Do you worship him too?"

"That's a little strong, but I consider him my friend. Without him we'd never finish our project on time. He really knows his stuff."

"Quite a testimonial," he replied. "But is he a good National Socialist? Surely as his close buddy you know that. You share things, don't you? Have a little fun and get drunk? Let off some steam and talk? You know what I mean?" His eyes had become sharp.

"Not exactly. I suppose you know he lost his right arm in Russia."

"So what? That traitor Stauffenberg who almost killed the *Führer* was a wounded hero too, wasn't he?"

"I think it's an insult to Leiwitz to compare him with a traitor," I protested.

"I hope so," he said, "for his sake. But you still haven't answered my question. Is Leiwitz a good National Socialist?"

"He doesn't belong to the Party, but neither do most officers his age. (Fewer than five percent of the *Wehrmacht* officers were Party members, as compared to more than nine percent of the general population.) I haven't the slightest reason to doubt his loyalty to Germany."

"That touches me deeply, *Unterbannführer*, but it could well be a heap of *Scheisse*. Just make sure you never forget your obligation to report any remarks against the *Führer* or Germany to the proper authority."

"Do you doubt my loyalty to the *Führer*?" I demanded, suddenly incensed. "I was decorated by him just a few days ago."

"You were?" That impressed him. "Did he give you that War Service Cross himself?" I nodded, doubting very much that the *Führer* had ever spoken to *him* in person.

"You'll keep this conversation to yourself, *Unterbannführer*. Do I have your word on that? Also, of course, this mishap with the V 2 is not to be mentioned. The enemy does listen in, doesn't he?" He was almost cordial now, but it seemed silly not to talk about the explosion. It must have been heard at least 20 kilometers inside France.

"You have my word," I said. "*Heil Hitler!*"

There were many times after the war that I wished I had not kept my interrogation by this *Gestapo* official a secret from Hans Leiwitz. If he had learned through me, his friend, that the *Gestapo* was interested in talking to him, it could possibly have saved his life. After all these years, I still don't know if he had any inkling that he was under surveillance. His occasional frivolous talk would indicate he didn't; but then, he trusted me.

I had one more chance to warn him, and I let that slip by also. By then, I too had begun to suspect his loyalty to the *Führer*. The *Gestapo* officer's admonition not to forget my duty in reporting enemies of the state, came back to haunt me sooner than I anticipated.

A few days after the explosion of the V 2, I unexpectedly witnessed a gruesome execution. In hindsight, this event might have become a moral turning point had I not been so fanatic. What it did was awaken in me a deep sense of pity for one of our victims. Ironically, though, by the standards of warfare, this victim was guilty.

The bridge at Remisch was a major supply artery between Germany and the front. Nobody crossed it without being thoroughly checked, which doomed three partisans who were caught trying to disguise themselves as foreign workers on their way to Germany. The two young men were French, but their driver and the owner of the car was a Luxembourg physician in her 30s. Shooting the two Frenchmen caught with German weapons didn't bother me in the least; it was her death that touched me.

Toward noon that day I had taken a brief cigarette break in the inviting stillness of the local cemetery on my way to the construction site. As I sat amid the solitude, an *SS Untersturmführer*, a second lieutenant, and three soldiers marched in with the partisans, placed them against the cemetery wall and methodically submachine gunned them. Unlike the two men to whom she was handcuffed, the woman did not die instantly. As she lay on her back, her wide eyes focused on me for several seconds in an unmistakable, terrified plea for help. I felt a surge of relief when the *SS* officer blew off the top of her head with a single pistol shot. What had she expected of me?

Long after the soldiers had left, I stared at the bloody mass from which her small nose and chin protruded, the only recognizable features of a face which would, for years, return so often in my nightmares. Sometimes the face assumed a familiar, beloved voice and I occasionally woke up screaming, "What do you want from me, Fabianne? Why did you have to get mixed up with partisans?"

That evening, after a disturbing conversation with Hans Leiwitz, Fabianne took me for the first time to her uncle's boat shed along the winter-deserted shore of the Mosel. I could not bring myself to tell her of the execution of her countrywoman. Our relationship was still fragile and could not have withstood the strain of an accusation, which the woman's brutal death might well have caused. But it would have helped my guilt to tell of my feelings of pity for an enemy of the Fatherland.

"You're not your usual, exuberant self, Ali," said Fabianne, as we spread the blanket on the stern of the small fishing boat.

"Did you have a tough day? You weren't near that V 2 that exploded were you?"

"You're not supposed to know it was a V 2, Fabi. That's top secret, but I bet it rattled windows all over Remisch. No, I was in no danger." The face of the dead woman still swam before my eyes as I traced every feature of Fabianne's face with my finger and rested my cheek against hers.

"Ali," she whispered, "the war will be over soon. Whether you win or lose, just survive for me, will you please, *Liebchen*?" I felt the salt of her tears.

"Don't cry, Fabi," I said. "We won't lose and I won't die. We'll be married and live on a *Luftwaffe* base somewhere in Greater Germany."

"Ali," she smiled, pulling me on top of her, "you Germans don't have much territory left." Seeing the look on my face, she laughed aloud. "I don't care if you become *Herr* Hitler's private pilot, *Liebchen*. I'll follow you anywhere."

As it evolved, we had only two more evenings together in the boat shed, the tangy smell of which will forever be a part of my memory. It was near midnight when I reached my quarters on that long day of the execution and found *Oberleutnant* Leiwitz asleep in an easy chair. I shook his shoulder.

"What's the matter?" I inquired. I was still disturbed by our meeting that afternoon when I had stormed out of his office in a rage. Riled by the execution, I had gone from the cemetery back to his quarters instead of continuing to our construction site, and described to Leiwitz the scene I had witnessed. Leiwitz had not only laughed at me for being so shaken by a mere execution, but in a sudden outburst asked me if I were aware that our "glorious" *Führer* was embarked on a mission of genocide.

"Our regime is killing Jews and other so-called subhumans by the thousands every day, and you and I are going to be held accountable one day for this insanity," he had yelled, beet-red with emotion. With as much dignity as I could muster, I had stalked out of his office, severely shaken by this treasonous slander. My duty was quite clear: despite my personal attachment, I had to file a report to our headquarters in Trier. It was one thing to overlook a less than respectful attitude toward our leaders, or to laugh at a joke about *der Dicke*, our fat *Reichsmarschall* Hermann Göring, but this was clearly slander against the man who held the destiny of our nation in his hands.

Oberleutnant Leiwitz was no fool. Shortly after his outburst, he had come out to the tank barrier and requested to meet with me. It must have been humiliating for an officer of his stature to plead with a boy, but he had no choice if he wanted to live. His timing was excellent. The feelings of torment and ambivalence that the execution had evoked in me, combined with the love of a beautiful woman who was non-German had, for the first time, opened a slight breach in the wall of unquestioning fanaticism that governed my actions.

Now, as he crawled out of his chair, I could see that there was more to discuss. "Despite the late hour, I hope you'll listen to me, Alf," said Leiwitz. "If you want to have me shot later, so be it," he grinned, not really joking.

"Go ahead," I said, already relieved by his sincerity. "We have all night." And so it happened that *Oberleutnant* Hans Leiwitz became the first man in authority to risk his life by telling me the truth and trying to shatter my naive image of a powerful, humane Fatherland. He didn't succeed completely on that night or the few that followed, but I was relieved that his disillusionment with Hitler had not tainted his feelings for the country we both loved.

"What I resent so much, Alf," he said, "is that all our· very genuine enthusiasm was so badly abused." He pointed to the stump of his arm. "I'd gladly give the other one and my head if I could deny what I saw with my own eyes." He then told me unemotionally of a mass execution of Jews that he had witnessed near Kiev in Russia shortly after our invasion of 1941. At first he thought it might have been an isolated incident, but unlike tens of thousands of German officers who closed their eyes to the more brutal aspects of the war in the east, Leiwitz began to question and to investigate. He never mentioned Auschwitz, but he spoke of "*SS* killing centers in Poland" to which hundreds of transports were sent from as far away as Paris, Amsterdam and Budapest.

I couldn't accept the enormity of what he was trying to tell me. For one thing, much of his evidence was based admittedly on hearsay and on undisclosed sources. For another it didn't make sense to me that we would kill masses of people when we were so desperately short of labor and had already impressed millions of foreigners into our work force. Most important, though, I did not want to believe that Germans were committing genocide. Brutal warfare, yes. Our enemies were equally adept at that. This had become a total war, waged on civilians and soldiers alike, but still it was not total, programmed annihilation.

When Leiwitz and I parted near dawn, he no longer had to fear that I would report him to Hitler Youth headquarters or the *Gestapo*. At the very least, I reasoned, his heroism entitled him to a case of battle fatigue. If he had been a traitor, he could have deserted on numerous occasions. Our relationship did, however, change. I did not like being disillusioned and I developed a nagging resentment toward him. That may have been the reason I never mentioned to him my encounter with the *Gestapo* official.

Paranoid suspicion of everybody was a *Gestapo* trait. Before I had been accepted as an officer cadet for the *Luftwaffe* in 1943, a uniformed *Gestapo* captain had questioned me about my feelings toward the Pope, because I had been an altar boy. It had never occurred to me that there might be a conflict of loyalty. He wasn't too amused when I pointed out that not only the *Führer* himself but 25 percent of the prewar *SS* had been baptized Catholics. He was undoubtedly miffed that I preferred the *Luftwaffe* to his Black Knights. The soldiers of the wartime *Waffen SS* were fearless, elite fighters and possessed by a great sense of camaraderie. Their officers and men mingled as equals despite their discipline, a marked departure from the Prussian tradition of a distinct, socially superior officer caste much like that of the British. Hitler, the lowly corporal of World War I, wanted his *Wehrmacht* to be an army of equals despite necessary differences of rank, but only the *SS* and the Hitler Youth reached that degree of social assimilation. At every promotion it was impressed upon me that we were only leaders, not superiors, despite the dogma of unquestioning obedience by which we lived. It was not surprising that one of the most suicidally aggressive *Waffen SS* divisions was named *Hitlerjugend*. It consisted largely of teenagers, former leaders of the Hitler Youth, of whom only 500 of the original 10,000 were still able to fight when Germany surrendered.

Our work on the *Westwall* was ending and it appeared that we could move out before our unarmed units fell prey to a sudden enemy offensive. Night after night our own forces were moving up to the bunker line under the perfect cover of the miserable weather. There was a general air of optimism, a nearly palpable feeling that after the disastrous summer, the snows of winter would signal the turning of the tide.

My orders to return to my hometown arrived with my district leader, whom I hadn't seen since leaving Wittlich. *Bannführer* Wendt was in the entourage of Dr. Robert Ley, head of the German Labor Front, which had replaced all workers' unions by 1934. The heavyset, blue-eyed Ley, a Rhinelander like myself, was also the Party Organization Chief and controlled the appointments of thousands of local Party officials. He was close to the Hitler Youth and had founded the *Adolf Hitler Schools* in which promising members of the Hitler Youth between 12 and 18 could prepare themselves for careers in the Party. His most popular achievement, though, had been the huge *Kraft durch Freude* (Strength through Joy) enterprise. This program enabled tens of millions of workers to travel to foreign lands for minimal prices on government owned railroads or luxury liners. It also opened cultural vistas like the opera, concerts and lectures, previously the province of middle and upper classes.

Despite his reputation as an alcoholic (which hardly diminished his stature among working-class males) Dr. Ley was popular for the "bread and circuses" he dispensed to compensate for the dissolution of collective bargaining and strikes. The German Labor Front professed a paternal socialism which made the worker an equal member of German society. In exchange for economic security and social welfare, the monolithic organization of nearly 25 million members controlled all hiring and firing and set a low wage scale. That, of course, kept the big industrialists happy with the regime.

The German Labor Front owned vast properties including the Volkswagen factory. The "People's Car" was a classic example of fraud against the German people. It cost only 999 *Reichsmark* in 1938, but could be paid only in installments. Consequently this affordable and excellent car was never available to any German worker, for by the time the first purchasers had made full payment and were ready to take delivery on their cars, the nation was at war and total production facilities were turned over to the *Wehrmacht*. The payments were frozen in a "trust," which became worthless after the defeat.

I received a duplicate of the War Service Cross I. Class with Swords from Dr. Ley. He apparently didn't notice I was already wearing the one Hitler had given me. Secretly I had been hoping for the Iron Cross, a more prestigious decoration usually given for bravery, but I had to admit that so far I had not committed any acts of bravery except for ducking strafing enemy aircraft. My unit, though, had shot down a four-engine B 17, an American Flying Fortress. The huge bomber had been damaged as it entered Germany, and like so many stragglers, became an easy target. After several bursts of our three *Vierling* cannons, it had exploded over the horizon on French soil. Robert Ley pinned the Iron Cross on the gun crew leader's scrawny chest. He was fifteen.

Despite its brevity, the Labor Front chief's visit made our spirits soar. It signalled a successful end to nearly five months of back-breaking labor and for me, a welcome relief from unrelenting pressure. Two nights later I climbed aboard a train with half of the units under my command. The others would follow within a week.

As soon as Fabianne had seen my face the night before, she knew it would be our last two hours together. The suddenness was a relief. We were both crying when we embraced for the last time before I started the motor bike in front of the boat shed. I gave her six tins of meat wrapped in my undershirt. "I shall sleep with it every night, Ali," she sobbed, "until you return to me." I tore myself loose, kicked the engine into life and biting my lips, wondered if I would ever suffer more pain.

"*Au revoir, mon amour,*" she called, a sliver of moon dancing in her hair. A few months later I heard that women and girls in occupied countries who had become intimate with German soldiers were publicly shaved, spat upon and made to run through town under the taunting cries of "German whores!" Some of these women shared the fate of thousands of males who were summarily shot without trial as collaborators, although the toll of women killed was much lower. Frenchmen outdid themselves in blood purges to compensate for their own deep feelings of guilt. Although near war's end, almost everyone claimed to oppose us, the truth was that many more had collaborated. The Resistance grew by leaps and bounds after D-Day when our defeat seemed inevitable, but not before. During the Klaus Barbie trial of 1986, it was revealed that more than 300,000 French were indicted as collaborators; 39,000 were sent to prison.

Had it not been for Fabianne's insistence on never being seen with me in daylight, I might have worried more. She had even refused to give me her address for fear I might contact her. "I'll write to you as soon as the war is over," she had said. "Nothing will separate us again." I was sure of it.

On December 16th, the same morning I arrived back in Wittlich, Germany launched its last decisive battle of the war. We named it the *Ardennes Offensive*; our enemies called it the "Battle of the Bulge." For ten days, it filled me with unrestrained elation. The promise the *Führer* had made to us was about to be fulfilled.

Reprinted from **Am Ende das Chaos**

Bridge over the Mosel blown up along with a train by the retreating *Wehrmacht*, 1945.

Chapter Seven:

THE NOOSE CLOSES

I once met a GI who had been fighting on German soil for three weeks and thought he was still in France. I didn't laugh at him because I was then a prisoner, writhing in such depths of paranoid self-delusion that it made this simple Nebraska farm boy look like a paragon of pure logic by comparison. "Once we get to Germany," he promised, furiously chewing gum, "I'll get a hold of this asshole Hitler and string him up by his balls from the Eiffel Tower. That'll pay him back for making me slog my ass through mud all over Europe." At least he had the continent right!

Despite the overcast winter weather, the week before Christmas had been exhilarating. General Hasso von Manteuffel, the diminutive commander of the *5th Panzer Armee*, had rolled out of the barracks of Wittlich, less than 30 miles southeast of the Trier-Monschau sector where the monumental battle began. Although his soldiers were a mixture of veterans and fuzzy-cheeked adolescents, much less imposing than the victorious gladiators of the 1940 *Blitzkrieg*, they soon produced impressive results. Long columns of American prisoners of war trudged silently back through the icy streets of my hometown. After a two-day rest, the *Bannführer* had ordered me to organize all able boys and men between 15 and 65 into cohesive units of the *Volkssturm* as quickly as possible. He had forewarned me during his visit to the *Westwall* that my fervent hope of getting into a *Luftwaffe* fighter squadron would be deferred again for several weeks. Our *Bann* was so close to the enemy that we had little time left to "man the barricades," as he put it.

Our surprising assault had caught the enemy with his pants down and eased the pressure enough to organize the remnants of an army. One morning as I instructed 200 elderly, bedraggled civilians of Wittlich in the use of the *Panzerfaust* (our bazooka), I compared them to the well-fed Americans being marched by, guarded by a few grizzled, stiff-kneed members of the *Landwehr*, the Home Guard. I immediately ordered an about face and marched them out of view of the prisoners, lest they see the "strength" of our armed forces. Only our Hitler Youth units exuded any fighting spirit, and I wondered how an American tank commander might react to a 14-year-old boy pointing a bazooka at his turret. Most elderly members of the *Volkssturm* had no uniform, but were identified as soldiers by a black and white (sometimes black and red) arm band with the inscription *Deutsche Wehrmacht*. Although I viewed these "troops" with deep suspicion, I had no doubt about the Hitler Youth. Most would fight to the death if ordered.

I spent Christmas Eve, a clear, bitterly cold Sunday in 1944, in my ancient hometown, originally a Celtic settlement which had been conquered by Roman Legions under Vitellius 50 years before the birth of Christ. During Wittlich's long history, it had ruled and it had been pillaged, it had been forgotten and it had been honored with the status of a city in 1291 by King Rudolf von Habsburg, at the request of Archbishop Duke Boemund von Warnesberg. The population of Wittlich had been decimated by the plague and by the religious zealots of the "Thirty-Year War." The town had been held in serfdom by greedy princelings, had blossomed under Ducal Archbishops of the Holy Roman Catholic Church, and had been subdued by Napoleon's troops, one of whom stayed behind and became my ancestor.

At 2:30 that afternoon, I was crossing the cobblestoned marketplace when the clock on the medieval city hall struck twice. The sound vibrated in the air, mingling with the ominous drone of approaching aircraft. As I looked west, I saw a wedge of American Flying Fortresses at an altitude of no more than 3,000 feet, heading directly toward me. I counted 18 of the B 17s before heading into a dead run toward the nearest public air raid shelter, in the basement of the *Hotel Klosterschenke*. The lead plane released a white flare which we called the "Christmas tree," and it cascaded gracefully to the ground. This signal led the start of a bombing run. What all of Wittlich's invaders throughout history had never fully accomplished, took American planes as much time as it would a soldier to smoke a cigarette. The shelter was filled to its oaken beams with screaming women and children. While it was still reverberating from the last roll of earth-shaking explosions, I stared in disbelief at the luminous hands on my watch. Only eight minutes had passed, but I suspected that most of my hometown had been obliterated.

The hotel had received a direct hit, splitting its facade down the middle like a wedge of cheese. Spurred by the flames roaring above us, we feverishly dug our way out, leaving behind the corpse of an elderly woman. Her head had been cracked by a brick dislodged from the ceiling. My elation at having escaped turned to misery seconds later, as I stared in disbelief at the destruction. Rounding the bend of the river, I saw our beautiful farm a raging inferno. I had no doubt that my grandmother, my Aunt Maria, Aunt Luise and her two small daughters had been incinerated with our entire livestock. Our French prisoner of war George had probably escaped, for he had mentioned at lunch that he was going to visit fellow prisoners at a camp on the outskirts of the city.

Small German towns were usually not the target of enemy bombers, but as I looked dry-eyed at the flaming grave of my family, I realized that our offensive had caused their deaths. Wittlich was not only a garrison town, but a major traffic junction and supply line to the front. How I cursed myself for not having foreseen that this first clear day since the launching of our attack would bring out the Allied air forces in over-whelming numbers. When I had glimpsed those first massive bomber hulks on their way into Germany that morning, I should have urged my family to take shelter. Swarms of fighter bombers this close to the battle would attack anything moving.

I was amazed at my own callousness in those first few minutes. It even crossed my mind that I didn't have to dig for their bodies. The intense heat of burning grain would consume all flesh. I was wrong. Two weeks later a squad of French prisoners of war dug through the layer of rubble and found the carcasses of 20 head of cattle and three horses, incinerated in their stalls. Lying next to a calf was the blackened upper torso of our 13-year-old land service boy Fred. He lived in another part of Wittlich, but as part of his daily duties had come to clean out the stable on this Sunday.

He became the only human casualty of our household, because a miracle had happened. Our neighbor, Hans Breuer, was home on furlough from the Eastern Front, shrapnel having sliced into his left upper arm. He had been given two weeks to recover, but alarmed by the thunder of approaching B 17s, he had run out on the street. As an experienced front line soldier, he didn't need to see the flare to realize the bombers were about to attack. He yelled at the top of his lungs to his family and broke the window to our living room with his fist. My grandmother confessed later that she had thought he was drunk, and then his words sunk in. "For Christ's sake, *Frau* Heck," he screamed, "drop everything! Get to the power station as fast as you can. Don't waste a second. Ami planes are about to drop a load on us!"

He, his family and mine made it into the city power station shelter directly across the street, but only by seconds. *Herr* Hollen, the man on Sunday duty, was caught by the first explosion as he was shutting the steel manhole cover to the shelter stairway. Hans told me that *Herr* Hollen had sacrificed his life waiting a few seconds for Fred, who had looked out from our stable door, apparently dumbfounded by the commotion. The delay had cost him his life and that of the man who was frantically waving his arms to attract him. It took us seven hours to dig our way to the 14 people trapped in the shelter. Like our farm, the power station had been caught in a "carpet" of bombs and collapsed, fortunately without burning. The raid had destroyed our only fire station and all its equipment, so the fires burned unchecked for days.

Our other neighbor, Andreas Kaspar, shook me out of my death watch and told me that our families were possibly alive under the twisted rubble of the power station. Minutes later, we were digging frantically. It was near midnight when we pulled my grandmother from the drainage canal into the bitter cold air. Tears of relief streaked the dust on her face, and then she looked around. The flames were roaring over the mountain of rubble that had been more than her life's work.

There was an unwritten, unacknowledged rule that the *Gestapo* did not arrest anyone for making remarks against the regime during the first hours after an air raid. People in their grief often lashed out at authority and then became silent, terrified of their sudden recklessness. The stream of vulgarity toward our *Führer* that flowed from my grandmother's mouth shook me to the core. For a full minute, she appeared insane, as if she had regressed into the body of a medieval witch; and then she sank to the ground wailing, clawing the frozen earth. That was her moment of truth and its very savagery restored her to her usual stoicism. I would never again see her in such despair. My moment of truth came two days later. We had been stacking bodies in the church for half the night and all day, some so badly mangled that no identification could be made. A few were children, even infants. One was my beloved nun Maria Aureliana, who had taught me to be an altar boy. I made the sign of the cross over her broken body, mumbling a quick "Hail Mary." There was no tear. Like a soldier, she had died for Germany.

Two days after the raid, much of Wittlich was still smoldering and most of its 9,000 inhabitants spent their days in the forest, fearing another attack. The air was filled with the sound of enemy aircraft, on the prowl for anything that moved. A dozen B 17s had returned on Christmas and demolished the railway station at Wengerohr, four kilometers south of us. Wengerohr, where I had spent my happiest flying days, was a small but strategic rail junction on the main line to Luxembourg and France.

Strangely, the American bombers that had blown up our farm had, despite perfectly clear conditions, missed the huge rectangle of *Wehrmacht* barracks. A complete infantry regiment numbering 900 men was stationed there, ready to move up to the front. While 69 townspeople lost their lives on Christmas Eve, no soldier received as much as a scratch. Many years after the war, I read a notation in the war log of the Eighth American Air Force which had been stationed in Britain. On that Christmas the contingent had launched an incredible 2,000 bombers against Germany, of which I had counted only the first 18 Flying Fortresses before diving into the shelter. Wittlich had been raided by 63, which bore out the story of our prisoner George, who had counted the planes from the trench at the prisoner of war camp. Surprisingly, the camp had lost only a few panes of glass.

I was out inspecting the smoldering ruins of our farm that Christmas day when the aircraft which had destroyed Wengerohr, unhampered by as much as a single cannon blast from our side, wheeled and headed west. They flew directly over my head at no more than 2,000 feet, as if they were on a sightseeing excursion. In a sudden, childish impulse, I pulled my pistol and fired the whole eight-round magazine at the lead plane. There wasn't the ghost of a chance that a single bullet would come close, but it made me feel better. And then I found the body of my dog Prinz.

A few minutes before the raid I had patted the shepherd, who went into happy hysterics every time I returned home. I had almost taken him with me, for dogs were always welcome in German pubs, but for some reason did not. The very first blast must have hurled Prinz more than 50 yards out of the farm yard, a place he never left on his own. The dog's body was partly covered by a smoldering beam which had incinerated it. I buried Prinz in the earth softened by the heat of the fire, then knelt alone beside the grave and sobbed uncontrollably for a long time.

Prinz's death had done to me what the loss of any human never achieved--because of its very senselessness, it momentarily cracked the armour of my soul. I had long since become immune to the brutality and death which were part of my daily life. But animals were not soldiers and they had not sworn an oath of unconditional obedience. Prinz and my horse Felix, now also charred to the bone, had been my closest companions.

As I staggered to an upright position, I looked around furtively, relieved that no one had observed my weakness. Beginning that bleak, cold Christmas day, I conceded to myself what was high treason--that Germany could no longer win this war. After the Christmas attack, I was prepared to write off my home province and all remaining territory of the Rhine. I later learned to my surprise that my *Bannführer* shared this opinion. I was not, however, ready to accept unconditional surrender or total defeat. I still harbored an illusion shared by thousands of German officers at the onset of *Götterdämmerung*--that the Americans would sustain so many casualties crossing the Rhine, that they might negotiate an armistice.

Two days after the devastation of Wittlich, our Ardennes Offensive ground to a halt. Under cover of night, ambulances transported hundreds of casualties into the barracks of my hometown. I had seen wounded soldiers before, but most of these men were broken in spirit as well. One morning as I marched a unit of elderly *Volkssturm* fighters past the hospital windows, some of the walking wounded stared at us and then tapped their foreheads with their index fingers. "Hey, *Opa*," yelled one to an elderly man carrying a World War I rifle without a bolt, "you going to hit the Amis on the head with your stick?"

That afternoon, *Bannführer* Wendt took me to a briefing with *Kreisleiter* Dr. Hurtger, the Party leader of our county, whose responsibility it was to assist us in the defense of our district. Dr. Hurtger always looked impressive in his gold-braided uniform, unlike the other "Gold Pheasants," for he maintained a trim, healthy figure. Today as he rose from his leather armchair, he nearly fell on his face. He was dead drunk. "*Heil Hitler*, gentlemen," he stammered, his eyes trying to bring us into focus. "How is the war going?" And with that, he crashed over the table and buried his face in his elbow. "My God," he sobbed, "what the hell happened since 1940? We're finished. *Alles Scheisse*." The blood shot to Wendt's face.

"You drunken *Schweinhund*" he growled. "Pull yourself together. If I find you like this tomorrow, I'll blow your head off." Wendt strode silently past two members of Dr. Hurtger's staff, barely returning their salute. They were packing crates.

"Do you suppose the *Kreisleiter* is planning to establish himself east of the Rhine, *Bannführer*?" I asked, not sure how the stern Wendt would take my question. Recently, he had started to single me out from the four leaders who held equal rank, presumably for my service on the *Westwall*. But Wendt had never invited easy familiarity, and to my surprise, he laughed.

"Of course he is. And when the time comes he'll have orders to that effect, so I won't even have the pleasure of putting him up against the wall for cowardice." No words could have demonstrated better the rift between Party and Hitler Youth, and our ascent to power. By 1945, we thought of ourselves as the elite of Germany, not the befuddled functionaries of a defunct apparatus. Our very fanaticism contained an ingredient of purity, for it was free of opportunism. "By the way," Wendt added casually, "it's likely that all of us will end up on the fortifications along the Rhine."

"We're fighting a rear guard action, then, and the Amis will take Wittlich?"

"I'm afraid so. Once they're through the *Westwall*, nothing can stop them from reaching the Rhine. It would be stupid not to face that fact." He put his hand on my shoulder.

"Don't advertise it to our units. We don't want to break their fighting spirit, such as it is. We must show the enemy that we're determined to defend each foot of German soil with our blood, even in retreat. Each Ami we kill here is one less at the final battle on the Rhine." There it was, out in the open.

"I wonder how the Amis will treat the people of Wittlich," I said, trying to get used to this once treasonous thought.

"It won't be fun, but they're not murderous Bolsheviks, Alf, and we'll be back before long." Suddenly, he chuckled. "At least you don't have to worry about your farm or your animals, do you? All you can lose now is your life."

He was right. Thousands of German soldiers had lost their families in air raids and returned to the front, no longer caring if they lived or died; they had already experienced the worst. I never quite reached that state, but I came close, and I was beginning now to understand the unofficial motto of the *Waffen SS*: "Let's enjoy the war while it lasts, comrades, for peace is going to be hell."

It became difficult to take seriously the training of the *Volkssturm*. The older men were openly cynical about their fighting qualities and highly critical of our poor equipment. Their attitude was so sullen that we separated our Hitler Youth units from them. Occasionally, news would be posted of some grandfather being publicly executed by the *Gestapo* for trying to dodge his duty. I had no illusion about our own senior men. They feared the *Gestapo* more than the approaching Americans. My suspicion grew daily that many of my fighters couldn't wait to surrender.

On the Russian Front, however, few Germans felt anything but abject terror at the thought of falling into Soviet hands. For Hitler Youth leaders it meant certain, perhaps cruel death. In the eyes of the Russians, we were no better and perhaps more fanatic than the *SS*. A secret circular from our headquarters stated that even the Americans treated Hitler Youth leaders above the rank of captain very harshly. I doubted we would all be shot out of hand or castrated, as one propaganda missive by Dr. Goebbels claimed, but I had no desire to become an American prisoner wearing my Hitler Youth uniform. Suddenly, that chance became remote.

Two days after New Year's my long-awaited orders for the *Luftwaffe* came through. I was to report immediately to a small base near Kassel for flight duty. I had to conceal my elation from Wendt; finally I was free of a duty which had become decidedly onerous. As a parting gift, the *Bannführer* gave me a brand new uniform complete with elegant boots and a leather great coat. (All my clothing had burned with our farm.) I left Wittlich at night on a hospital train loaded with casualties from the Ardennes. I carried a change of underwear and toilet utensils in the ample inner pockets of the coat, and felt like singing when the train began to roll east. Soon I would sit in the cockpit of an aircraft again, free from the worries of command.

The seven passengers in our compartment were lightly wounded, able to sit up. One wore a bloody turban around his head, and the others had their arms or legs bandaged. The compartment was blue with cigarette smoke and reeked of disinfectant, sweat and alcohol. The wounded were celebrating a "homeland bullet"--not bad enough to turn one into a cripple, but serious enough for evacuation back home. Only one of them bothered to return my salute, but they all stared at my brown uniform.

"Where are you going, *Herr Reichsleiter*?" asked a mean-faced lieutenant who wore the Iron Cross I. Class, mockingly giving me the very top Party rank, "to a conference in Berlin?"

"I'm on my way to flight training," I said. "I'm an officer cadet of the *Luftwaffe*. At least I will be, once I get to Kassel."

"Are you nuts, kid?" he laughed, handing me his cognac bottle. "Have you looked at the sky lately? All you see is *Scheiss* Ami planes as soon as you stick your head up. That's who stopped us during this little action, not their goddamn ground troops." He patted me on the knee and looked at his comrades. "What do you think, boys? Should I save him some time and put a nice, clean bullet through his leg?" They all laughed uproariously at what I considered a tasteless joke by a German officer, just short of treasonous. But the man had been wounded in the head; perhaps it had affected his judgement. The truth was, hundreds of German soldiers were summarily executed for self-inflicted wounds. Altogether 40,000 soldiers were sentenced to death for "treasonous" behavior, which could be as minor as advocating that it was "stupid" to continue fighting. Compare this figure of 40,000 to the sole American GI executed for cowardice, Private Slovik. I took a quick swig of the excellent cognac, handed the bottle back and settled into a corner. Within minutes after the train started to roll, their hilarity subsided and they began to doze as if commanded. Most front line soldiers had learned to snatch sleep whenever possible.

The train jolted to a halt two hours later in the pitch-black safety of the Kochem tunnel. I heard the drone of many aircraft engines and the muffled sound of explosions. Koblenz, the major transportation center at the confluence of the Mosel and Rhine rivers 20 kilometers east, was under attack despite the heavy overcast. The Americans were determined to stop our supplies to the front even if only one of 50 bombs found its target. It was near dawn and I wondered if we would make it to the other side of the Rhine before daylight. The air became thick with coal dust, which meant that our locomotive was inside the tunnel under steam. One by one the soldiers awoke and started to cough. A wine bottle circulated. Suddenly, two ghostly stabs of white illuminated the darkness outside our window and somebody yelled in a high-pitched voice: "Halt, or I'll shoot!"

The lieutenant pushed down the window and we crowded around him, just as a Field Gendarmerie Police soldier fired a submachine gun burst into the back of a man trailing a long snake of a bandage. The other policeman illuminated the scene with his powerful flashlight. "Just as I thought," we heard him call out to his comrade who had killed the escapee. "The *Schweinhund's* a deserter. Must have sneaked on the train. Hasn't got a scratch on him."

He rolled the dead man on his back and unwound the rest of the bandage from his head. Sure enough, there wasn't a sign of a wound. I was indignant that the deserter wore the insignia of a *Luftwaffe* antiaircraft sergeant. Was our morale so bad that non-commissioned officers of my own service were turning into cowards? To my surprise, the tough lieutenant almost seemed to regret that the deserter had been caught. "Poor bastard," he said to nobody in particular. "The *Scheisse* just got too high for him." And then he grinned at me. "You better have your marching orders ready for these assholes, kid. You don't have a scratch on you either. You sure you're on your way to a base? Not establishing a rear headquarters on the other side of the Rhine, are you?" he chuckled.

"How dare you?" I asked, but he merely waved his hand. "Forget it," he said, "you have all the makings of a future dead hero. *Heil Hitler!*" They all laughed.

When the train crawled out of the tunnel, we greedily inhaled the cold, snow-laden air. Not even hospital trains clearly marked with huge red crosses were safe from enemy strafing runs. But this one carried a number of American wounded who had fallen into our hands. It was bound for Heidelberg, the best possible destination for any soldier. The Allies knew that many of their casualties were treated there and didn't launch major bombing raids against the city. Heidelberg survived virtually unscathed and became the headquarters of the American Military Occupation after our surrender.

I changed trains in Koblenz which, like most other sizable German cities, was turning into a mountain of rubble. When I arrived in Kassel later that night, the degree of destruction was about as bad. If anything, the railroad station looked worse with its twisted beams of blackened steel pointing into the sky. Most of the vast, glass-domed roof was gone, but the maze of rails was intact.

The small *Luftwaffe* base, just a few kilometers west of the city, seemed like another, orderly world, as yet untouched by a single bomb. The dozen buildings were divided by a high fence. Each section had its own hangars and runway with quite different functions, my side being the less glamourous. My 40 comrades and I had been picked primarily for our expertise as sailplane pilots, but shortly we discovered that we were vastly over-qualified for our future mission. We who had soared in the swirl of giant updrafts, able to equal Icarus, were condemned to fly in plywood boxcars filled with 13 sweating soldiers.

I was shattered when I saw the ungainly DSF-230, a stubby plywood duck with a plexiglass nose, armed with a single machine gun poking through the windshield. I wasn't going to win the Knights Cross in this thing. Couldn't it have been a *Messerschmitt* 109, or even better a *Focke-Wulf* 190 with its menacing radial snout, six machine guns and two cannons?

What hurt even worse was to look across the fence. Here, a few lucky bastards no better qualified than I, were training on an ME-262, the incomparable *Messerschmitt Schwalbe*, the "Swallow," the world's first operational jet fighter. Professor Willy Messerschmitt himself had delivered this advanced design to the field on the day of my arrival. The camouflage-painted, single seater with its twin turbojets had already become the terror of Allied bomber pilots. At 540 miles per hour, it outflew any escort fighter aircraft, although it was limited by its operational range of 500 miles. Professor Messerschmitt supposedly had improved its less than sturdy landing gear. As I watched it climb at the incredible rate of 4,000 feet per minute, I cursed my fate.

My favorite flying buddy Rabbit, who had been in a *Focke-Wulf* squadron since September, had already downed two American bombers. He would laugh himself silly at our plywood ducks. I hadn't heard from him since before Christmas, but I was confident he was on his way to becoming a new fighter ace.

I would live to regret this childish envy of my best friend. Rabbit, I later learned, was already dead when I arrived in Kassel. He had died on New Year's day 1945, with what was left of the *Luftwaffe* as a viable fighting force. To stem the impending disaster when our assault faltered during the Battle of the Bulge, Hitler ordered the *Luftwaffe* to call out all available pilots, despite the consequences. Nearly a thousand German planes made it into the air in a suicidal effort to bomb Allied bases in France, Belgium and Holland. The enemy admitted to the loss of 300 aircraft, hardly damaging to its vast arsenal. But our loss of 250 planes was the last deadly blow for an already comatose *Luftwaffe*. Some of our pilots were so green that they became hopelessly lost and even rammed each other. Rabbit died trying to attack an American bomber formation through its escort of P 51s. That's all his mother could tell me six months after the war. Neither his plane nor his body were ever identified.

Had it not been for my roommate, the "mad Count" *Leutnant* Franz von Ebersfeld, an ancient navigator of 19, I would have gone into a prolonged bout of self-pity over my new assignment. But Franz pointed out the obvious; although it was true that a sailplane pilot might be better qualified for learning to fly a jet, he still did not have the immense advantage of combat experience of those chosen few. I took an instant liking to Franz, although his undisguised criticism of our top leadership, especially *Reichsmarschall* Hermann Göring, made me very uneasy. I quickly learned that many *Luftwaffe* officers were quite disrespectful of authority, particularly when they were drinking, but only Franz told me bluntly that Hitler should have asked for an armistice after D-Day. There was a fatal flaw in his reasoning, though. Franz proposed that we continue fighting the Russians for he firmly believed the Americans and British would join us at the very end to defeat the Russians. It was our common goal, he believed, to stifle the threat of Communist hegemony in Europe, which had already surpassed the danger of Nazism in the minds of some. Like many others, I heartily embraced that theory, for it promised the only alternative to our impending defeat. As the scion of an aristocratic *Junker* family which had supplied officers to kings and kaisers for centuries, Franz detested Communism as the rule of the common mob. His opinions were unabashedly arrogant, yet I couldn't fault his contention that American capitalism and British monarchy were threatening to the Soviets. Josef Stalin had, after all, still supplied us with oil and grain *after* we had defeated France and the British forces on the continent in 1940. Stalin, in particular, harbored an almost paranoid distrust of his American and British Allies. He maintained, for instance, that Rudolf Hess had embarked on his bizarre flight to Scotland in May of 1941 with Hitler's blessing. The aim: to free Germany from the threat of a British attack while launching the invasion of Russia in June of 1941.

On January 12, when Russia launched its long-dreaded final assault on Germany across a broad front from Leningrad to the Carpathians, Franz' father shot himself rather than leave his vast holdings in East Prussia. His wife and teenage daughter made it safely to their ski lodge in Bavaria. The idea of reclaiming his ancestral home within a year had become an obsession with Franz. Unlike most of us who dreaded any assignment to the Eastern Front, he was trying to avoid the west. Franz viewed our coming orders to glide behind the American lines and bring pressure on the Americans as nonsense; it would merely prolong them from joining us at the Rhine.

During the night of February 13, 1945, 773 Lancaster bombers of the Royal Air Force set historic Dresden on fire. Daylight attacks by a total of 600 bombers of the Eighth U.S. Air Force in the following two days, finished the worst devastation of any German city during World War II. We at the base received details withheld from the general population.

Although the first number of 200,000 people incinerated in the horrific fire storm has now been down scaled to 125,000, the raid still stands as the pinnacle of Allied mass murder by air. The city was not of strategic importance and, as the Allies well knew, was jammed with refugees fleeing the onslaught of the Red Army. If the intent was to destroy the resistance of the German people and thus save Allied lives, it achieved just the opposite. We at the base were obsessed to get at the enemy with anything that could fly. This raid had lent credence to Dr. Goebbels' exhortation that no German, Nazi or otherwise, could expect any mercy from the enemy.

We were still numb from the news of Dresden when our training course ended with the announcement that we would not be used after all on the Western Front. Franz and I were jubilant, if for different reasons. I was certain we would quickly be sent across the fence to do some real flying. During the last snowy days we had already put in several hours in *Messerschmitt* 109s. The speed of the *Messerschmitt* 109 *Gustav* was quite a switch from flying a sailplane, even in a steep dive, but we had the quick, natural reflexes of young pilots. The plane's severe torque to the right made take offs tricky in gusty wind conditions, but the craft's quick turning ability was very reassuring. With the insolence of youth, I was sure I could take on any American P 51 after a few more hours of training.

Then, for the second time in three weeks, my hopes were crushed. It appeared the Fatherland wasn't impressed by my potential as a future ace. Despite my almost tearful plea to be assigned to flight duty, any flight duty, I was unceremoniously detailed back to the Hitler Youth. I wasn't alone; most of my comrades ended up in antiaircraft units or infantry trenches, but Franz got lucky. He was assigned to a *Messerschmitt* 110 "Destroyer" squadron near Berlin. The slow but powerful two-seater fighter aircraft were mainly used in night combat, not quite as one-sided as taking on swarms of daylight enemy fighters. Franz was so eager to engage the Russians that he left a day before the rest of us. In addition to a leather suitcase, he gave me a couple of silken uniform shirts and his ceremonial dagger, since I was still not completely outfitted.

Despite our relatively short time together, I felt as drawn to him as I had to Rabbit, for in spite of his cynicism, he loved Germany above all else. One evening I had caught him glancing at a picture of his hound dog with tears in his eyes, an emotion I understood very well. So many of our comrades had been killed that a bond to a dog was more permanent. Franz died in the skies over Berlin a month later, no doubt still under the illusion the Fatherland would live. His fate could well have been worse.

Ironically, I reached my highest rank in the Hitler Youth when our forces were beginning to evacuate Wittlich. Just two days after I returned home, still resentful that I was back rounding up units for the *Volkssturm*, the *Bannführer* was promoted to Hitler Youth commander of the entire mid-Rhine section, itself an indication that our territory had been written off. The paper strength of our *Bann* exceeded 6,000, of which 3,000 were girls exempt from fighting. In reality, the more than 50 villages and two towns of our district had no more than 900 Hitler Youth boys organized into the *Volkssturm*.

The major reason for this low turnout was the massive breakdown in communications after the Christmas air raid. Families dispersed in panic into the surrounding forests and could no longer be reached by radio broadcasts. We sent out teams to round up all males over 14, but the haul was meager. The *Gestapo* had its hands full looking for suspected adult deserters, and they let us do our own enforcing. I spent days signing orders to Hitler Youth members with detailed instructions to report to one of three training camps, but most remained undeliverable. In Wittlich, in particular, the homes were empty. Many years later in Chicago, my former classmate Rudolf Hein showed me the same form signed by my predecessor. The last paragraph stated that no excuse, even an enemy air raid, would be grounds for failing to report within 48 hours. Failure to comply would "draw the gravest consequences," a euphemism for the death penalty, clearly understood by every German. Rudolf decided to report to Camp Gillenfeld.

My meteoric rise from a rank comparable with an army captain, to that of *Bannführer*, equivalent to general, in a mere eight months was the best indication of our disintegration. There were no longer any seasoned leaders around. Had it not been for the caliber of Wendt, a tough army veteran, I might have suspected I was merely a scapegoat, doomed to die with a forlorn band. The *Bannführer* was brutally honest when he made me his "acting" successor. "I expect you to do what you can on our western perimeter, Alfons, but don't hang around longer than the last *Wehrmacht* units. When they head for the Rhine, you do the same, understand?" He laughed as I nodded glumly. "I'll bust you down a couple of ranks after the war, but this will give you a hell of an advantage should you decide to give up the *Luftwaffe* and make the Hitler Youth your career; you know that, don't you?" He handed me two silver oak leaves, the shoulder board insignia of a full *Bannführer*.

"I think I'll stick to my four pips," I said, slipping them into my pocket, "but I'll keep these as proof in case you get killed." He understood gallows humor and grinned appreciatively.

I used the few days remaining before his departure to visit our neighboring Hitler Youth district of Bitburg, which extended to the border of Belgium. There were no longer any German troops on Belgian soil, Bastogne having long since fallen to General George Patton. Bitburg itself was about to be overrun by the Americans. Unless a miracle happened, we were next in line of assault, and this was the only chance I had to gather some experience in deploying Hitler Youth forces against the enemy. When I returned after three days, I had fired a machine gun at American soldiers and tasted seconds of panic so intense that I now understood how soldiers could turn and run. But I had also overcome the natural feeling toward self-preservation, the taming of what we called "*der innere Schweinhund,*" the animal of cowardice.

The American attack by a few tanks and infantry platoons had been merely a probe of our defenses, but I was deeply impressed by the Americans' willingness to die as recklessly as we. I fired wildly at a GI who stood defiantly on the turret of a tank, coolly shooting his sub machine gun from his hip. And I felt a strange pang of regret when we cut him down from the comparative safety of our trench. His death seemed just as heroic and needless as those of the two Hitler Youth boys who had climbed atop our trench to aim their bazookas against the tanks.

The mood in the Hitler Youth headquarters in Bitburg paralleled my own. We were walking a tightrope, trying to decide when a quick march toward the Rhine would become strategically acceptable to our superiors, whoever they were. Whenever possible, Hitler Youth units were to be interspersed with seasoned *Wehrmacht* troops. The problem was that the front line fluctuated so crazily that the bunkers were the only way of identifying a line of defense. Armored troops moved in all directions, provided they had any fuel left. Soon the roads and fields were littered with hundreds of tanks and armored vehicles that had run out of gas. Frequently, the crews crowded together on a few trucks and headed east toward the Rhine for "re-assignment," but they were not about to stop for *Volkssturm* units, which they rightly considered more of a burden than an aid. As February drew to a close, the retreat of our troops from the Ardennes sector turned into a panicky rout, unless a commander were able to keep his units intact. The *Waffen SS*, with its *esprit de corps*, did not fall apart despite suicidal losses and units stayed together even when routed. The first soldiers to surrender usually belonged to the poorly trained green forces of the *Volksgrenadier* divisions which were hurled against the numerically superior enemy after just a few weeks of training. There was a certain safety in numbers when a whole platoon or company, or even a regiment of several hundred surrendered (which quickly became a daily occurrence on the Western Front), but it was deadly to be picked up as a straggler. Within minutes, a drumhead court of field police would pronounce and carry out the death sentence, usually by bullet but sometimes by hanging, as an added deterrent.

Fittingly, my last deployment of *Volkssturm* members of the Hitler Youth took place against the grisly backdrop of German soldiers dangling from trees. They had been caught, one by one, in a net of the *SS* Field Police just a few kilometers behind the front line. During these last grim months before the end, when a soldier could not produce orders justifying his presence away from his unit, the death sentence was imposed on the spot, usually with a *Genickschuss*, a single pistol shot in the neck. The bodies were often strung on trees with a sign "Deserter" or "Coward" displayed on the chest.

On the first or second day of March, I passed such an execution scene with 50 or 60 hand-picked members of a unit specially trained in firing the bazooka. The youngest was under 14. We all rode bicycles, with the long stems of the weapon tied to the frames. The lead rider carried the flag of our *Bann* as if we were on a camping trip. We reached the bunker line near the village of Hetzerath, about 18 kilometers west of Wittlich, in less than two hours and at a crossroad there, encountered the carnage. The faces of most boys turned pale as they gazed at the bodies dangling in the wind, and their lips moved as they read the inscriptions below the grotesque heads. Several retched.

The *SS* soldiers watched us calmly, but their sergeant called out, "Don't let this happen to you, boys! Fight for the Fatherland. *Heil Hitler!*" That made me angry.

"We don't need your goddamn lectures, Sergeant," I yelled. "You'd just better come with us to the bunkers yourself." He turned red, but his companions laughed and saluted us as we passed. Under the scrutiny of these executioners, we were like gladiators filing into a Roman arena for the fight to the death. Our option was to dangle from a tree in disgrace.

To these selected Hitler Youth fighters, the threat of execution for desertion was insulting; they had volunteered to form a special "alarm unit," a sort of commando group to be thrown into the breach at especially hazardous sections of the front. The bunker line near Hetzerath was sparsely manned by remnants of a *Volksgrenadier* division which had been driven into defense by an armored spearhead of the American Third Army. An attack was imminent within 48 hours, and what was needed most were men or boys trained in firing bazookas to stop the tanks.

The captain in charge of the two center bunkers overlooking the road was relieved to see us. Many of his soldiers were also teenagers and, unlike many *Wehrmacht* officers, it didn't bother him to sacrifice more children, if only to halt the enemy temporarily. He listened approvingly as I exhorted my charges to die if necessary so the Fatherland might live. That command would haunt me for many years, although as my duty, it seemed perfectly justifiable at the time. The shining eyes of those fanatic children, feverish with a mixture of fear and bravado, and consigned by me to be captured, wounded or killed, are still edged indelibly in my mind, especially since I didn't stay long enough to share their fate.

As they split up and filed into the steel mouths of the bunkers, they waved at me, flattered that I had shared their journey here on a bicycle. At that moment the deep, sensuous alto voice of Zarah Leander, one of our most popular torch singers, waved soothingly from a radio inside the bunker in her theme song which had consoled homesick German soldiers from occupied France to Stalingrad.

"I just know some day soon a miracle will happen...and we

will meet again...." I swallowed hard, touched by the schmaltzy sentimentality of the song's fake promise. As I pedalled away toward safety, I felt guilty for not having to face the American tanks with them. This unit was as good as dead, but its sacrifice might buy time. If fate had a miracle left for Germany, it had better produce it fast.

Two days later, the front of Hetzerath was pulverized by a massive American artillery bombardment, and the Sherman tanks began to roll. Most of our men were killed or wounded, although (I learned after the war) an estimated 400, including some Hitler Youth boys, fell back and did make it to the Rhine.

On the day of the assault I relinquished command of *Bann* 244 Wittlich to my unenthusiastic successor who was preparing to flee with the last soldiers of the garrison, many of them wounded. By nightfall, a single antiaircraft battery was left next to the main bridge over the Lieser river, not to defend Wittlich, but to keep the road open for an intermittent stream of fragmented units hurrying toward the Rhine. Explicit orders to report to the *Luftwaffe* base in Frankfurt had finally freed me from the Hitler Youth at its nadir. I boarded a truck heading south to the Mosel and then east across the *Hunsrück* Mountains to the Rhine crossing at Bingen.

The sky to the west occasionally flashed into a violent spectrum of color, but the growl of artillery fire was muffled and so distant that I couldn't distinguish detonations. Unlike the roads in East Prussia and along the Russian Front which were so jammed with panicky refugees that they hindered troop movement, here I did not see a single civilian fleeing from the Americans. Occasionally I spotted a vehicle flying the brown standard of a Party functionary, apparently authorized to retreat.

I had not bothered to say good-bye to my grandmother and aunts. They were now living in a wooden hut on a piece of our land three kilometers out of town. I had ordered a Hitler Youth team to excavate a slit trench behind the structure and cover it with oaken beams in case of artillery fire. Since Wittlich would not be defended, their chances of surviving were excellent, even if the Americans decided to level the town. But I no longer cared what happened to anybody, including my family.

Decades later I was asked if I had been afraid of getting killed during these last weeks of the war. "I think I was more afraid of living in a world I could not envision," I answered, "the terrifying world of a defeated Germany." Thousands of Germans about to fall into the hands of the Red Army committed suicide, often killing their families first. Many were not even Party officials, let alone Nazi war criminals, just ordinary people horrified by the tales of abject cruelty perpetrated by the conquerors. A quick bullet or a poison pill was preferable to rape and torture.

We on the Western Front had the advantage of facing a generally humane enemy with whom we had signed the Geneva Convention for the treatment of prisoners of war. Our conquerers here were people whom we had not treated as "racially inferior," and whose country we had not ravaged.

Some Nazi families still, however, chose death over American conquest. At one point near the end of the war, I did reach for my pistol, slide a round in its chamber and shove it in my mouth. But when the cold steel touched a gold filling in a tooth and sent a spasm through my body, instead of pulling the trigger, I heaved the weapon against the wall. By that time, I was in the deepest pit of desperation.

My moment of truth, the final admission that Germany and I were headed irrevocably for disaster, should have come during that night of the 80-kilometer journey to the base. I had just abandoned my own *Bann*, relieved that orders from the *Luftwaffe* had extricated me honorably. My successor, Peter Geisbüsch, stated it succinctly when we parted. "You have a knack Alfons, you lucky bastard, for getting out of the *Scheisse* just before it reaches your mouth." His point didn't sink in until a week later when, faced with imminent capture, I reached for my automatic, convinced my luck had finally run out.

I crossed the Rhine near Bingen at dawn on March 6, 1945, and made the remaining 20 kilometers to the base in the car of a taciturn *Luftwaffe* captain. Ordinarily anyone not attached to a sizable unit headed for a specific location was directed to a waiting truck for deployment along the trenches near the river's edge. An *SS* Field Police captain seemed amused by my orders to report to the Frankfurt base of *Luftflotte* III *without delay*. "Your flying days are over, my boy," he said almost kindly. "They'll ship your ass back to us anyway. We're all in the infantry now."

A motley assortment of men from various branches of our

armed forces, several junior officers among them, were about to board the next truck. I shrugged; like them I was in no position to challenge the _SS_, who performed a task that had become routine close to the front. I grinned at the unhappy face of a low-ranking Party official among the soldiers. The three uniformed bodies of executed soldiers dumped into the roadside ditch had apparently convinced him not to protest. The _SS_, like the Hitler Youth, regarded most Party functionaries as opportunistic wind bags.

For reasons that I never understood, I was exempted from boarding the _SS_ truck by the interception of a _Luftwaffe_ captain. My _Luftwaffe_ orders had come directly from Field Marshal Walther Model, the last military commander of Germany's forces on the Western Front and a brilliant defense tactician. I had met him during his brief inspection of the Wittlich garrison after Christmas, when we were still elated by our progress in the Ardennes battle. Before being appointed as Supreme Commander West in August of 1944 Model (called "the _Führer's_ fireman" for his ability to avert military disaster), had done the incredible. At least briefly, he had stopped the Soviet onslaught toward Warsaw and even stabilized the Eastern Front. Like most of our best generals, his authority was limited by Hitler's interference, especially the insane order not to withdraw under any circumstances. Model, however, was one of the rare commanders who had Hitler's trust. It was apparent in his remarks to us that he was a Nazi who supported the plan to hold out at all costs. The graying, stocky field marshal with his incongruously cherubic smile practiced what he preached. When his desperate efforts to coordinate our defenses on the right side of the Rhine failed, he disbanded headquarters, walked into the woods near Wuppertal on April 21, and shot himself rather than surrender.

During the half-hour ride to the base, I noticed that the _Luftwaffe_ captain wore the Knight's Cross and wondered if this were why he had been able to override the _SS_. He spoke only a few words, asking that I watch the cloudy sky for enemy aircraft through the rear window of the Mercedes. When he dropped me at the gate, we saluted each other and I thanked him. "Forget it," he smiled bleakly, "at best I bought you three days, Comrade. The _SS_ stallion is right; we'll all end up in the trenches. _Auf Wiedersehn!_" He was off by two days.

That evening I enjoyed superb food and wine in the luxurious officers' mess, deep in the bowels of the base headquarters. The serene, orderly bustle was in stark contrast to the frenzy a few kilometers west. Nobody seemed apprehensive that the enemy was literally knocking at the gate.

The spotlessly attired major who was to send me on my first and last wartime action for the *Luftwaffe*, was taken aback by my age. There were many 17-year-old officers in the *Wehrmacht* by 1945, but few had reached the rank of Hitler Youth *Bannführer*, albeit "acting." A brief conversation about my recent experiences must have convinced him that I was one of the dangerously fanatic adolescents who had been steeped in the Nazi ideology from the time he could walk and was thoroughly trapped in its power. Conditioned to follow any order, no matter how senseless, I was a walking time bomb, potentially fatal to myself and others. I would have unhesitatingly flown a *Messerschmitt* against a formation of enemy bombers or directed children to clear a minefield. This sensible officer made sure I did neither. Despite the odds, he had made up his mind to preserve me for whatever future there might be. He wanted me to be captured by the Americans as soon as possible, a notion so startling I never suspected it, although I should have become alerted by his final order.

He outlined on his map a small radar station just 12 kilometers west of Wittlich which was in imminent danger of falling into American hands. The 14 men were not as important as the advanced sensitive equipment, he stressed; unless a vehicle succeeded in getting to the station, the top secret machinery had to be blown up. Since I knew the area as well as the backyard of our farm, I was the logical man to attempt the rescue. "There's an Iron Cross in it for you, *Fähnrich,*" promised the major, "most likely the First Class if you can pull it off in time." We were still in radio communication with the station, he said, but the front was fluctuating so wildly that the Amis were already north of them in Bitburg. "You'll have to reach them before dawn tomorrow at the latest, but you may well find your way blocked even then. You game?" I desperately wanted to earn the Iron Cross I. Class, but his question implied no choice.

"Let's get started," I said, stepping up to the map to note the exact location. My total force consisted of three soldiers in a sturdy Mercedes truck with a heavy machine gun mounted beneath the tarpaulin on its flatbed. The hood was armor plated and able to withstand rifle and machine gun bullets.

"Don't take on any Sherman tanks," smiled the major when he handed me my orders. "If you run into them, you've either taken a wrong turn or gone too far."

"Then what?" I queried.

"Use your best judgment," he shrugged, "but don't become a dead hero. Get my drift? You don't have to fly into the ground."

I nodded, suddenly excited by the chance to retrieve our men from certain captivity. It still didn't compare to flying a fighter, but here was perhaps my only opportunity to earn the Iron Cross I. Class before the war ended. "By the way, *Fähnrich*," said the major, out of earshot of the three soldiers, "if you should succeed in getting the men out in time, (and between you and me that's a big 'if') get off in Wittlich and have the men proceed without you. I'm giving you four days furlough to look after your family." I was dumbfounded; the last thing on my mind at that moment was my family. When I started to protest, he became angry.

"I have given you a direct order, *Fähnrich*, clearly stated on page three of your documents. I don't want to see you back here before March 11. Is that understood?" I merely stared at him.

"Why March 11, *Herr Major*?"

"For Christ's sake boy, take the goddamn rest while you can. There's still time to die for the Fatherland after the eleventh. Besides, I don't know what the hell to do with you after this mission. Take off!"

"*Heil Hitler!*" I said, snapping the mandatory straight-arm greeting. But he merely lifted his hand silently to his cap, a hint of a smile on his lips, as if he were pleased with himself.

It was cold and drizzling as we set off toward the west. The setting sun broke through for a few minutes as we crossed the Rhine, tinting its small waves with a hint of red. "Blood," I thought. That weather extended into the morning of March 9 and stopped all enemy aircraft along the entire front. Consequently, the roads were alive with retreating German columns; nobody seemed headed toward what remained of the battle lines. Here and there an abandoned tank was ablaze, its gun barrel split by an explosive charge. With the surety of a sleepwalker, I directed the sullen corporal who was driving our vehicle across the Mosel river to a secondary road past Wittlich and into the Eifel Mountains. There was an occasional detonation of an artillery shell several kilometers west of us, but by the time we reached the burned-out village of Spang near midnight, we had only encountered one of our own *Panzers*, lying in ambush for the Americans under a camouflage of fir trees powdered by snow.

Three hours later we were headed east in a straight line toward the Rhine, 18 happy men perched on crates of radar equipment. The sullen corporal, who would just as soon have shot me in the back earlier, offered me a cigarette. "You sure know these roads, *Herr Leutnant*," he said, smiling ingratiatingly. "You'll be a hero back at the base."

"Sure," I said, "if I ever get there."

As I left the men at the crossroad near Wittlich and instructed them to drive on, it occurred to me that I had given the sullen, obsequious corporal the idea that I was a coward, about to desert. "I'm merely following my orders, you bastards," I yelled after them, as if they could have heard me. "I'm not running away!"

The following morning around six, I awoke in the dark basement of my Aunt Tilly's house to a strange sound. It was the whistle of American shells tearing into Wittlich at random. I jerked fully awake, my heart racing in sudden panic. The unthinkable was about to happen: I was at the mercy of the enemy. It was then, in that moment of wild despair that I shoved the barrel of the Walther automatic into my mouth, shuddered from its impact on my tooth and slammed it against the wall. And then I started to cry, with the inconsolable abandon of a six-year-old, in the sure knowledge that Germany and I were headed for slavery. We had lost.

Volkssturm civilians surrender in Trier, March 8, 1945

Photos reprinted from **Am Endes das Chaos**

Heck farm in April, 1945

Chapter Eight:
OUT OF THE RUINS

When I arose from the stone benches of the demolished Nuremberg stadium on that October day of the verdicts, I was alone in the vast oval where once the enthusiastic shouts of a quarter million people had hailed their savior. In the darkness I took one last look at the jagged top of the huge pillar which had held the German Eagle. Turning toward the ruins of the city, I became clearly aware, for the first time, of the immense moral responsibility heaped on our nation.

It crossed my mind that I should have pulled the trigger the day the Americans arrived in Wittlich; at least I would have died with my innocence intact. To lose a war after the most unimaginable sacrifices was one thing, but to be shouldered with the irrefutable genocide of millions was an intolerable burden. Like most of my countrymen, I wasn't ready for that; I myself had not laid a hand on any civilian, Jew or Christian. Unlike West Germany's present Chancellor, Helmut Kohl, who ended the war as a 14-year-old Hitler Youth member, I could not claim "the mercy of a late birth." Probably the Chancellor *was* innocent, but I knew plenty of 14-year-olds in my own units who had killed Americans. Still, that, did not make *them* culpable; only the people who instructed them to kill. Was I a victim like my younger contemporaries? To ask myself that on the day some of the leaders I had met were sentenced to hang, seemed like tempting fate.

On this, my last evening in Nuremberg, *Herr* Friedrich produced two bottles of wine. As usual, his wife quickly disappeared into their bedroom. "I'll be sorry to see you go, Alfons," he smiled, lifting his glass, "although I still don't understand why you came here."

"Trying to lay a few ghosts to rest," I said. "Maybe I have." At that he shook his head. "I hope so for your sake, but they'll come back if you let them, believe me."

"You're saying there's no redemption then?" I asked. He pointed to the moonscape outside, unending piles of reeking, decaying mortar.

"I don't know about you," said Peter, "but I've been redeemed enough. I never even voted for this Austrian house painter." He leaned forward and we touched glasses. "*Prost*," he said, "to survival. That's all the morality there is."

He put down his glass and looked earnestly at me. "Go home, Alfons, and put this *Scheisse* behind you. Get on with your life, man, and count yourself damned lucky. That American lieutenant who thought you were a boy could just as easily have blown your brains out when he found out you were a *Luftwaffe* officer in disguise." Earlier, I had related to Peter the story of my ludicrous capture by the American Third Army.

As I prepared to leave, Peter said, "Let me give you a piece of good advice, boy, although I don't think you'll take it." When I didn't reply, he went on, "From now on, for Christ's sake, hide in the middle of the herd like most of us. Don't stick your head out like some dummy in the trench when the bullets are flying. Play it safe and play it smart, and don't fall for this glory crap again."

"In other words, Peter, I should join the railroad like you."

"Why not?" he said, "it's the safest branch of the civil service. Hitler took it over straight from the Weimar Republic and never touched it except for kicking out the Jews. Our conquerors can't do without it either. It's immortal, see, no matter who's in power."

"Since you mentioned the Jews, Peter, how about the hundreds of trains filled with them that were sent efficiently to points of no return by our railroad?"

"I didn't load them," he said unperturbed. "I don't have to lose any sleep over that, do I? Let them hang the ones who did."

Mellowed by the wine, we parted company as good friends. *Herr* Friedrich's realism was tinged with cowardice, I thought, but it worked for him as for millions of others. Soon, I too would adopt this outlook, simply because I could find no other answers.

I was about to climb to my room atop the rubble when I ran into Renate, *Herr* Friedrich's voluptuous, blonde daughter who rarely even nodded at me. Compared to her GI boyfriend, I was a mere pauper. When I told her I would be gone by morning, she offered me her hand to say good-bye. "I was a *Scharführerin* in the Hitler Youth," she said, chewing gum and looking at me coyly. "Does that surprise you, *Herr* Heck?"

"Should it?" I asked. "We all have to survive, my dear *Fräulein*, even if it means assuming a horizontal position for the conquerors." It was a cheap shot in that time of bitter privation when hundreds of thousands of girls and women were selling their bodies for food, a few "luxuries" like nylon stockings and soap, or the only valid medium of currency--the American cigarette.

"Up your ass, buddy," she said in English. Not even raising her voice she continued, "hasn't it sunk in yet that you arrogant assholes are dirt now?" She actually laughed, and I noted with envy her perfect American drawl.

I never regretted having gone to Nuremberg in 1946. Renate's statement and dozens of other comments I heard on that trip evoked the feeling of the era more unforgettably than any photograph, and it marked the beginning of a new phase in my life. I resolved to accept my situation with as much equanimity as I could muster.

My classmates were much too occupied with their own survival in this hungry winter of 1946-47 to question and reflect with me. It was so cold that all classes were suspended for two months. Our starvation ration for a *Normalverbraucher*--a "normal user" without any privileges--was less than a quarter pound of bread per day, enlivened by one potato, one ounce of margarine or lard and a tablespoon of marmalade. There were allotments for hard workers engaged in construction, but those few jobs were usually done for the occupiers. It was particularly hard on infants, children and the sick. If the United States had not started with shipments of grain and milk, (which only raised the daily calories to a meager 1,100) and if the Swiss had not helped the children, that winter would have been worse than the previous two and consigned many thousands to their deaths.

Because of our land we fared better. Our harvests had been meager, and like all farmers we were under constant scrutiny by the French as well as by our own administrators, who had the unenviable task of filling ever increasing demands of the greedy French at the expense of our own starving citizens.

Wittlich 1945,
showing destruc-
tion of the
inner city.

Helmut Hagedorn

Beginning the
clean-up in
Wittlich in 1945,
six months
after VE Day.

Still, our family belonged to that privileged class, the upper three percent of the population which not only had enough to eat but was able to hoard supplies, especially tobacco. There were penalties including prison terms for stockpiling grain or even for not reporting all livestock, but there was no farmer with a clear conscience and some supplied those who came to their door offering their last piece of jewelry or themselves. Skilled craftsmen, such as cabinet makers or carpenters who had returned from prisoner of war camps, fought for the chance to build the finest furniture or the sturdiest barns merely for a full belly and some food for their families. We ourselves bought a former *Wehrmacht* hut for 200 pounds of potatoes and five pounds of tobacco. For the next four years, its three shabby rooms were our home. Over 50 of the best undamaged houses of Wittlich and 40 additional apartments had been seized by the French, but no occupier would ever give our tawdry hut a second glance.

Our most precious possession by far was a four-year-old Holstein cow, given us by my Uncle Hornung after we lost all of our livestock in the Christmas Eve air raid. The cow was housed in the fourth room of our hut and watched by everyone in the neighborhood, because her substantial milk output furnished the meager ration to nearly 60 people. She was vital to the nourishment of the children.

On a freezing March day in 1947, at the end of an unusually severe winter, two French soldiers led by a corporal knocked on our door and presented us with a confiscation request. My Aunts Maria and Luise and her children Marika and Marie-Luise stood there silently, tears rolling down their cheeks. Only my grandmother raised her voice in protest, waving the piece of paper which entitled her to a ludicrous compensation of 100 *Reichsmarks*, equal to three pounds of butter on the black market.

I was filling in one of the bomb craters near the river when I saw the soldiers leading the cow away. I rushed toward the hut with the shovel in my hand, while my grandmother was yelling, "Stop you idiot! They'll kill you." The corporal lowered his rifle and pointed it at me with an eager look of anticipation. I dropped the shovel and his lips curled in a sneer. I would gladly have killed all three.

This miserable year did end on a note of hope caused by

international developments, the importance of which I only dimly perceived. For over a year now we had gotten the *Rhein Zeitung*, a newspaper which was strictly censored by the military authorities. At first it was no more than six pages, published three times a week. A radio station with a severely limited program of music and local and world news operated from Koblenz. But again, no criticism of military authorities was ever voiced. Unfortunately, few radios were left. Like weapons, cameras and binoculars, they were confiscated by the Americans whenever they seized a German city. While the soldiers had a keen eye for the first three items, most couldn't be bothered to pack unwieldy radios, inoperable in the United States because of the different voltage. On the day of my capture, the Americans disposed of a pile of radios in front of city hall by running a tank over it.

I read President Harry Truman's March 1947 proclamation to the Congress--a reaction to Communist agitation in Greece and Turkey--with the amused cynicism of a slave. I was restricted to my hometown for another four months, subject to possible forced labor in France or incarceration in their infamous camp for political prisoners in Dietz. For any former Nazi, a relatively trifling offense such as selling butter on the black market, could warrant instant arrest. The President's words, the now-famous Truman Doctrine, signalled the beginning of a new era, of the utmost importance to us, the vanquished. "It must be the policy of the United States to support free peoples who are resisting attempted subjugation by armed minorities or outside pressures," was his stern warning to the Soviets to stem expansion beyond the huge territory President Roosevelt had so generously given to them at Yalta and Potsdam in 1945. So immersed was I in my own tribulations that it was of no consequence to me if more of Europe turned Communist. Indeed, it might have been sweet revenge for the American refusal to join us against the Russians in the waning days of the war, but neither did I want any more German territory to fall into their hands.

The notion that Germans would someday carry weapons as allies of the western world was positively outrageous. "Not for generations will we trust you *Boches* with anything more dangerous than a hunting rifle," the French school liaison officer told us when our class was shown documentary films of

Buchenwald and other concentration camps. Yet just eight years later, hundreds of former *Wehrmacht* officers would become the nucleus of the fledgling *Bundeswehr*, the purely "defensive" army of democracy.

That long winter was followed by a rare period of dry, hot weather which withered the meager crops already endangered by a severe lack of fertilizers and pesticides. Summer produced the worst food crisis ever, flooding the country with hordes of hungry city dwellers who literally combed the fields with their bare hands for leftover grains. Scores of farmers were arrested for withholding food and for eating their own seed potatoes. We formed nightly patrols to guard the harvests, and when our precious tobacco ripened we took turns sleeping in the fields. Because tobacco was such an easy medium of exchange to conceal, the stalks would have been ripped bare by people whose hunger drove them to steal. Again, only the largesse of the Americans averted disaster. Continuously into 1948, the French plundered their zone with relish, ignoring the suffering it imposed. They were paying us back tenfold for our pillage of their land during the four years of our occupation.

"At least we don't shoot you like the *Gestapo* did us," said an unmoved French commandant when our courageous mayor protested the endless confiscations. In the daily struggle to subsist, few people were impressed when the French military governor, General Koenig, allowed general elections for the state legislature of our *Rheinland-Pfalz*, (an artificial creation of the French which is now one of the most prosperous *Länder* of West Germany.) At 19, I was too young to vote; besides I considered this merely a French colony.

The three Western Allies now began to encourage the formation of political parties, provided, of course, they were not tainted by the slightest Nazi sentiment. Most citizens viewed this privilege with amused cynicism. We were still totally at the mercy and capricious whims of the military government, which passed its orders to the few German administrators who were considered political innocents. Some of these administrators were very able men who had opposed Nazism; others had merely convinced the conquerors they were clean.

The three major parties which had been outlawed by the Nazis--the Christian Democrats, the Social Democrats and the Communists--established themselves falteringly at first. The

Communists, though, were better organized and had clandestine support from Russia. In our predominantly Catholic zone, the Christians quickly dominated and became the powerful CDU (Christian Democratic Union). Within two years this, the first ruling party of the new Federal Republic, was organized under the wily but brilliant Chancellor Konrad Adenauer. The Social Democrats became the strong opposition, and the Communists quickly faded, placing a single member in parliament.

There were many Communists in the French military government who strongly favored our homespun Communists, but to no avail. They always fared badly in the polls and soon became impotent. Our Communists' connection to the Soviets who had chased nearly 10 million fellow Germans from the east (murdering an estimated two million in the process) was an anathema to all but a few fanatics who clung to Communism as a form of salvation. Every emaciated German soldier released from Soviet captivity was an eloquent witness to life in the "Workers Paradise." As it was, only a few of the estimated two and a half million German soldiers listed as captured or missing in Russia ever made it home. In the relentless carnage it was impossible to say how many died fighting or were captured, but the number remains at a million and a half more than 40 years later. Hundreds of thousands undoubtedly ended their lives as slave laborers. All of the last 10,000 released by the Soviet Union in 1955, testified that many of their comrades stayed behind. The Soviets could not be moved; they insisted that only war criminals under life sentence remained, and that their names and alleged crimes would never be made public.

Again, our family had its share of blessings. My Uncle Franz returned from Russia in 1946, weighing 95 pounds and barely able to walk, but after three months of bed rest, he was over the worst. Miraculously, Uncle Gustav returned home in 1949 from Siberia, having been listed as missing in action since 1943. Only my grandmother never gave up hope that he was still alive. Amazingly, he was in excellent physical condition, having been employed in his trade as master barber in the administration of a huge *Gulag* camp which contained a rare mixture of Soviet political prisoners and German soldiers. Gustav had accepted the inevitable--that he would end his days in Siberia--and he made the best of it. The idea of running into the electric fence only occurred to him once, on the day, nearly six years after his capture, when he was told he could send a 50-word post card home. He considered it a cruel hoax and the long repressed hope it awakened, shattered his composure. It was a Russian who saved his sanity by telling him that only those selected to return home were allowed to write. When he did return, the mayor and hundreds of townspeople met him at the station in a spontaneous outpouring of compassion for the very last soldier of Wittlich to make it home alive.

Decades later I thought of Gustav's triumphant homecoming when I compared it to the cruel indifference, rejection and outright hostility that greeted returning Vietnam veterans in America. Despite the fact that our soldiers had fought for an evil regime which had brought the most horrendous suffering to our own people, their return was eagerly awaited. Aside from members of the *SS* convicted of war crimes, our veterans received nothing but compassion for the miseries they had endured as prisoners. Germans understood that the blame, if any, had to be shared by all. Even when the populace was starving, any appeal to help our captured soldiers in France always produced the last crust.

The year preceding Gustav's deliverance, 1948, was the most decisive in postwar Germany history, for it would set the basic political configuration between East and West for a generation and beyond. In a Fulton, Missouri speech in March 1946, Winston Churchill had, in front of President Truman, predicted the coming confrontation between the United States and its Allies and the Soviet Union with the unforgettable phrase: "An Iron Curtain has descended over Europe." The astute Churchill, who had been turned out of office by the British people in July of 1945 in a show of rank ingratitude for the rallying of his nation in its darkest hour, never trusted Josef Stalin as naively as President Roosevelt. Churchill continued to protest, albeit from the sidelines, the Russian enslavement of all countries within its sphere of influence.

The pot began to simmer in March of 1948, when the U.S. Congress passed the Foreign Assistance Act proposed by former General, then Secretary of State, George Marshall. The Marshall Plan encouraged the formation of strong economies and free institutions, and was also offered to countries under Russian control. Stalin immediately forced his satellites to reject the proposal for fear it would establish economic as well as political independence, and again set Germany on its way to a quick recovery and thus a potential threat. As a counter measure, he established Cominform, his version of an economic organization for Eastern Europe.

When I read that the U.S. Congress had included us, the land of the Nazis, in its generosity, I was stunned. I wondered if the French would allow us to receive some of the five billion-plus dollars initially intended for European recovery. The powerful French, as well as the strong Italian Communist parties had actually voted to join Stalin's version, the Cominform. But I need not have worried. For once the United States proved who had really won the war. The Marshall Plan did much more than spark an astounding recovery; it turned millions of Germans like myself into close allies of the United States. It was the opposite of the the harsh Treaty of Versailles, that victors' revenge which produced a towering resentment and made Adolf Hitler successful.

Before the actual money began to flow into Germany, the currency needed to be reformed. The *Reichsmark's* only buying power was for items allocated on the ration cards. That created particular hardships for old people and the hundreds of thousands of war cripples whose pensions had become a mere pittance. I sometimes lit a cigarette with a 10-Mark note, at one time three days wages for a farm laborer.

The new money, henceforth called *Deutsche Mark*, was printed in the United States under the strictest secrecy, so as not to destroy the *Reichsmark* completely. The miracle occurred simultaneously in all three western occupation zones on Sunday, June 20, 1948. That day, every German received in an even exchange for 60 *Reichsmark*, a payment now of 40 new *Deutsche Mark*, and the remaining 20 a month later. Every single German, then, infant or man, Black Marketeer or farmer, started out exactly even, with the equivalent of $10. In the following months, half the amount in *Reichsmark* bank accounts was frozen; on the unfrozen portion, the rate of exchange was 10 new *Deutsche Marks* for 100 *Reichsmarks*. That was the beginning of our road to capitalism which led from total chaos to a standard of living that would one day surpass that of the United States. The day of the currency reform was more important to most Germans than that of the founding of the *Bundesrepublik* the following year. We received our 40 marks on Sunday and by

Monday, stores displayed items we hadn't seen since before the war. Within a month, despite the French occupation, the laws of supply and demand had asserted themselves. The black market was a memory, the American cigarette just another smoke, and the farmers started to look for customers again. It was truly a miracle.

The equality of that first day didn't last, for it never really had existed. The people who had hoarded for the day of the new money quickly accumulated more, but nobody minded. There was plenty of food, and although ration cards continued to be printed for a few months, nobody claimed them. From that week in June, the clearing of the mountains of rubble changed to a boom of construction that would fuel the *Wirtschaftswunder*, the economic miracle, for the next 15 years until the housing needs were met and West Germany began to export in earnest. Unlike the United States with its vast domestic market, export was the only way to sustain our new prosperity, an affluence which quickly became the birthright of a generation that knew ruins only from yellowed photographs.

Four days after the "Sunday of the new money" the Soviets closed the border between their zone and Berlin; the new currency was gaining strength so rapidly that it threatened the Soviets' economic control over their zone. The Berlin blockade had begun. The Soviets were confident that they could break the city and the will of their former allies, forcing them into negotiations. Millions of Germans in the three zones were shaken by the likelihood of an armed confrontation between the two super powers. I believed the Americans would have to back down to some degree. But instead, they launched the Berlin airlift.

When the Soviets called off the blockade in September of 1949, an incredible 14 months later, the Americans had proved to us that they were willing to go to war if necessary over the fate of Berlin. The airlift was an enormous logistical feat, unsurpassed in air transport. An unending stream of aircraft, often flying under dangerous weather conditions and threatened by Russian Migs in the narrow allied Berlin air corridor had fed a beleaguered city of millions. American, British and French pilots had died so Germans would not starve. The United States no longer had to doubt the loyalty of most Germans, including many former Nazis. The Soviets had turned West Berlin into a huge American fan club.

Few Germans regarded the French on the same level as the Americans, the true victors. In our zone, their harsh treatment did not gain them any friends. In the first two postwar years, I lived in constant fear of our occupiers, for so many people had ended up in French internment camps, having been denounced by fellow Germans. The first dangerous wave of arrests had occurred when I was seized, in July and August of 1945. Nearly all low-level Party members such as *Ortsgruppenleiters*, officials in charge of small villages, were imprisoned and sent to the large camp of Dietz without any pretext of a trial. Very often, smoldering grudges led to the incarceration of men whose only crime was that they had joined the Party. Our penitentiary in Wittlich held 84 at its peak in 1947. Some internees were beaten repeatedly during interrogations, despite the fact that only a few had held a rank comparable to a leader of a county. There was never any defense provided, and the "justice" dealt out was so capricious that it created a deep resentment throughout the population. When the French turned over the de-Nazification commissions to Germans, the damage was done. In the entire county of Wittlich in 1947, not a single German could be found who was willing to be public prosecutor. In the end, a committee reluctantly reviewed the files of all former Nazi Party members, and in a single afternoon session in November of 1948, pronounced 700 blameless. That was the end of the de-Nazification era--a true farce since so many of the Nazi mass murderers had long since vanished and would never face any judge.

Had it not been for my age, 17, I would certainly have ended up in slave labor, despite the fact that membership in the Hitler Youth had been compulsory since December of 1939. There was no escape for me or any other Nazi from a small town. We were known to everybody. Not only had I drilled senior citizens for the *Volkssturm*, I had been the last highest-ranking Hitler Youth leader of the entire county. When my restriction to the limits of my hometown ended after two years, I began to breathe easier, but I didn't feel entirely safe until completion of the hearings in November, 1948.

By the end of that summer, I no longer daydreamed of ambushing any Frenchmen. Conditions were improving and we now had the choice of two daily papers. Although neither risked any open criticism of the military authorities, German political parties became more and more visible in their pages. The Cold War was the major factor in returning local power to democratically elected German officials. Military authorities began to loosen their grip, although it would be nearly a year before incarcerated Nazis or prisoners of war in France were released, with the exception of those convicted of war crimes. France's fury had spent itself and the law once again dictated that French soldiers could be brought to trial for mistreating Germans.

Throughout my years in the *Cusanus Gymnasium*, we studied no German history after World War I. The Nazi era remained off limits to us. We had been an integral part of the Nazi era, and with Gallic realism, the French decided we were probably beyond redemption. On one occasion, we were made to watch documentary films depicting the horror of the concentration camps, particularly Buchenwald and Bergen-Belsen, where living skeletons meandered through heaps of bodies. Some of the soldiers guarding us became so incensed at our stoicism throughout the film, that they drove us back into the truck with blows of their rifle butts.

It wasn't that we weren't moved (although at that point I still thought that some of the scenes might be staged); we just could not identify with the victims and how they had perished. Someone advanced the theory that most had died of typhoid aggravated by starvation, like our prisoners in Russia. Besides, he suggested, they were "enemies of the *Reich*". To my embarrassment, I was the only one who threw up, for the pictures brought back the nauseating stench of that hellish day when I had excavated French corpses with a shovel and my hands.

By 1948, no one in my class could deny the full scope of the mass murder. But acceptance was always accompanied by the disclaimer that 1) we ourselves had not committed any atrocity, and 2) that a monstrous punishment had already been exacted from our people, ourselves included. Not only had we been duped, we had been betrayed and sacrificed. Half our class of 1939 never reached its eighteenth birthday, fallen on "the field of honor." Without exception, all of us followed the dictum of most Germans during these years--*ohne mich*, "without me." That became our new ideology. *"Ohne Mich"* was much more than a slogan; it expressed the conviction that you can't trust anybody, particularly any authority. That was a radical reversal for a people who had once obeyed so readily. It became the "credo of the duped;" from now on, we would concern ourselves only with our own narrow interests--survival of the individual, not the Fatherland nor even the larger community. This thinking contributed in part to the drastic decline of West Germany's birth rate as well as to its materialism. Although the young of Germany are involved today in the affairs of their country, the hallmark of my generation is skepticism.

I was convinced that no one would ever again succeed in winning us over to any cause, no matter how noble. After Hitler's deceit we could never again believe in anybody--politician, priest or educator. *Herr* Friedrich's cynical obser-vation that survival is the only morality became our credo. We had become so hardened to death and suffering that we could sit next to a corpse and eat a sandwich without a second glance.

One afternoon, a member of the youth branch of the emerging Christian Democratic Union invited about a dozen of us to a pub after school to drink some beer at his expense in return for listening to his pitch. He was a one-armed veteran of the war, which was the only reason that we didn't throw him out of the place in the first ten minutes. Despite his injury, this fool apparently had not learned the same lesson we had. When he announced that soon, young Germans like us would have to involve themselves with rebuilding the democratic, political structure of Germany, half of us sarcastically shouted "*Heil mein Führer*", while the other half sang the *Marseillaise*, the anthem of our French masters. He blushed angrily, but he stood his ground.

"You have no right to forsake a new Germany," he yelled, "just because you have been misled by an evil genius. What do you expect out of life anyway?"

"Nothing except your free beer, asshole," somebody shouted. "Leave your money and get the hell out while you can still walk."

While the hapless young man couldn't begin to start a dialogue since we didn't trust his judgment, we did listen respectfully to Dr. Schneider, our Latin teacher who was also a Catholic priest. He was the only one of our teachers who had been arrested by the *Gestapo*, his crime being that he had criticized Hitler Youth leaders for letting us get away with no homework twice a week. (On Wednesdays and Saturdays there had been no school assignments because rallies took up both afternoons.) In a moment of exasperation, Dr. Schneider bitingly observed that the Hitler Youth had made us physical supermen but mental dwarfs. That very evening, the _Gestapo_ knocked on his door.

What we liked most about Dr. Schneider was his rueful confession that the _SS_ men in Dachau didn't have to torture him to turn him into jelly. They merely threw him into an open septic tank and told him to renounce God before they'd let him out again. "In less than three minutes I not only renounced God, the Pope and my bishop, but volunteered to serve on the Russian Front despite my age of 62." Dr. Schneider had every right to apply for special consideration given to victims of Nazi terror, which would have entitled him to much more food and decent housing during the postwar hunger years. But the idea revolted him.

"Like so many of us, I should have opened my mouth in September of 1935, not in 1943. When the Nazis deprived German Jews of their citizenship and we didn't rise in massive protest, we set the stage for a mass murder which, God help us, included our children."

I was embarrassed by Dr. Schneider's vociferous insistence that _all_ of us boys were innocent lambs who had been turned into potential killers because our priests, teachers and parents had abandoned us to the state. Yet he maintained, chopping the air with his powerful hands, "We are to blame. We intellectuals are even worse than most storm troopers, for we knew better." He considered me a victim of both the Nazis and the French, and treated me as if I were a gravely wounded soldier. When I admitted to him reluctantly that I had enjoyed much of my Hitler Youth career, including the power I had been given, he became angry. "Don't apologize for that. My God, there were times in the early '30s that I wished I weren't a priest. I was so enamored with the promise of this new Germany that I shouted 'Heil Hitler' with the best of them."

If Dr. Schneider's stance hadn't been so uncritically forgiving, he might have been more effective in helping us understand the depth and meaning of our involvement. To be assured I had been merely an ignorant pawn was momentarily comforting, but also somewhat demeaning. I had attained my high rank because of ambition and drive as well as circumstance.

Even after I began to understand the brutality of our regime, I still served it to my utmost. But Dr. Schneider had offered me a painless way out, and I took it willingly, with only a slight gnawing around the edges of my conscience. Still, I knew my accounts had not been settled.

Dr. Schneider occasionally celebrated a Sunday mass in our parish church. His sermons generally were superior to those of our monsignore and his chaplains, who carefully avoided any offensive themes. But the Sunday Dr. Schneider castigated the role of the church under Hitler, was the day of his last sermon to our parish. His claim that not a single German Catholic or Protestant prelate with the rank of a full bishop had ever been sent to a concentration camp was the truth. But it offended not only our monsignore and the Catholic hierarchy, but the parishioners as well, including my level-headed grandmother. Driving home his point he shouted, "Our shame is that Dachau was filled with all kinds of Hitler's enemies who risked their lives to speak out, but it was glaringly empty of our spiritual shepherds, our bishops."

"Just because he was there on his own stupidity gives him no right to insult our bishop," said my grandmother indignantly, echoing the general sentiment. Dr. Schneider became unpopular overnight. The very last thing our people needed was the brutal truth about their only source of solace and comfort. Strangely, church attendance during those years of redemption rose considerably. I couldn't explain why I went to mass every Sunday, full of cynicism and yet finding moments of peace listening to the soaring notes of our grand organ. My grandmother held out, hoping that now that the Nazi "idiocy" was over, I might reconsider and become a priest after all. There were times that I envied her simple faith, which had survived the Nazi era without the slightest chip.

Toward the end of 1948, the construction of our farmhouse was well underway and the partially finished barn held two horses, four cows, a couple of pigs and a flock of chickens. It wasn't a good wine year because of a rainy summer, but our tobacco harvest had been substantial. Despite the setbacks, my grandmother's new account of *Deutsche Marks* quickly began to grow. When I suggested laughingly that she blow it all before it became worthless again, she gave me a disapproving look. The only luxury she allowed herself was a bar of fine bittersweet chocolate every Sunday afternoon when she returned from her visit to the cemetery. But she was quite tolerant of my spending habits, citing one of her dictums that few males gain any sense before age 48.

Despite our hardships after our defeat, we males were spoiled in one very agreeable sense. We had become a rare commodity. So many young men had died that the girls outnumbered us three to one. After the Hitler Youth, with its nearly exclusive male companionship, most of us had a difficult time regarding girls as equals. To a surprising degree, we continued the close camaraderie of our Hitler Youth years.

We shared a bond of openness that excluded our families as well as our educators. We neither asked for guidance nor accepted it, and although we were not, as a rule, ill-mannered toward our elders, we no longer trusted their judgment. How could we? These were the same sages who, as mature adults, had fallen for Hitler.

Nearly all our teachers were sensitive to our cynicism because of their own feelings of guilt. No fanatic Nazis were still around, of course, since all party members had been dismissed from teaching positions. The occupiers were relentless in purging them, afraid they might contaminate our minds again, despite the fact that most had joined under pressure or merely out of opportunism.

Ironically, some of the real Nazis had been excellent teachers, driven by the same enthusiasm that had made them good Nazis. The conquerors never fully understood that the Nazi movement, like no other political force in history, died completely with the demise of its leader. Aside from a few thousand die-hard fanatics who were unable to face reality, most former Party members wanted nothing more than to forget the whole Thousand Year Reich.

I can recall not a single discussion about Nazi Germany during these important years of physical reconstruction. Most of us who had lived the Nazi era so thoroughly were vengeful that it had robbed us of a normal childhood. To my friends who had not wielded any power, the past exerted anything but nostalgia. They had been mere pawns who had survived a deadly game that they played without choice, and not a single one ever professed the slightest personal guilt. The notion that they needed rehabilitation from the Nazi brainwashing was insulting.

The total defeat and its aftermath had been as effective as a lobotomy. For them, despite the magnitude of Nazi atrocities, Germany's punishment seemed out of proportion to their own meager involvement. That more Germans than Jews had been killed, seemed to them to even the score.

At this point, enlightened discussions of the origins of Nazism and the phenomenon of German enthusiasm would have helped prevent the near total repression syndrome which seized Germans for years to come. But in fairness, it was nearly impossible for anyone to reach us. There was no one we trusted. And so we debated the ancient Greek and Roman civilizations and history ended with the Weimar Republic. Even that era was not interpreted for its importance in the rise of Nazism, but fleetingly mentioned as the first commendable exercise in democracy. The assertion that we were now engaged in the second noble experiment with democracy, after a regrettable lapse of barbarism by some former Austrian, evoked hollow laughter at a time when we still had to doff our hats to the French tricolore on the turret of city hall. No wonder "*ohne mich*" became our cry. In a purely political sense we were the first "flower children."

The economic rebirth of West Germany owes more to the fierce materialism spawned by the currency reform than to the seed money of the Marshall Plan. The desire to possess things went far beyond our basic need for food and shelter in a landscape of bomb craters, but no foreigner could have foreseen our grim determination to rise to the economic level of the victors. When our cities and factories began to rise, so did our self-esteem, somewhat assuaging our unacknowledged awareness of guilt. Our generation could not only destroy, it could create.

The *Wittlicher Tageblatt*, this headline of May 11, 1940, announcing the invasion of France, Belgium, Holland and Luxembourg: "The Battle Has Begun."

This bunker near Wittlich served as shelter to townspeople who had lost their homes in the fighting after the *Wehrmacht* had withdrawn on March 9, 1945. The U.S. Army allowed the people to stay, but later that summer the French blew up the bunkers.

Chapter Nine:
THE SILENT YEARS

For three years after the war, the memory of Fabianne shone like a beacon through the pall of my darkest days. I often looked toward Luxembourg at sunset, which might as well have been across the ocean instead of an hour's drive away. As long as I was closely supervised by the French, restricted to the boundary of my hometown, I didn't dare contact her. When we parted, she had promised to write as soon as it was "safe."

Initially I wasn't alarmed when I didn't hear from her; she was intelligent enough not to bring attention to our relationship. Women who were discovered were shorn bald, publicly branded as collaborators, sometimes driven through the streets of their towns in their underwear for having slept with Germans; more serious offenders were severely beaten or even executed. Thanks to Fabianne's realization that Germany's defeat was imminent, we had always met in secret, although I found that demeaning at a time when we were the masters of Luxembourg. She had been so careful that I knew only the name of her uncle's pharmacy, not her home address in the city of Luxembourg. I received one post card from her a day after I arrived home from the *Westwall*, but it went up in flames with our farm on Christmas Eve.

Despite her silence, it never occurred to me that she no longer loved me, or might have found somebody else. Our relationship had been so dangerous for her that I never doubted its intense purity. I was humbled by her willingness to be vilified for me, especially when I later realized how much she had risked.

Six months after all restrictions against me had been lifted, and a few days after de-Nazification proceedings had been halted, I sent a brief, carefully worded letter to her uncle's address in Remisch. After six weeks, I began to imagine that her uncle, recognizing my German address, had opened the letter and thrown it away in disgust after reading of his niece's shameful attachment to a young Nazi. After a sleepless night, I decided to risk it all, even if her family should turn against her. I contacted the German Red Cross in Baden-Baden with the request to find her. Hundreds of thousands of people were looking for family members across Europe, and the Red Cross was hopelessly overburdened. Every newspaper was filled with the description and last known location of loved ones; every railroad station was plastered with despairing notes like:

> "Dear Soldier! Have you served with my missing son Heinrich Schmidt, 1. Company, Second Regiment of the 82 Artillery, in Russia? Last letter dated May 1944? Please contact me urgently at..."

Miracles seldom happened, and I opened the Red Cross note printed on shabby paper with shaking hands. It had taken less than three months for the agency's reply, which could mean only good news. Tiny, orderly Luxembourg with a population of 350,000 was not vast Russia where millions disappeared without a trace.

The message was an impersonal obituary: "According to the records of the Red Cross search service of Luxembourg, Fabianne Mercurier and her mother Madelaine Mercurier were killed as a result of Allied air action on a train near the city of Luxembourg on December 28, 1944." The typist didn't add a word of regret; it would have been hypocrisy.

I didn't mention Fabianne for many years. Neither my grandmother nor my closest friends ever knew of my love for her. Fabianne's death was the final irony of this insane war: she was killed by her liberators. My world became a few degrees colder, but paradoxically her violent death helped relieve my own feelings of guilt. The loss of the only perfect woman I had ever known, was, I thought, my last penance. It occurred to me then I probably would never marry. No other woman would ever measure up to Fabianne.

Despite the rapid improvement in their lives, the 24 members of my class of 1949 faced some tough choices. Spaces were at a premium in the few universities because tens of thousands of former students had returned from captivity and had first option to resume their studies. I wasn't quite sure what to do with my life anyway. The study for the priesthood was out, despite my grandmother's silent reproach. I was astounded when my classmate, Paul Müller, who had partied with the best of us, disclosed that he was going to enter a seminary, despite his no longer solid faith. He had been a minor leader in the Hitler Youth, but such was our taboo concerning the past that I didn't ask him if becoming a priest was a kind of atonement. Personally, I no longer wanted to lead anyone, and had become so indifferent to my studies that my last history teacher (*Frau* Dr. Fein) frequently predicted I would become a bum. The truth was that I had peaked emotionally at 17, and despite my resentment toward Hitler, I couldn't visualize anything as exciting and seductive as my past had been. I might have become a good veterinary, since I liked animals better than people, but the wait for admission to the few veterinary schools was at least four years.

Unexpectedly, my long friendship with Wolfgang Knopp lead to a job offer which might have turned into a satisfying life. His father was the publisher of our daily newspaper, for many years known as the *Wittlicher Tageblatt*. The plant had burned in the air raid of 1944 but had been rebuilt in time to become a branch of the *Rhein Zeitung*, the major daily established in Koblenz which had gradually acquired small papers. *Herr* Knopp's eldest son Erwin had been shot through the head by a sniper a week before the end of the war, which perhaps explained why he let Wolfgang and me get away with a lot. Knopp was a veteran of World War I as well as an aging major of the *Wehrmacht* during what he called "Hitler's war," as though he had never been a part of it. Although he stopped short of accusing his own generation of cowardice, he did remark that "we shouldn't have stood by idly while the barbarians took you in." There was no doubt that Nazi atrocities deeply offended his sense of honor, but he offered us no remedy. He sensed that I was more preoccupied with the past than were my classmates, but he saw no point in dwelling on something that would probe his own conscience. Knopp and his family had paid heavily, especially with the loss of Erwin who had never given him any trouble. Wolfgang, on the other hand, was always challenging authority and usually in trouble at the *Gymnasium*.

After a week of instruction in newspaper bundling at the plant in Koblenz, I came home and was installed as the packing supervisor, with a team of one man and 12 women. The actual printing on the restored rotary press began shortly after midnight and, on trouble-free nights, ended at 5 a.m. when 28,000 copies were shipped to the town and 60 villages by train, truck and even motorcycle. My principal duty was to direct the counting and sorting of the bundles, which quickly became routine. But when the press broke down, usually due to inferior newsprint, the shipping schedule went awry. Soon, dozens of irate distributors from three counties demanded their papers from me personally. My performance was closely watched from Koblenz, since we were in direct competition with the *Volksfreund*, the major paper of Trier and a well-established news source.

The management in Koblenz wasn't receptive to my excuses for shipping delays. "Start printing earlier," was their suggestion. Unfortunately, I didn't have the authority to arrange that. Soon, friction developed between myself and the men who ran the press. While I paced, looking at my watch and my idle packing team, the printers took their 15-minute break prescribed by union regulations, whether I missed the first train or not. This was no longer the Hitler Youth where orders were carried out instantly.

The packing procedure was boring, but I liked the atmosphere of the newspaper business with its challenge to provide information to masses of people. One afternoon, I submitted a couple of paragraphs dealing with market day activities to *Herr* Schmidt, the editor of our branch paper who alone determined the make-up of the local news. The next day I asked him to let me become an unpaid writer. Schmidt was no fool. He had found himself an eager reporter and he used me shamelessly for nearly a year. I thoroughly enjoyed this unpaid apprenticeship, and was satisfied that I had found my calling, a reporter.

To a large degree, I invited my own downfall. Our Sunday supplement from Koblenz featured a writing contest, and in a moment of recklessness, I entered. I won the 200 *Mark* award, which was nearly my monthly salary, but was fired as a writer as soon as I asked for a job as a full time reporter. It seemed that by winning the contest, I had brought myself to the attention of the head office in Koblenz. *Herr* Schmidt was uncharacteristically diplomatic when he sacked me, explaining that the editor-in-chief had told him emphatically that all reporting responsibilities were to be assumed by him and not by some underling in the provinces. Within a day, I had talked myself into believing that Schmidt had made up the whole story and called the editor-in-chief myself. He not only fired me again, but told me that I had entered the contest illegally, since it wasn't open to anyone affiliated with the *Rhein Zeitung*. "You're damn lucky we let you keep the money," he reminded me, and hung up.

Supervising the expedition of newspapers might have been a prestigious job to many 21-year-olds, but I had held the power of life and death over thousands as a teenager, and my distribution work paled in comparison. My reluctance to supervise anybody stemmed from my years as a Hitler Youth leader. I had become a loner, perfectly suited to journalism where solitary perform-ance is more important than team work. Had I possessed the patience to wait, I might have found a satisfying life as a reporter for the *Rhein Zeitung* or another newspaper, and wouldn't have left Germany. That would have been my loss, despite nearly 30 years in jobs that posed little challenge and left me feeling that I was squandering my potential. These silent years eventually propelled me into what would become my life goal--to write and talk frankly about Nazi Germany as I had lived it. I could not have achieved that through a newspaper career in Germany, for here all of us were insulated from the past by our reluctance to talk about it. Very likely, my well-educated classmates never did read harrowing accounts of extermination camps, let alone talk to victims of Nazi terror.

In a country where nearly all became victims, few claimed special attention. Within the neighboring counties of Wittlich and Bernkastel, only 17 people had, by 1948, applied for the status of "Nazi Victim." This designation gave them special privileges in food, housing, and monetary restitution. Most of their fellow citizens didn't look kindly upon them, for the main criterion to qualify was "substantial deprivation of freedom," which most people had experienced to some degree.

A farmer's son in Wittlich had spent three years in Dachau, arrested when he was overheard criticizing Hitler's conduct of the war. He had been pardoned to fight on the Russian Front. My Uncle Gustav was furious when he found out the man received restitution as a victim. He reasoned that his own six years in a *Gulag* camp in Siberia certainly qualified him under the same criteria. Was the anguish of a farm woman who had lost all four of her sons in battle less than that of former *Gestapo* prisoners? Before long, the comparatively few Germans who applied for restitution payments did so secretly. The ones who had an irrefutable claim to restitution had virtually disappeared.

More than four decades after the end of the war, the Federal Republic of West Germany has a total Jewish population of about 30,000. There are twice as many Jews in San Diego County, California, which means that the average German doesn't even know a Jew on a personal basis. In this atmosphere, I never could have written frankly and extensively about the Nazi era. I quit my job as the packing team manager when I heard on the radio that Americans were hiring German interpreters in Frankfurt. *Herr* Knopp didn't try to change my mind and gave a glowing reference about my work as a supervisor. I think he was relieved that my move would break up the close friendship between his son and me. I was so confident the Americans would hire me, that I packed my bags.

Compared to our wartime partings where each one might be the last, this one between my grandmother and me was casual. I confessed to her that my real goal wasn't working for the Americans, but finding a job as a reporter in Frankfurt. The Frankfurt of 1950 was in the full boom of reconstruction and despite its many bomb scars, was a bustling metropolis that had something to offer to every taste. Since the proclamation of the *Bundesrepublik* in August 1949, the former occupation zones had disappeared, with the exception of Berlin. The former capital of the *Reich* is still divided into the four sectors of 1945. Germans were once again governed again by German authorities, although we regarded this new land as an appendage of the United States rather than a sovereign state. The GIs must have been dazed by the flocks of very pretty women who chased them, usually not out of true love but with the cold calculation of landing in the USA, the land of opulence. Many German women of marriageable age had lost their boyfriends to the Third Reich. To find an American husband meant economic security, or so they thought. Compared to the *Deutsche Mark*, the American dollar of the 1950s was so strong that even an ordinary soldier could afford to live it up with his girlfriend. A glass of good German beer was 15 cents.

The horse-faced Military Police captain who interviewed me spoke only a few words of German and barely glanced at my documents. I had arrived on a good day; he needed two more interpreters to accompany MPs on their rounds through Frankfurt. That same evening, I cruised through our assigned sector of Frankfurt in the back seat of a jeep behind two muscle-bound MPs on the lookout for hell-raising soldiers. But I was only needed if GIs got into trouble with Germans, which was rare.

My work was in a Labor Service battalion through the German employment office. The unit divided into squads, platoons and companies like the U.S. Army. My fluency in English saved me from having to stand guard duty in front of any of the hundreds of American posts throughout the city, ranging from motor pools to American civilian settlements. Only a handful of the Labor Service members spoke some English; even fewer could write a report in English or translate simultaneously. I was astounded that the Americans equipped these Germans, many of whom had fought in the *Wehrmacht*, with U.S. Army carbines and trusted them with the safety of their families. They had, however, thoroughly checked our backgrounds and excluded any former *SS* members. Each one of us had to produce complete German identification documents, including a police report with fingerprints and the mandatory registration form required when a German changes his residence.

The $60 a month I received as an interpreter was a fortune. I boarded and ate free in the American barracks in the *Gutleut Strasse*, and on my salary, I could party three nights a week. Work was so fascinating that I didn't get around to presenting myself for a newspaper interview for two months.

One of the most prestigious German dailies, then and now, is the *Frankfurter Allgemeine Zeitung*, perhaps a mixture of the *New York Times* and the *Wall Street Journal*. It took several calls before I persuaded the assistant executive editor to see me. He read through the folder of what I considered my best articles and handed it back to me without a smile. "There is absolutely nothing in here that would persuade me to give you preference over the hundred former journalists who are still waiting to get their jobs back. We are only beginning to regain our former circulation, and it'll be years before we add anybody new, unless it's an unusual talent. Besides, we seldom hire anybody without a graduate degree in journalism. Your chances with us are almost nil, but try again in two years. That'll give you a chance to finish your studies. Good Day!" He didn't even bother to shake hands. I was devastated but he was right. I had very little to sell, especially in a country that attaches great importance to formal training and degrees. I had blown one chance; now it was back to school or back to asking *Herr* Knopp to rehire me. I couldn't do either.

For the next eight months I amused myself in Frankfurt. Apart from an occasional visit to the first-rate opera, I spent a lot of time in the sergeant's mess of the Military Police to which we interpreters had access. I was fascinated watching the Americans in their dedicated pursuit of leisure. Few of them ventured among the German population, and not one ever engaged me in a serious conversation about Germany's recent past. They had won and we had lost, but now was party time.

Even the CIA official who delved into my file didn't seem interested that I had belonged to the Hitler Youth for seven years. Our mutual enemy was now Communism, and my past made me his ideological ally but not his equal. Until the establishment of the *Bundeswehr* in 1955, most American officers stationed in Germany displayed a Master Race syndrome--they considered themselves superior not only to us but to the British and the French. Indeed, no one could dispute the American claim that they had rescued their wartime allies from us.

Until August 1949, the United States was the world's military as well as economic superpower. And then the Soviets exploded their first atomic bomb. The "balance of terror" began, heralding the gradual decline of American might and prestige. The proud GIs of 1950 were the symbol of a virile country at its peak of world dominance, while GIs of the '70s were (in the eyes of many Europeans) representatives of a bully nation which had found its well-deserved comeuppance in Vietnam.

In 1950 I would have scoffed at such a bleak prognosis. Despite the Soviet atom bomb, this was the century of America. There were times when I thought the United States had been foolish in not pushing Russia back to its prewar borders, but I was learning that most Americans don't think like Nazis. In my view, the 1948 Berlin Blockade would have given the Americans a legitimate reason to attack Russia. The immense advantage of their atomic bombs would have assured virtual victory, but the Americans could not bring themselves to wage war on their former ally, now their only mortal enemy. Still, there was something noble in their pacifism. It's not likely that Josef Stalin would have hesitated had he been the sole possessor of atomic power.

Hitler had predicted this confrontation between fundamentally opposing ideologies. The only hindrance was an ingrained streak of fairness which prevented Americans from using their advantage to win. I wasn't surprised when the U.S. repeated and compounded its mistake in Vietnam.

By the summer of 1950, I had become so enamored of what I falsely assumed was the carefree "American Way of Life," that I resolved to emigrate to the United States at all costs. The problem was that although the Americans hired me to guard them in Frankfurt, they didn't want to see me on their own home ground. The MP captain who took my daily reports held out little hope. "Every goddamn D.P. (displaced person) on this continent wants to get into the USA, and honestly I don't think you stand a chance. You're not a victim, see, but a perpetrator, as far as our short-sighted government is concerned."

Unexpectedly, the Canadians came to the rescue. My roommate Peter, who had fled from Breslau in what by now was the East German Democratic Republic, found an announcement in the paper by the Canadian consulate in Karlsruhe. "Germans! Come to Canada and start a new life in a friendly country. If you meet stringent requirements, we advance your passage." That same afternoon I wrote for further information, without much hope. I mentioned that both of us had been members of the Hitler Youth, and I assumed that would stop us right there. Within a week, we had not only a reply, but a long application form. The instructions were quite detailed: in addition to a three-page questionnaire, we had to furnish identity cards with photograph and fingerprints, police reports from Frankfurt and our home town, proof of residence for every year of our life, employment records, health certificate, chest x-ray, and a processing fee of 50 *Marks*.

We arrived at the consulate long before our appointment at nine. Throngs of people were waiting to pick up forms; the news had spread quickly. The processing took the better part of the day. A stern matron in her late 50s checked my documents with hardly a word, occasionally wrinkling her brow. She then directed me to an army physician who gave me a quick checkup and looked at the x-ray.

Next came the first of two interviews by higher officials. An elderly gentleman in a tweed jacket went over my documents again, repeating the questions on the form. I wondered if he thought I had lied and wanted to catch me in a contradiction. I was surprised by the youth of the consul. He was a tall, lanky man in his late 30s, and spoke with a clipped British accent. He gazed intently at me for a few seconds, studying me. His first question took me by surprise. "Do you still like Adolf Hitler?" This must be a trap, I thought. It was unlikely that anyone would say yes, ensuring a denial of the coveted visa.

"I once followed him fervently," I said, "but now I resent him for what he did to Germany." His brows went up.

"Only to Germany? Not to yourself?"

"Not really. There were times I enjoyed myself."

"Doing what?" he shot back. "Killing Jews?"

"I never laid a hand on a Jew. I was 12 years old when the Jews from my hometown were deported. I was talking about my time flying. I thoroughly enjoyed that."

"So you don't claim to be a victim like so many of your buddies who come in here and hope we'll buy their crap?"

"Maybe I was an enthusiastic victim," I said, no longer caring much what he thought. I wasn't going to get a visa from this man anyway. I wondered if he were Jewish.

"Well, not everything was bad, even with Hitler," he said, suddenly almost conciliatory. "Under Hitler you Germans introduced some good animal protection laws. Do you like dogs?"

"Better than most people," I said, astounded at the strange turn of his questions. He leafed through my file again and then looked me full in the face.

"This whole Hitler mess didn't turn you into a Communist, did it? You aren't planning to overthrow our government, are you?"

"I want to get as far away from politics as I possibly can," I said. "I wouldn't even join a bowling team again, here or in Canada."

He laughed, got up and held out his hand. "Welcome to

Canada. We're still awaiting the report from the Americans about you, but I assume that's going to be all right or you wouldn't be working for them. If you can afford to pay the passage of $180, you can choose your own destination. If not, we'll advance the money but you have to go to a processing center near Toronto called Ajax."

When I told him I had the money and that I would like to go to British Columbia, he asked why. "The scenery is supposedly beautiful and I hear the climate is milder around Vancouver."

"Right you are," he said.

Dazed by my good luck, I waited impatiently for Peter. When he finally came out of the building, he looked glum.

"The bastards turned me down, at least for the time being."

"How come?" I asked, astounded. Peter's high rank in the Hitler Youth had been much lower than mine, yet they had accepted me.

"Christ," he said, "the Americans and Canadians are so paranoid about Communist infiltration. You ought to have a great future with them; they actually trust Nazis. They turned me down because I fled East Germany."

"That's ridiculous, Peter. That proves you don't like Communists. Didn't you tell them that?"

"Of course I did," he said. "I guess it's because my family got killed by the Russians that they think I might be a Soviet spy. I don't know, it's nuts."

A month later I received the visa for permanent entry and the transportation tickets from Bremerhaven to Vancouver. I immediately quit my job and went home, afraid of how my grandmother would take the news. Both my uncles, no doubt relieved, assured her that I had done the right thing. How many Germans were lucky enough to escape this blood-soaked country with so little left to offer? Canada, with its smaller population, might even be better for me than the United States. Besides, I could always come back after a couple of years. The experience of the new world would easily qualify me for any newspaper job, especially with my perfected English.

On a cold October morning at dawn I went into my grandmother's bedroom and hugged her for the last time. I had no doubt I would see her again, but when I tore myself loose from her, the only member of my family I truly loved, she cried out, "I'll never see you again. Oh please, don't leave."

"I'll be back, *Oma*," I choked. "I promise you." It was one promise I didn't keep, and it would haunt me. On the way to the harbor, I stopped for two days to see my parents in Oberhausen, and in contrast to my grandmother's good-bye, I left them with a good feeling. After the war, my father had helped us for a few weeks in the summer when the farm was still in ruins. The magnitude of my own defeat was so great that he refrained from rubbing salt into my wounds, but we were not close. We both evaded the subject of my former allegiance to Hitler. Once he had asked me in front of my grandmother if I had learned my lesson, or still thought ordinary working stiffs like himself were stupid. I had walked away, avoiding a confrontation.

My twin brother Rudolf had worked very hard helping to rebuild the farm, and he later resented more than I that our Uncle Franz's children, who had never seen the ruins, would inherit the property. That was my grandmother's fault, for she didn't bother to leave a will. But I had no reason to complain-- she had provided me with a carefree childhood and a good education. I had chosen to go to Canada instead.

I hadn't told my parents I was coming, let alone that I was on my way to Canada. When she heard the news, my mother started to cry. Unknown to me, my brother had recently moved several hundred kilometers away to a new job. And now I was going to journey across the Atlantic and she would lose us both. I didn't quite see it that way; I was more disappointed that I couldn't spend my last two days in Germany with my brother. I had even planned to ask him if he wanted to join me in Canada after a year or so. With my legal residency there and his clean political past, obtaining a visa shouldn't be hard. Despite our rivalries as children, he was the only person from which I kept no secrets. My first reaction to his absence was to have dinner with my parents and get back on the next train to Bremerhaven. But for the first time in my life, my father asked me to stay. "I'm going to take a couple of days off," he said. My mother dropped her spoon. He was obsessed by his huge steam shovel, and although he complained about his bad back, nobody could have dragged him off the three-story high machine which ran on broader tracks than a Sherman tank. I sometimes wondered what his thoughts were as he looked up to the mountain of slag he was attacking, protected from the shattering din by ear muffs.

For a working man, he had some unusual habits, as my

brother had told me. He loved the opera and serious movies, and he never took my mother with him. He also secretly ate filled chocolates and chain-smoked four packs of cigarettes every day; by German standards he wasn't a heavy drinker. I thought of my father as a loud but solitary man, both fearless and cold. He was the master of the house in the German tradition; my mother wouldn't dream of asking him where he was going when he left on weekends, sometimes with one or two of his long-time friends. Sunday afternoons, though, were reserved for a family walk, weather permitting.

An hour after dinner that first evening, he told my 57-year-old mother to go to bed, and she obediently kissed me good night. For a time we sat silently across from each other at the kitchen table, drinking the wine I had brought from our farm.

"I think you're making a mistake," he said, puffing on a smoke, "but not as bad as when you fell for that goddamn magician from Austria." I looked at him, sure that this was the opening shot of a long barrage, but he was smiling. "Do you know that I was actually proud of you when you rose that high in the Hitler Youth? Me, a Social Democrat who had hated the bastards ten years before? I'd even told my buddies then that we should make common cause with the Communists against the Nazis or they would bury us both. They almost kicked me out on my ass, but I was right."

"You were," I said, "and for what it's worth, I'm very sorry I thought times had passed you by. You were smarter than I."

"Come on," he chuckled, "you and your brother may have your mother's brains, but the three of you together don't have much common sense. You know, don't you, he left a good job in the *Krupp* factory office? And now you take off for Canada just when this country is going to get on its feet again. In a couple of years you kids could pick and choose. Christ, boy, you could end up in the *Bundestag*."

"You're kidding," I said. "I heard you were so fed up with your Social Democrats that you refused a paid position with them after the war. As the genuine enemy of the Nazis, you're the one who could be a big party wheel today. You're one of the rare untainted."

"To hell with that," he said, lifting his glass. "I burned myself out fuming at the Nazis for 12 years, then worrying about what the French would do to you for another three." In my whole life, it hadn't occurred to me that my distant father might worry about me.

"That's right," he continued, almost belligerently, "I did care what happened to you even if I let your grandmother take you." I stared at him, amazed. That subject had never arisen. "You know yourself you were much better off with her than with us," he nearly pleaded. "Believe me, boy, I did you a favor." He had tears in his eyes and I was embarrassed.

"Come on, Old Man," I said. "I've had a hell of a ride so far, and I never really missed you until today. Let's get drunk before I decide to stay here and climb on your steam shovel."

"You could do worse, you bastard," he grinned, "but that would be a waste of your grandmother's money, wouldn't it?"

That was the first and last time that my father and I drank much together, simply to hide our newly-found affection for each other. He missed my brother, although he had never told *him* that. In his guilt, he showed a side of him I had never seen. He was 58, and when I reached that age I looked startlingly like him, still with full hair but weary eyes. The following evening, after a quiet day together, he took me alone to the station. There was another first and last--he embraced me, and achieved what my mother hadn't done despite all her warmth. I loved him then.

In Canada with first car, a 1937 Packard

In Canada, 1952, with dog

Leaving Canada on Canadian Pacific Ferry to mainland and U.S., November, 1963

Chapter Ten:

IN THE MIDDLE OF THE HERD

The gleaming white M.S. *Fairsea*, a converted Liberty ship sailing under Liberian registry, was only four days into the gale-whipped Atlantic when all the beer was gone. The purser had underestimated the thirst of the 600 Germans aboard, who were joined by 300 French in Le Havre and 250 or so British at Dover. Despite the cramped quarters (men and women were separated into sleeping areas of 30 bunks) there was the carefree atmosphere of a carnival cruise.

For me, that feeling had started the minute we weighed anchor on the brisk, sunny October afternoon in Bremerhaven while the band played, "Must I Then Leave This Little Town?" a tear-jerker that had survived kings, kaisers, Hitler, and two world wars. The women cried openly and most of the men looked into the wind wiping their eyes. I swallowed a couple of lumps, not because I was homesick or feared the unknown, but out of triumph: I had escaped my past. Of course I no longer had to fear French or American occupiers--the age of persecution had ceased in 1948. The books were closed on all Nazis except those still slated for trial as "major offenders" on the Allied war crimes list. These were either fugitives, criminals in custody, or those who had been released by the authorities pending trial, which might be five to twenty years from now, if ever. Particularly in West Germany, the mills of justice ground as sleepily as the dripping sand in an hour glass. The prosecution of Nazis, which had never been popular in the *Bundesrepublik* (why foul our own nest), ranked in importance somewhere below traffic offenses in public opinion polls. German politicians, like those of other nations, saw no future in espousing unpopular causes. Only a handful preferred courage over reelection.

As the *Fairsea* heaved from one gigantic trough into another on the wild Atlantic, I often clung to the ropes and sang happily into the gale. With the whole North American continent awaiting me, I was freer than as if we had won the war. I had no idea how the French or British passengers felt, but I doubted they were escaping their political pasts. Canada, with its small army and less than 20 million population, wasn't a superpower, but it had other advantages. For one thing, we weren't likely to be drafted into its volunteer army, and for another, the vast country was very sparsely populated--one could easily get lost. There was no obligation to report a change of address as in Germany. I had lived under the strictest supervision throughout the Nazi era, not knowing what freedom was until the French deprived me of it. For three years after the war, I felt as threatened as the French must have under the *Gestapo* rule.

Crossing the Atlantic took 12 days. The weather was so rough that only a handful of us clung to the tables and chairs bolted down in the cavernous dining hall. We served ourselves from a row of containers held by steel bands and pinned our plates down on water-soaked table cloths. If I ate quickly and ran up on deck for fresh air, I could keep my stomach from churning.

The party atmosphere returned for the last three days of the voyage when the gale abated. Most French, British and Germans mingled freely with each other. The competition to dance with the numerous young French women was intense. This wasn't the "Queen Mary" where elegant ladies and gentlemen in evening clothes flirted under the glitter of crystal chandeliers and slipped discreetly into state rooms. This was a drunken sailors' ball. Whether former friends or deadly foes, we were now literally all in the same boat.

The rails were crowded with hushed passengers when the thin line of Canada's coast appeared, as fragile as a pencil stroke on the gray horizon. Gradually, as the wide mouth of the St. Lawrence narrowed from an ocean to a river, the New World emerged. I wandered from bow to stern most of the day, taking in the shore that was as rugged as any that I had seen. Despite the numerous, vividly painted wooden houses, the small settlements were overpowered by the wilderness. And this was the settled part of the country!

The continent's immensity struck me fully after we departed Quebec, which reminded me of a European city, in a Canadian Pacific train. About 60 of us remained, all bound for British Columbia. With the exception of two master carpenters, nobody had a job waiting. I had $28 in my wallet and Canadian Pacific meal tickets for 6 days, but I wasn't worried. Neither did I have any illusions; chances were I would end up on a farm, or if I got lucky, in a logging camp, where, I had heard, princely wages were paid. After 14-hour days on a German wine farm, lugging a hundred pounds of manure up steep slopes in a wooden backpack, I was ready for any kind of physical labor.

During the three-day journey, I sometimes awoke at night, climbed down from the bunk which folded into the ceiling, and looked at the endless, moonlit prairies of central Canada. Occasionally, the mournful blast of the locomotive sent a shiver of loneliness down my spine. Until three weeks ago, I had never seen the ocean, and now I couldn't wait to return to it again. The monotony of the land was in such contrast to the steep vineyards and green meadows of the Rhineland with its vista of rivers and ancient castles, that I felt a sudden stab of homesickness. I missed the endless action of the sea and its clean, tangy smell. If possible, I resolved to live close to the beach, the one plan that didn't dissolve into a mirage.

My uneasiness fled as soon as the breath-taking peaks of the Canadian Rockies mirrored themselves in the windows of the train. The most spectacular regions of the Alps looked tame compared to these craggy mountains that appeared totally wild, with no sign of man-made roads, huts, or ski lifts. The train snaked wearily through the gorge of the Fraser river like a long silvery worm, dwarfed by the precipitous walls of rock that cut off the rays of the sun. When it emerged into the rain-soaked, cool greenery of British Columbia's Okanagan Valley, I felt as if I had held my breath for a long time. At last I was seeing the wonders of the world, in addition to its horrors.

My life in Canada was not materially different from any of a thousand other immigrants. As a preparation for the decisive later years in the United States, it was largely a waste. Contrary to our expectation, the immigration officials in Vancouver had no jobs for us. It was November, and the logging industry was beginning to close down for the winter. The unemployment rate hovered close to nine percent, and nobody was keen on hiring foreigners. For $2.50 per day we could spend the winter in the clean bunks of the immigration building with plenty of food and company. Everybody assured us things would open up in the spring, and we could then repay our debt. To me, it seemed like a bad beginning. Again, my knowledge of English saved me. On the third morning at our sumptuous breakfast of cereal, fruit, bacon, eggs, muffins and mountains of delicious white bread and butter, I overheard an immigration officer say to another that the Canadian Railroad had six openings for an "extra gang" on Vancouver Island. I immediately volunteered and was asked to pick five others at random. None of us had any idea what an "extra gang" was, but it paid 74 cents an hour plus room and board. That meant a used car was no longer out of reach.

One of the immigration officers took us down to the ferry dock in Vancouver and bought us tickets on a ship which was larger than the M.S. *Fairsea*. The voyage through the San Juan Islands on the *Royal Princess* with its teak dining room and luxurious lounge is still a scenic highlight of a British Columbia visit today. This memorable trip ended in a far from glamorous railroad car, lit by kerosene lamps and filled with eight bunk beds, a coal stove and a dirty wooden table with two wash bowls.

We had been driven straight from the dock in Victoria to a siding deep in the woods. Nobody welcomed us at the work train. The driver pointed to one of the cars, strikingly like a cattle car with windows, and left. It was around ten at night, but everybody in the other cars seemed already asleep. We soon found out why. At five o'clock the next morning, a gong woke us and a man yelled: "Get up!" at the top of his lungs. I was still in my underwear, lining up at the wash bowls when the door tore open and a bearded giant in heavy rain gear strode in. "Get your asses to the dining car and worry about your toilet tonight," he said, "this isn't the goddamn Empress Hotel." Thus we were welcomed to our new career.

Boss Schultz was a decent guy despite his mountain man exterior. Within days he had advanced us rain gear, boots and gloves, and also supplied us with a new bunk car to replace the reeking mattresses in ours. We were the first "Displaced Persons" he had been sent, and he quickly realized how different we were from his 60 or so other workers. An "extra gang" consisted of men willing to lay and repair tracks and trestles and clean away underbrush from roadbeds for a very low wage. It was a way for most to get through the winter before returning to better-paying jobs in the lumber industry.

We six immigrants--four Germans and two Austrians--immediately irritated everybody because we actually worked. Boss Schultz and his foreman Ivan, a big Russian who spoke the wildest English I ever heard, spent a part of their ten-hour work days looking for men who slunk into the underbrush for card games. On the second day, as we were unloading kerosene-soaked wooden ties from a flat car, a delegation of three ruffians approached me, since I was the only one of us fluent in English. To my surprise, they weren't looking for a fight, but almost pleaded with us. "You D.P.s work too damn hard," said their leader. "You're screwin' up things for all of us. No Canadian busts his ass for 74 cents an hour. So take it easy before we gang up on you."

"What did you have in mind?" I asked, "burning down our bunk car?"

"Just take it easy, for Christ's sake," he spat, "and we'll get through the winter." To us, it seemed easier to use a shovel than to lean on it, but he had made his point. We were hopelessly outnumbered in an alien country. I decided to ask Schultz for advice. He let out a stream of truly inspired obscenities, but the next day he segregated us into a rail-drilling crew. From now on we trailed hundreds of yards behind the other men, joining the tracks they had laid. That was about the only skilled job, since the rails had to be adjusted to an exact width. The oldest of us was a 35-year-old Austrian from Graz, a former *Panzer* sergeant and mechanic by profession. For Othmar, who had fixed tanks under Russian fire, this was child's play. When the Canadian National Railroad engineer arrived to inspect our first day's work as drillers, he whistled in admiration. Not a single joint needed to be redone; from that day on we could do no wrong. To every visiting official, Schultz bragged about us as his "Nazi supermen."

Othmar was one of those gifted men who understood anything mechanical. He'd sooner spend time under a car than in it. Soon, he had Schultz's 1946 Buick purring as if it had just left the factory. As a reward, Schultz let us pick up the mail in it every evening at the nearest settlement. He later cursed himself for that. We became friendly with the couple that ran the post office and country store near an Indian reservation, and they told us that a major sawmill had job openings at twice the pay we were getting on the railroad. By then, however, it was early March, and we felt so much at home in the train and with Schultz, that he almost succeeded in persuading us to stay the summer at 25 cents an hour more, the highest rate he was authorized to pay. When we wouldn't budge he offered me a job as section foreman in charge of four men including Othmar, patrolling 30 miles of track near the west coast of the island. With the position came a two-room foreman's house next to the workers' bunk house. He was astounded when I turned him down; I would have been set for life with the Canadian National Railroad, an enterprise owned by the government.

There were times in later years that I regretted my refusal. Othmar made the decision for me; we had become friends and resolved to stick together. With his expertise, he could have had work in any car repair shop had it not been for his ignorance of the language. Night after night I taught him English, but it was tough going--he had no aptitude for learning a language. That wasn't much of a handicap to our future plans, however, for we intended to save some money and open a car repair shop together, with me doing the selling.

When I explained to Boss Schultz how we saw our future, he not only gave up graciously but drove us the 30 miles to Youbou, a mill town on the shore of Cowichan Lake in the tall fir country of the central island. Here, the British Columbia Forest Products Company operated its largest sawmill and three logging camps. I sweated during the interview, but I needn't have worried. When I told the personnel manager we were Germans, he hired us on the spot. "Germans are supposed to be the best workers," he smiled.

For the first two years with B.C. Forest, Othmar and I commuted 20 miles to work, for we still lived close to the Canadian family who owned the post office and store. When we told them we had been hired but had no place to live, they immediately offered us a three-room cottage behind the store. Thanks to Mr. and Mrs. Loyd's kindness, we got a good start and had an opportunity to immerse ourselves in the Canadian way of life. All that the Loyds knew about me was that I had been one of the youngest sailplane pilots of the *Luftwaffe*. That impressed Othmar, although he had no idea of my Hitler Youth rank. By some of his terse remarks about his service in the

Wehrmacht, I gathered that he was still sorry we had lost the war. As an Austrian, he had a soft spot for Hitler, believing *SS* leader Himmler had been the real culprit in organizing the persecution of the Jews. But he couldn't accept the scope of the extermination. "There just weren't that many Jews," he said once, "nobody who has seen chaos in Russia like I have can tell me there were exact figures." My own equilibrium was still so shaky--I hadn't liked it when Schultz had called us "Nazi supermen"--that I didn't want to open my soul to Othmar. We were all here to forget, not to remember.

Othmar and I shared our cottage and life with the Loyd family for two years. By then he had saved two thousand dollars and brought his girlfriend over from Austria. Canadian girls with their independent ways made him uncomfortable, especially when they corrected his English. He accepted that only from the Loyds and me. Two days after Hildegard arrived, I moved the 20 miles to Youbou.

Among the 500 workers of the sawmill I had risen to the top layer after a hard year pulling lumber from a moving "green chain" in the company of Chinese and East Indians. Six months later the company put me in a three-month training course grading lumber. Shortly after our exam, I belonged to the elite team of twelve inspectors who spent their eight-hour shifts grading lumber as it moved by on the chain at top speed. I was making $2.50 an hour in a time when a family of four could live on $300 a month, so I was well off. But soon, the monotony of the work became so oppressive that I dreaded getting up in the morning. Only the quiet, deep, 15-mile long lake, set like an amethyst in a crown of forests, kept me at the mill through three more years. Before long I acquired the reputation of an eccentric, for I neither hunted nor fished, but drifted for days on the silent lake with a book in my hands. My co-workers didn't understand why I willingly accepted their venison but wouldn't go hunting with them. They hadn't seen what I had; the only way I could ever again point a gun at any living thing would be in self-defense.

The personnel manager who had hired Othmar and me five years earlier had started to drop hints that I was in line for supervisor. I left him speechless, therefore, when I walked in one noon and quit. "For Christ's sake," he stammered after I assured him that Othmar would stay on, "you better think this over. In just 15 years you can retire from here with a good pension."

"I'm sorry," I said, "you were decent to us, but the smell of lumber makes me gag by now. I'd sooner become a bum in Victoria than stay another month."

In retrospect, I don't have much to show for my twelve years in Canada, although I was the minor partner in the Harbor Taxi Company, which operated six cabs in Victoria. Two of these, a beaten-up Chevrolet and a black Cadillac limousine, the pride of our fleet, belonged to me. For two years, I was also the general manager of Johnson's Cafe, a busy 24-hour eatery which catered to dock workers and sailors of the Victoria waterfront. When the operator offered me a partnership *and* volunteered to put up all the money for the purchase, I decided I had nothing to lose. Sandor had recently made several thousand dollars working in a gold mine in the Yukon. I still had my cabs to fall back on if things went sour, but they didn't. We worked 12-hour shifts, he at night and I during the day, and we soon showed a good profit in the refurbished cafe.

As happens to so many partnerships, ours ended over a woman. Sandor, who was a refugee of the 1956 Hungarian revolt, fell for a British seamstress in her '30s, who owned a tiny shop next door to us. She was a quick-witted attractive blonde, divorced and with a ten-year-old girl. Unlike many Hungarian and German immigrants (Othmar included) who eventually returned to their homelands, Sandor never suffered from homesickness. His main interest was making money. When the lady offered to work as a cashier on busy Saturdays for no pay, I should have become suspicious. By the time I did, it was too late.

When she began to show up during my shift and work as if she owned the place, I confronted an embarrassed Sandor. "We're going to get married," he said, in decent German, "and she wants to work with us as a third partner and manager."

"Not over me," I said bluntly, "not a woman. It won't work, Sandor; the fun is over." We embraced, and the next day he handed me a generous check for $2,000. Since we had never signed a written agreement, he wasn't legally obligated to pay me beyond my salary and the profit split for each month. I decided to sell my cabs and go home.

Two weeks later I met my wife. She was a cashier at the civic arena of Victoria, and I was a cab driver searching for customers. What better contact for my taxi business than an employee in the entertainment center which drew the largest crowds in Victoria? When I could neither entice her to go for a cup of coffee, nor accept a free ride home, I wondered if I had lost my touch. This woman didn't even fall for my two most effective lines: one, that I wasn't the marrying kind; and two, that there were more important matters in life than sex. After a final confession that indeed I *had* hoped to gain some customers through her, she relented and we went on a series of unusually chaste dates.

I was quite vulnerable at that time; I had been ousted from my promising restaurant partnership by a woman, the same week my beloved grandmother died unexpectedly at 81. My Uncle Victor had berated me for writing to her only once or twice a year, and once even had the Canadian Red Cross searching for me. After his last letter, in which he minced no words about my "brutal indifference," I called my grandmother for only the third time in nine years and promised I would come home, perhaps for good. "Make it soon," she had pleaded. "I miss you so much." I then let another eight months slip by with only one letter. During the war, I had seldom written her, but she knew I loved her. Now she was dead, and with her, my chance to make amends.

During one long evening, I tried to tell June what my grandmother had meant to me, and before I knew it, I had touched on the Nazi era and admitted my former fanatic adherence to Hitler, something I had never mentioned to Othmar in our five years together. I was dumbfounded that June was not in the least perturbed. At 26, she had little concept of the war era; like her brother Ken and many other Canadians, she harbored not the slightest animosity toward Germans. That was exactly what I needed in those weeks of self-recrimination about my grandmother--not to be judged for my past failings. Overwhelmed by the understanding of this family at a time when I badly needed it, my resolve to remain a bachelor crumbled. We were married quietly without benefit of clergy.

Before our marriage, I had gingerly broached the subject of children, which I didn't want. What I didn't then admit was that my complicity in the death of so many Hitler Youth adolescents played a large part in my feeling. To my relief, June felt the same, albeit for other reasons.

Within a year my wife had me out of the taxi business, which she did not consider suitable work for a married man because of the long night hours. I enrolled in a journalism seminar through the University of Victoria, the purpose of which was to prepare aspiring free-lance writers to sell their material. The professor was impressed that I, a foreigner, had sold a political opinion piece on immigration to the *Daily Colonist*, Victoria's major paper in October 1956. I didn't tell him that I had been so exhilarated by this, my first article in English, that I had applied for a job at the paper. Understandably, the editor hadn't been eager to hire a German with no knowledge of the city, let alone a solid grasp of Canadian politics. He advised me to frame my eight-dollar check, since there might never be another. Even Canadian journalism graduates were having trouble finding jobs in Canada. "Try your luck in the United States, young man," he said. Thirty-one years later, his newspaper did a feature on the article which had launched me on a writing career when I returned to Victoria to autograph the Canadian edition of my first book. He was dead by then, but his advice to go to the United States had been sound.

During my 12 years in Canada, I left Vancouver Island only five times, twice for visits to Vancouver and the mainland, once for a weekend in Seattle during the 1962 world's fair, and later that year for a three-week trip down the west coast to San Diego. That visit paved the way to my last good-bye from Canada. Prompted more by my wife's insistence than by my own desire, I applied for a permanent visa to the United States. June, born and raised in sheets of refreshing downpour on Vancouver Island, had discovered the lure of southern California's eternal warmth. By the time I discovered I preferred the cool rain of the northwest with its various moods, it was too late.

After we returned from our vacation to California, I still had no intention of leaving Victoria. Determined to become a writer, I entered a one-act playwriting contest offered by the Ottawa Little Theatre. I was elated when my 30-page play "Choice of Evil" was selected as one of the three best entries in the Canadian-wide contest. As the only immigrant among the budding playwrights, I exacted brief, but nationwide attention. That fall, an amateur theatre group in Toronto proposed to stage the play, which dealt with the capture of an *SS* officer by a

Jewish Canadian Army captain. This might well lead to Broadway, I speculated. And then my play came back; the company had gone broke. Instead of a check, I received a letter of praise by a high-ranking immigration official. Disgruntled, I applied for a visa to the United States, the bastion of capitalism, where I assumed even writers were paid.

Many times later, hostile questioners demanded to know how and when I, an admitted former Nazi, had made it into the United States, implying that there was something sinister about my entry. Perhaps I had been assisted by a network of ex-*SS* fanatics, as in *The Odessa File*. I had made no effort to obscure my past. All of my wartime Hitler Youth activities had taken place either in my home county where thousands of people knew me, or in one location in Luxembourg where I had stood out like a virgin in a brothel. Before the French finished with me, they were convinced I hadn't committed any crimes. But it no longer puzzles me that some people are skeptical about my past. Hatred, I have learned, is bound neither by logic nor reason.

We were in Nogales, Arizona, preparing to visit Mexico, when President John F. Kennedy was assassinated on November 22, 1963, just nine days after we had entered the United States. The murder of the President, who had stood up against the Russians during the Cuban missile crisis of October 1962, shocked me into the reality of the United States. I briefly wondered if we shouldn't return to Canada. During his visit to West Berlin, Kennedy had been wildly applauded when he said: *"Ich bin ein Berliner,"* after his inspection of the infamous Berlin Wall. He had been safer among the throngs of Berliners, which surely contained many former Nazis, than in his own country. And yet, democracy had functioned flawlessly; nobody had used the days of national trauma to seize power. This was the land which, despite its lunatic contradictions, determined the fate of the Western World. Those first two weeks fuelled a lasting excitement which neither Canada nor Europe could hope to match. I belonged here.

After our four-week vacation through the western states, I returned to Seattle and found the perfect job to still my insatiable curiosity about Americans: I became a Greyhound bus driver. In those pre-deregulation years, Greyhound drivers received excellent wages, often better than middle level executives, but my incentive was the unexcelled opportunity to meet America in its undershirt. Every day I was a part of real American life, with all its prejudice and indifference, as well as with its tolerance and genuine friendliness. I occasionally grinned as I watched my passengers in the mirror. They would have been surprised that "leave the driving to us" included an ex-sailplane pilot of the *Luftwaffe*.

From Seattle I transferred to San Francisco for six years and then to San Diego, my wife's favorite city. Neither one of us missed our birth places. After my father died of cancer, induced by his four packs of cigarettes a day, I seldom thought of Germany except at Christmas. I missed the snow. Gradually, all correspondence with my former classmates stopped; our lives ran in different channels. Two or three times a year I wrote my family in Wittlich, but I kept in close touch only with my brother Rudolf, who had also left Germany. He worked for a French-German corporation in Paris and had married a tiny French woman. He was puzzled that I was content driving a bus in the United States, which despite the good income was a step down the social ladder for an educated European. During these years, we didn't mention the Nazi era; he ascribed my revulsion with management positions to my past.

Our only close friends in America were Jacques and Sarah. She was an American but Jacques was French. Our European backgrounds drew us together. Possibly because we were the same age, we never discussed details of the war, although we occasionally got carried away at parties and sang the *Marseilleise* and German marching songs. Jacques' village had been occupied by the Germans and mine by the French. Times, presumably, hadn't been pleasant for either one of us.

At least twice a month we shared big meals with plenty of good wine. On such occasions, Jacques extolled the virtues of French culture while reminding us that we were living in the midst of barbarians who actually mixed the finest French cognac with Coke and drank aged Burgundy ice cold. Jacques had witnessed this travesty in a restaurant and never gotten over it. He kept admonishing me to return to Germany since I wasn't "trapped" with four kids like he, and still had a choice.

Jacques' reminiscences of Europe and my brother's letters were beginning to have an effect on us, but what made me decide to visit Germany after 16 years was the news that my

Aunt Maria, who, next to my grandmother, had been closest to me, was dying of bronchial cancer. She had always lived moderately, never smoked or drank more than an occasional glass of our wine, and lived in a valley famous for its clean air. Her condition seemed a particularly cruel blow at 64. The war had robbed her of the only man she had ever loved, and when my Aunt Luise called me to say she was hanging on only long enough to see me again, I couldn't do to her what I had done to my grandmother.

Despite that moral obligation, I still wondered what I was doing in Europe as our Lufthansa jet descended into Orly airport at dawn. The gray, drizzly skies suddenly reminded me of the *Westwall*, an image which hadn't flickered across my mind for years. I had a sinking feeling this trip had been a dreadful mistake. I couldn't have been more wrong.

The next three weeks were some of the best of our lives. My brother and I fell into each others arms, while his wife spontaneously embraced mine. Three days later, all of us, including the Siamese cat Oreste and our dachshund Cindy, were on our way to Germany in my brother's Peugeot. After the immense distances of Canada and the United States, Europe seemed strangely miniaturized, as if I were looking at it through the wrong end of binoculars.

The trip to my hometown in Germany from Paris took less than seven hours, including a brief visit to Verdun, the blood-soaked killing ground of World War I where a million and a half young Frenchmen and Germans died within an eight-mile radius. I wanted to see Fort Douamont where our father had fought Frenchmen underground, sometimes with bayonets on the staircases leading from one level to another. My brother claimed it was here that our father's hatred of war and disrespect for government began. I wondered why it hadn't had the same effect on Corporal Adolf Hitler. The battlefield of Verdun was a sobering contrast to the glitter of the Champs Elisees. My wife grew quiet as she gazed at the piles of human bones heaped in the "bone house" of the Verdun war cemetery monument.

Before lunch in a Verdun restaurant, my brother cautioned us not to speak English until he had ordered our food. "They raise the prices for Americans," he grinned. The spring of 1967 wasn't a good time for Americans to visit France. General de

Gaulle had just withdrawn his country from NATO's military alliance and ordered American troops to leave France, despite the loss of tens of thousands of French civilian jobs. The General's prickly honor couldn't stand American bases on French soil. "Would you believe," smiled my brother, "that we Germans are better liked in France than the Amis?" I could see that with my own eyes. While it seemed like the rankest ingratitude, since Americans had saved the French from us Germans, the Vietnam war had played a large part in creating the animosity toward the United States. The huge Communist Party of France saw the Americans in Vietnam as mindless killers, especially since France had pulled out of Indochina.

Two hours later we had crossed the German-French border, once the deadliest obstacle in the world, merely by showing our passports. The polite customs officials were more interested in an American-born dachshund than in us. When we reached the Mosel river valley, I pointed across the stream to the Luxembourg shore. We were only ten minutes from my former Hitler Youth headquarters of 1944. It seemed like a century had passed.

As we followed the river into Germany toward the Rhine, I grew silent. I had forgotten how beautiful my home province was. In the waning light, my wife saw her first castle high atop a steep vineyard above the river. "My God," she gasped, "how could you have left this?" From that moment, she was in love with Germany.

It was dark when we approached Wittlich from the south. I recognized the silhouette of the church and the buildings that now marked 23 years as the barracks of the French garrison. Far from hating the French as I had done in those bitter postwar years, the people of Wittlich now considered the thousand soldiers a valuable financial asset to the community. Since 1955, they had been the military allies of the *Bundeswehr*.

Fifteen family members met us at the gate of the farm. My Aunt Maria ran forward and we held each other for a long time until I could trust myself to speak again. I was home. My wife felt uncomfortable that first evening, for the whole family stood around the dining room table and examined us as if we were prized cattle. It didn't help when Uncle Gustav demanded to know why we didn't have any children.

We were on a whirlwind of parties almost nightly, but I did

spend many hours with my aunt who, despite her frailty, didn't seem close to death. One afternoon we stood silently before the family grave. The last name engraved on the black marble was that of my grandmother. As I bent down to place a dozen roses in the vase on the flower bed, my aunt made her only remark to me about her illness. "I'm glad you came," she said. "I'll soon join her." When I started to protest, she silenced me with a wave of her hand. "Let's not talk about death again while you are here. Life can be worse." Three weeks after we returned to California, she was dead.

My wife saw much of the beauty of the Rhineland in these few days, but almost no scars from the conflagration of the war. As we looked at the spires of the Cathedral of Cologne from the main railroad station, she found it hard to believe that these lovely surroundings had been a vast heap of rubble in the fall of 1945. The physical resurrection of West Germany was a powerful testimony to the industry of the German people, but to my amazement, no one except me seemed interested in the past.

"What's wrong with you?" asked my *Westwall* buddy Wolfgang Knopp, who had succeeded his late father as the publisher of the popular *Wittlicher Tageblatt*. Wolfgang, three other classmates and I had met in Rex Friderichs' wine restaurant, Rex being one of the original *Cusanus Gymnasium* gang. "Are you still pondering the follies of our youth? The *Wirtschaftswunder* doesn't leave us time for useless reflections, my boy. We paid the piper long ago."

After that, I didn't ask him to accompany me to the *Westwall*, as I had intended. Even my brother wasn't interested. Wittlich had a couple of blown-up bunkers overgrown by grass. Wasn't that good enough? My wife and I made the circle to Luxembourg and back in half a day. We lunched in Trier, within view of the 2,000-year-old Roman Porta Nigra, the huge black gate erected before Christ. About mid-afternoon, I halted the car on the bridge to Remisch where I had once met Fabianne. The retreating *Wehrmacht* had blown up the ancient stone bridge, and this new, modern steel span evoked no memory. I couldn't even find a trace of our huge antitank barrier, although I recognized the farmhouse where it had started. The young farmer I questioned about the war shrugged. "Sorry, I was two years old when the Americans drove out the Germans. I vaguely remember my father filling in a ditch in what's now my orchard."

When I asked if the parish house and cemetery were still there, he looked curiously at me but without animosity. "The cemetery was moved close to our new school right after the war. A bunch of shells had ripped it up pretty badly on the last day of the fighting and it wasn't used again. The parish is still there, but the old priest and his sister died a few years ago. Did you know them?"

When I explained that our command post had been in the parish and that we had dug up his orchard to stop the American tanks, he grinned. "Didn't do much good, did it? God, what a waste of everybody's time." As far as World War II was concerned, that Luxembourg farmer summed it up more succinctly than most historians. Whether Frenchmen, Germans or Luxembourgers, the prevailing sentiment in 1967 was that the only war of interest was being waged currently by Americans. My teenage cousins greeted my few references to the Nazi era with an indulgent yawn, but questioned me closely about the ethics of the American involvement in Vietnam, and about race relations in the United States. They had seen the Watts riots on television. Watching our Sunday evening meal be preempted for "Bonanza" was the last straw. With that jolt into the 1960s, I too forgot the shadows of the past and enjoyed our vacation thoroughly.

I was an anachronism, as my friend Hans-Josef Fabry laughingly observed when we spent a day with him and his family in his hotel at Dudeldorf. He was very fond of Americans; the U.S. fighter base in nearby Spangdahlem had made him a millionaire with its influx of local workers who patronized his hotel, butcher shop, and cinema. American officers met each Wednesday noon in one of the hotel conference rooms for a big German sausage dinner and then went bowling in the hotel's alley. While the four of us were drinking exquisite champagne in his luxurious private dining room tiled in Italian marble, my suggestion to make a quick visit to the cemetery at Bitburg where some of my former Hitler Youth charges were buried, was quickly brushed aside by everybody, including my wife. She remembered that 18 years later when President Reagan's visit there unleashed a storm of controversy. The day and night faded into a pink haze of alcoholic nostalgia.

My mother, then 74, was still in excellent health. When she saw the four of us together she dissolved into tears and laughter, hugging and kissing us time and time again. I was thoroughly embarrassed by my mother's unbridled affection, despite the fact that she hadn't seen my brother and me together for 18 years. I was relieved when we left Oberhausen the next day for the 200-kilometer drive home to Wittlich. Wittlich and my family there were home, not where my mother lived.

After a tumultuous evening of good-byes, which included my family and school friends, I looked back through the car window at the roofs of Wittlich nestled in the green valley of forests and vineyards just as the sun was rising. Suddenly I was seized by such a feeling of impending doom that I broke into tears. "I'm never going to see this again," I sobbed. "I'm going to die in America." My sister-in-law Josiane wasn't as embarrassed as my wife who had never seen me cry in public. While I buried my face into my dachshund's fur, Josiane reached for my hand.

Not only had I made peace with the past, I had planned for the future, but paradoxically, I still felt cornered. We had enjoyed Wittlich so much that in a long family discussion we had decided to retire here in 15 years. Uncle Franz would furnish us with an apartment on the farm for very reasonable rent. It seemed the ideal solution to the problem of aging in the United States, where sickness and debility often mean poverty and degradation. Germany, to be sure, had higher taxes, but like all developed countries with the exception of the United States and South Africa, it cared adequately for its elderly and sick. Not that I thought much about old age; I was nearing 40 and, I assumed, in good health, according to Greyhound's mandatory annual checkups. My pension would allow us to grow old comfortably in the beautiful town that I had come to miss again during this visit.

As the half empty Lufthansa jet climbed into the Paris night, bound for San Francisco, my wife and I toasted each other, our dog between us slinging down a slice of lox. Our life had never been more promising, especially after the warmth of this vacation. During the following year, we talked so much of that first trip that its lure proved irresistible. We returned for another three weeks, which reinforced our first impression and was made even better by my wife's feeling thoroughly at home. We had bought the tickets for our third trip in 1972, when our world crashed. Without any warning, I suffered a devastating, disabling heart attack.

ALFONS HECK & HELEN WATERFORD

Chapter Eleven:

THE BURDEN OF HITLER'S LEGACY

My wife almost certainly saved my life on that January evening when I doubled over with searing chest pain, but still I wouldn't let her call an ambulance. I couldn't imagine that my heart was about to quit at the age of 43. She had me in our car when the second wave hit, making me slump against the dash board. I was barely conscious when the emergency team at San Diego's Mercy Hospital lifted me out of the front seat, still with my dachshund Cindy on my lap. The next thing I remember clearly was a young priest standing over my bed while doctors and nurses attached tubes and hoses to me. By then I had been injected with morphine and was drifting in and out of consciousness with little pain.

The feeling of impending doom was gone, and I wondered what the priest was doing there. When he made the sign of the cross over me and opened a small vessel containing holy oil, I realized with a start that he was about to perform the Last Rites of the Catholic Church; I hadn't been an altar boy for nothing. His presence, however, struck me as wasted effort. I had no intention of dying, which, at that hour, was an optimism not shared by anyone else. My wife had been told to gather the family--of which there was none within 2,000 miles--because I would likely expire before morning. The young priest had sneaked into intensive care against her wishes; she feared his somber appearance might trigger the final, fatal shock.

On the contrary. "It won't work," I whispered through caked lips, "unless you give me an unconditional absolution. I haven't been to confession for years." He almost dropped his oil.

"Please don't strain yourself," he urged. "You've had a coronary and you need absolute rest. We can do the confession later, if you make a brief repentance now. Are you sorry for all your sins?"

"Sure," I murmured, not wishing to offend. "I regret whatever I did wrong, including in the war."

"What war?" he asked, and that's the last I heard or saw. Apparently I passed out smiling. But that was the last fun I had for a long time. The blow fell a month later, the day I left the hospital. The doctors had told me that the infarct had not only produced an aneurism but had caused so much damage to the heart muscle that my activities would be severely limited henceforth.

I prepared myself for a long recovery, a just punishment for the careless life style that had put me into this predicament. I was a heavy meat eater, 35 pounds overweight, and smoked two packs of cigarettes a day along with an occasional cigar. My compulsive "Type A" personality seldom allowed me a real rest. I had never been a minute late in nine years at Greyhound and often worked on my days off, despite my wife's dire warnings that I was headed for trouble. Now it had come, surpassing our worst nightmares. On the day of my hospital release a company physician, in a master stroke of insensibility, told me I would be retired on permanent disability. Greyhound wouldn't even allow me to sell tickets unless I could pass an impossible physical. Worse, I was one year short of claiming any kind of pension. My monthly disability income--less than one fifth of my former wages--didn't even cover the rent; we would be broke in a year. I was through at the age of 43.

For three days I lay on my bed, mechanically stroking my dog who sat patiently beside me. I refused to eat or talk, except for occasionally berating my wife for having rescued me. I demanded that she return to Canada and her family. The only time I had felt so hopelessly cornered was the night the French threatened to execute me.

When my wife went to work at the age of 40 to feed and house us, I was emasculated, merely an impotent invalid, a burden to everybody. I couldn't understand why she wanted to stay with me. She was still young and could find somebody else. I would make an "honorable" return to Germany where I could die. The urge to flee to the farm where I had been born became such a fixation that I wrote my Uncle Franz without my wife's knowledge, begging him to let me come home. I wanted to be buried next to my grandmother. Weeks later, his wife explained awkwardly why they couldn't help me. As an American citizen, I was not entitled to any medical coverage in Germany, so there was no room on the farm. Besides, they said, my loyal wife didn't deserve to be deserted. She could ship them my ashes, though.

Strangely, that nadir of humiliation and my wife's contemptuous remark that only cowards give up, saved me from sinking into the last, suicidal depression. I considered buying a pistol and cursed the French for not having shot me in 1945.

My heart pumped so inefficiently that I landed in emergency a dozen times that first year. An angiogram showed that I was a risky candidate for the still experimental cardiac bypass surgery because of the damage the muscle had sustained. Additionally, doctors discovered, I had diabetes and high blood pressure.

Day after day I sprawled on the bed, listlessly watching television. Most of it was a numbing waste, but the war movies sent my blood pressure soaring. Few had anything in common with the war I remembered. Even some of the most expensive productions commonly confused the German uniforms, such as putting SS rank insignia on *Luftwaffe* tunics. What these antiseptic, modern horse sagas needed was reality, the unforgettable but inimitable smell of war.

"Do Americans really believe this nonsense?" I demanded from my wife. "It's an insult to their dead as well as to their intelligence. The war was hardly like 'Hogan's Heroes.' Somebody ought to tell them the real story."

"Why don't you do it then, instead of petting the dog all day?" she shot back at me. "What's your excuse now that you have all that time on your hands? I'll support you forever if you'll only do something." Two days later, I enrolled in a creative writing course at a nearby community college.

During the next four years, I suffered a second heart attack, an embolism, and a stroke followed by brain surgery to relieve some of the paralysis it had caused on my left side. My recovery, however, began that first evening in class. My saleable asset was my unparalleled view of Nazi Germany, where I had risen to a high rank in its most victimized organization, the Hitler Youth. I began to realize that the vague uneasiness I had often felt was an urge to attend to this unfinished business. During my innocuous life as an American, I studied the enigma of Nazi Germany in hundreds of books, most mediocre or severely slanted to the view of the victors. Now, seasoned by the awareness of my own mortality, I plotted to describe with cold objectivity how I had been ensnared and then recovered from the fanaticism of my youth. I soon discovered that no one is that capable. The most honest evaluation is tinged by self-serving emotion, especially when greeted with skepticism and hostility.

Aliton was a stimulating teacher as well as a tough, incisive editor with the gentle soul of a poet who shuddered from all violence, but her instincts were sound. I wasn't ready to expose myself to America as a former fanatic Nazi. What better solution than to hide behind a novel? Nobody is punished for committing fictional atrocities. It didn't work for me, but my two years and 500 pages of a sex and violence-peppered war novel were a valuable apprenticeship. This exercise cured my black depression.

I put the manuscript in the closet and began to write articles of a general nature, some dealing with health issues. Eventually, my tenacity began to pay off; I sold an article here and there, usually to small publications. In December 1978, the *San Diego Union* accepted my first article mentioning my Nazi past. It was entitled "German Loss Finally Set Me Free." Two hours after the Sunday edition was on the streets, the phone rang and a male caller inquired politely if I were the author of the article.

"Yes," I said, "did you like it?"

"We liked it so much, you Jewish pimp," he said, "that we are going to kill you on New Year's Eve." He hung up, and I stood there with the phone in my hand and the blood pounding in my ears. The second call came 20 minutes later, but this time I was prepared.

"Yes, I wrote the article," I answered. "Would you mind giving me your name?"

"Never mind the social stuff," he shouted. "You have just two weeks left to live."

"I know," I said as calmly as I could. "You're going to kill me on New Year's Eve, but would you mind telling me why?"

"Sure, I'll tell you why," he said. "You're pimping for the Jews and you've insulted the memory of the greatest man who ever lived."

"Who's that?" I asked.

"You know goddamn well who I mean, you Judas. Adolf Hitler, the man you betrayed." Suddenly, the lights went on. In the closing paragraph of the article, I had questioned how otherwise sane Americans were parading around in Nazi uniforms vowing to preserve white supremacy by separating whites and blacks.

"Are you guys members of the American Nazi Party?" I asked, not really expecting a fervent 'yes'.

"Never mind who we are," said the man calmly now, as if he had gone beyond his original message. "We're going to kill you within two weeks." He hung up. I didn't know whether to laugh or update my will. My wife didn't have to think twice; she was badly shaken.

"Why did you have to make people mad enough to kill you?" she said accusingly. "You could have omitted that paragraph."

"Why should I?" I yelled. "This is a free country and this is the way I see it, and nobody is ever going to shut me up again, understand?" I did, however, allow my wife to call the police. Anonymous phone threats are commonplace, but after a brief interview the police notified FBI agents, who didn't dismiss the calls out of hand as I had expected. They not only suggested a number of precautions, but kept us under discreet surveillance for some time.

During these weeks of apprehension, I decided that no threat would stop me from writing what I perceived to be the truth. The Nazi conquest of the German people had started exactly like that: with intimidation. If I allowed myself to be silenced now, I had learned nothing from the past. No rational person likes to die violently, but a few things are worth taking the risk. I was glad that my wife understood that.

I wrote other articles about current issues that occasionally found praise, but whenever I interpreted a snippet of the Nazi era, I drew fire, not always anonymously. When a German war veteran wrote that I had glossed over the suffering of the population during the air raids, I sympathized, but it had nothing to do with the impetus of the Marshall Plan, which was the focus of my article. What amazed me was that I never heard from a Jewish reader. I began to imagine that I was so fair-minded that only radical right wing extremists found me offensive.

And then in October 1980, Helen Waterford called. Not only was she Jewish, she had survived Auschwitz. Most surprising, she sounded genuinely cordial. She complimented me on an article I had written for the *San Diego Union*, in which I had admitted my former enthusiasm for Hitler. My honesty had been her impetus for calling me. For a few seconds I was totally bewildered by her remark that she was curious about "our side." Former adherents of Nazism and its Jewish victims didn't talk to each other; there was something unnatural about that. The wall between us was too high for friendly talk. And then I felt a twinge of shame. This lady had the courage to do the impossible, something I wouldn't have dared for fear of being rebuffed: she had held out her hand to a once deadly foe. That deserved a civil response. I, too, was curious; despite my extensive research into all facets of Nazism, including the fate of its victims, I had never *talked* to a death camp survivor. It would be awkward to be sure, despite the easy politeness of this call, but I would gain valuable insight and enough material for a couple of articles.

After Mrs. Waterford explained herself, I readily accepted her invitation for a meeting. She, and a half dozen other survivors, had volunteered time to speak about their ordeals under the Nazi regime, usually in schools on behalf of the Jewish Federation of San Diego. She was about to chair a meeting of the speakers and wondered if I would like to attend. I was touched by her understanding; these people could apparently surmount their hostility. It would have been churlish not to accept.

The only problem was that Mrs. Waterford neglected to tell her fellow speakers that I was coming, let alone who I was. Their friendly, smiling faces turned to pinched masks when she introduced me. "This is Alfons Heck," she said as calmly as if I were a fellow Jew they hadn't met before. "He was a member of the Hitler Youth, and he is a writer now." I was dumbfounded. Had she done this to embarrass both myself and the other speakers? If so, she had certainly succeeded. I felt like a child molester in a police line-up. Indeed, a repentant child molester would have been more welcome in this group. The stigma of Nazism in the minds of its victims is so strong that I didn't have to wonder if anybody but Mrs. Waterford would shake my hand. We didn't get far beyond the introduction. Two members left the room abruptly and the others avoided looking at me while I talked with my hostess.

Our acquaintance might have ended there, had it not been for our mutual discomfort. Far from intending to embarrass anyone, Mrs. Waterford had naively assumed that her fellow speakers would be as interested in meeting me as she had been. She was indeed an anomaly--a survivor who didn't loathe Germans, even those who had served Hitler willingly. Not only that, she assured me that she had never hated any Nazis, even the *Gestapo* men which had arrested her and her husband in their Dutch hiding place. I had trouble believing that, but I compared my experience to hers. Long ago I had stopped hating any former enemy, not only the French who had imprisoned me, but the anonymous Soviets who had annihilated all 22 members of my mother's branch of the family in Pomerania. I would have shot them all in 1945, French and Russians, but in retrospect I realized that we had started the war and we must reap its harvest. Apparently Mrs. Waterford had undergone a similar metamorphosis, realizing that unrelieved hatred is self-destructive. For a victim, though, that seemed to be a singular feat. I could accept that she didn't hate now, but surely she must have hated in the past, unless she was a saint! Her mind was undoubtedly playing tricks with her memory to preserve her sanity. Nevertheless, to voice to other survivors what I considered (falsely, I learned much later) a blanket absolution to all Nazi miscreants, took a lot of courage. But Helen Waterford *didn't* forgive; she just didn't hate.

When I said good-bye to this short, plump 71-year-old grandmother with her gray hair cut short in a no-nonsense style, we agreed to meet again in more neutral quarters, her home. She had made me an intriguing proposal. The San Diego School District had invited her to speak to a workshop of teachers about the Holocaust, and she thought I should join her to give a brief account of my side. I was captivated by the idea, mainly because I wanted to listen to her impressions of the Nazi regime. I sensed that she wasn't going to recite endless, gruesome details of torture, salted with outbursts of hate against all Germans, because in our brief conversation I learned that she had visited Germany several times after the war and still admired its beauty. That was an indication of her open-mindedness. On May 12, 1965, Israel established formal, diplomatic relations with the Federal Republic of West

Germany which, over the years, has led to a large volume of trade with many favorable concessions to the Israelis. Still, there are thousands of American Jews who wouldn't visit Germany if the trip were free. They echo the newly appointed lady rabbi recently quoted in a San Diego newspaper who said she could do anything socially acceptable except wear a bikini in public or drive a German car. I can understand that a *Gestapo* torture victim might shy away from anything German, but when a 20-year-old claimed that while he admired the quality of a Porsche, he wouldn't buy a "Nazi" car, I couldn't take his anguish seriously.

This time, Helen Waterford took the precaution of clearing my participation with David Vigilante, an official of the school district's Race Relations Committee which had arranged the symposium. Mr. Vigilante wanted to assure himself that I no longer harbored or advocated pro-Nazi opinions. After he scanned my recent articles in Helen's home, he not only gave his assent, he tried to allay my misgivings. What I had to say addressed the theme of his own work--the eradication of all forms of prejudice.

During that meeting at Helen Waterford's home we agreed on the sequence of our presentation. We planned to take turns talking about our radically different lives under Nazism, to give our audience the view from both sides. Beginning in 1933, we would proceed in chronological order to the end of our respective wars in 1945. David's enthusiasm seemed premature to me. Mrs. Waterford was assured of our listeners' sympathy, but I might well encounter hostility. I planned to deflect the worst of it by emphasizing my age. Despite my rank in the Hitler Youth, I had been only 17 when Germany surrendered on May 8, 1945.

Mutual honesty was, we agreed, the only criterion. I was certain of my facts, but could we hold our emotions in check and refrain from preaching? I worried, too, that the stark contrast of our stories would confuse the listeners. There would be a question-and-answer period determined by the interest of the audience that could become a nerve-racking finale for me. I made up my mind to give a no-holds-barred, straightforward account of my indoctrination, in an attempt to put the teachers in my shoes.

I had now taken an irrevocable step; it was one thing to write about Nazism, but quite another to expose myself publicly as a former fanatic. Despite the potential for danger, I experienced an uncanny feeling of relief. By publicly confronting my past 35 years after the war, the burden of repression was beginning to be lifted. Whatever the audience might think of me, I was doing this for myself.

I needn't have worried about the audience. Helen's strong voice, unlike my rather soft one, doesn't need a microphone to penetrate a hall. My attention was so focused on what she said that it was some time before I noticed how attentively the 60 or so teachers listened. Her unemotional account of the advent of Nazism was so unaccusingly honest--as if she were coolly performing an autopsy on her own life--that it had an impact no hand-wringing lament could have matched. I could only follow with an equal absence of theatrics.

There were two other symposiums being conducted at that time, but after the first break our room was jammed with hundreds of teachers who had deserted the other workshops. Word had spread of this unlikely combination of speakers, former Nazi and victim. Even in this first lecture, I made the point that while Helen spoke for her dead, I also did for mine: the children of the Hitler Youth who had been sacrificed.

Seven years and nearly 200 nationwide lectures have passed since this first presentation to the teachers of San Diego, but few have equalled the excitement and satisfaction of that first one. We were there all morning, answering questions. Some were simple, some were complicated, all were interesting in their newness. I was relieved that none of the questioners showed any open hostility toward me. On the contrary; people commended me for my "honesty and courage." But I felt that David Vigilante had shown more courage by inviting me. From that day on, he jokingly referred to himself as our "midwife."

The format which we established in that first speech never changed; neither did our feeling of trust for each other. Unlike Helen, it hadn't occurred to me that our relationship as speakers would go past this first meeting, but the interest at the symposium had been so infectious that it led immediately to more invitations, first locally on the high school level. None of these first talks evoked the hostility I expected, but one 17-year-old asked me a question that tested me as no other before or since.

"Sir," he began politely, "would you have killed Mrs. Waterford 40 years ago if you had been ordered?" I could feel my blood pressure rising, and I silently cursed the brazen, pimple-cheeked kid for putting me in such a dilemma. Not daring to look at Helen, I took a deep breath.

"I'm afraid, young man, the answer is yes. Unconditional, unquestioning obedience was the first iron-clad rule by which we were raised. A refusal of any direct, specific order in the course of duty, no matter how distasteful, was unthinkable." A collective gasp of shock rose from the packed auditorium. The question-and-answer session ended. On the way to the parking lot, I turned to Helen. "I'm really sorry you had to listen to that, but the kid deserved an honest answer. I hope you're not too offended."

"If you had said anything else," she replied quietly, "our association would have been over; I couldn't have trusted you to tell the truth." After that, we had our disagreements, (especially regarding American domestic politics--I consider her much too liberal) but there was never any doubt about the strength or merit of our partnership.

There were occasions later when I wished Helen Waterford had never called me. The constant recital of my past began to take its toll. I could easily deal with my own emotions, but soon I needed a respite from the disturbance I evoked in some listeners, who reacted as if they had come face to face with the sadistic Dr. Josef Mengele.

We gained our first national attention in February 1982, after the *Los Angeles Times* ran a feature story about one of our high school lectures. Two weeks later we were guests on "Good Morning America." By then well-seasoned by adversity, we were no less committed to what had become a mission. Helen's naivete had suffered with the realization that not only members of the Jewish Federation of San Diego but many Jews in the community, looked upon her association with me as collaboration with the enemy. Confronted with an ultimatum (it was either me or them) she severed her ties as a speaker with the Federation.

I was astounded by the Jewish reaction toward my partner which, although there were some remarkable exceptions, ranged from indifference to hostility. Our seven-minute appearance on "Good Morning America" made us more acceptable, particularly on the college circuit, but it still didn't convince influential Jewish groups of something Helen had recognized long ago. The uniqueness of former Nazi and Jewish victim sitting side by side at a table would attract more attention than a thousand survivors. People seemed to appreciate hearing both sides of the Nazi era. Not infrequently, it was put more bluntly. "All you ever hear is the Holocaust, as if there had been only Jewish victims in World War II. Finally, there is another view."

I agreed with that sentiment, but not because I thought the annihilation of the Jews of Europe should be forgotten or its importance denigrated. The attempted eradication of the Jewish race was an unsurpassed atrocity, perpetrated not in the darkness of the Middle Ages but in the Twentieth Century, and in the name (if not with the consent) of an educated, highly developed nation. If it could happen in Germany, "land of the poets and thinkers," the land that had seeded the world with genius as well as prosaic workmanship, it could happen any-where. Seen in the broadest interpretation, the Holocaust was a failure of all civilization. The Nazis, spurred by the obsession of one man, Adolf Hitler, carried out the "Final Solution," but not without the help of non-Germans all over Europe. In addition, most of the world including the United States had abandoned the Jews before the war when determined action could have saved millions. In view of that dismal record, I couldn't blame the Jews' attitude. Their fate was worse than Josef Stalin's murder of at least 16 million Russians during the purges and collectivization of the '20s and '30s. Stalin's aim was not genocide, and he had eventually stopped. The unanswerable question is, 'Would the Nazis have stopped if they had won the war?' I would like to say yes, because the SS had already taken measures to eradicate traces of the extermination sites when they were caught by the advancing Allies. But it's unlikely that even after Hitler's death his racial policies would have changed. We, the children raised in his ideology, might well have continued the course of the Master Race. We would have stayed Nazis.

Despite its enormity, the death of six million Jews was an event on the periphery of a raging inferno that caused at least 50 million casualties. Fewer than 300,000 were American which, as a Soviet journalist once pointed out to me "was a ridiculous bargain to attain the role of super power, measured against 20 million Soviet deaths." If Germany had won, those Russians--as well as the six million Jews--would have disappeared without a trace as "missing in action," which is exactly what happened to at least three million Germans in the wake of the Soviet conquest. Who would have dared to ascribe the Jewish fate to organized mass murder? Who would have believed it?

Jewish listeners in particular, see World War II in the flaming letters of the word Holocaust. They find it both offensive and incredible that I lived through the rise and fall of Nazism without any awareness of the fate of the Jews, except for what I myself had seen--harassment, forced emigration, loss of citizenship, the destruction during the *Kristallnacht*, deportation. After 1940, I don't recall ever seeing a Jew except for an elderly couple adorned with yellow stars sitting forlornly on a bench in the city of Koblenz.

On a visit to the Holocaust Memorial Center in Detroit, I looked at the casualty numbers listed for each country. Of approximately 600,000 German Jews, 160,000 had been killed. A few feet further, there was a view of devastated, burning Berlin. It struck me again what a terrible price had been exacted from us Germans for this insanity. There wasn't much point in exchanging casualties, but of an estimated nine million Germans who died, about five and half million were civilians. At least two million, in and out of uniform, had been mere teenagers. I had sent some of them to their deaths myself. Although no tribunal ever blamed me for that (what victor cared how many Germans had died) I owed them restitution. While one can make a solid case for the mass guilt of German adults mesmerized by Hitler's persuasion, their children had been innocent, even most who wore the *Führer*'s uniform. I had to speak for those children, as Helen Waterford had to speak for her dead, but with a difference. Although I carry a lingering resentment against Hitler and our educators who allowed us to fall into his grip, I have forgiven all of them for what they did to me personally, partly because I am guilty of having enjoyed much of my life in Nazi Germany, but mainly because unceasing hatred is too heavy a load.

When Helen is asked when she began to forgive (often the follow-up question to her courageous statement that she never hated) she answers that "only the dead can forgive." Here, she echoes Elie Wiesel, the Nobel Peace Price winner and fellow

Auschwitz inmate who became the most eloquent writer on the Holocaust. While I concede that those who paid the ultimate price--the dead--should be the ones to forgive (if this were possible), the living victims cannot claim this immunity if they hope to escape the debilitating punishment of hatred. To forgive is to gain peace, and it may well be too much to ask. But does that preclude a willingness to understand? Does it justify blanket condemnation of every Nazi? I hope not, but I was never in a death camp.

Our delicate partnership works because we don't interfere with each other's interpretations, although we do discuss what stirs an audience most. I suggested that Helen should describe her harrowing experiences more explicitly. It's one thing to say women and children were segregated at the ramp and soon died, but students are much less likely to forget if they hear that the victims died choking and writhing naked on the cement floor of a gas chamber. Helen, though, purposely refuses to dwell on the details of the horror, because she doesn't want the audience to become overly emotional and forget her message in a flood of tears. She prefers that her listeners think, not cry.

While there is extreme sensitivity among the Jewish community to Helen's presentations, there is almost no reaction to my appearances from the German side. As part of my work as a writer, I have followed German politics avidly, and a few times received mild comments about my articles, usually with the complaint that I dredged up a past which was better forgotten. I wondered whether these Germans were aware that while they may have forgotten the past, the Jews of the United States had no such intention.

Although I had become steeled to this unconcern, I was dismayed by the reaction of my family in Germany when I sent them clippings of our lecture coverage. At first there was no response. This wasn't unusual; I seldom received more than a couple of letters a year. But when I asked my cousin, a high school teacher, to try to find some Hitler Youth photos for my first book, I received a brusque refusal. "I think the time has come to let the Jewish horror stories rest," wrote this highly educated young woman, born after the war. "The so-called Holocaust was the doing of the Nazi generation, and I resent that my tax money is being used to make restitution to so-called 'victims' who are always attacking us Germans. I also resent that every administration, beginning with Adenauer in 1953, has burdened us with these payments until every last one of these 'victims'--some of whom were criminals--have died."

My brother Rudolf who, along with only two of my former classmates, helped me with research on my first book, was sympathetic to her view. He pointed out that "you Americans" had neither compensated nor even formally apologized to the more than 110,000 Japanese-Americans which had been deprived of their property and freedom in 1942 when President Roosevelt consigned them to internment camps by executive order. He also explained that our cousin's distaste stemmed partly from a visit in England. When she toured the cathedral of Coventry, a British tour guide had castigated her for "what you Germans did here," knowing that she was not yet born when the *Luftwaffe* bombed England.

I never wrote her again, but I was often reminded of her bitter lines when I was berated by survivors as "once a Nazi always a Nazi." In light of what they were hearing from me--that I had looked upon Hitler as my God--their skepticism wasn't surprising. Still I wondered how many of them were receiving checks from Germany, as my cousin had suggested. The Nazis confiscated so much Jewish property that some restitution seems just. In the budget of the *Bundesrepublik*, each taxpayer pays a few *Marks*; East Germany doesn't share that moral obligation. Never once, however, have I heard a victim admit to receiving any compensation.

There is little awareness in the United States of the genuine sensitivity that Germans exhibit toward world opinion. The *Bundestag*, which contains a number of former Nazi Party members, passed a law in 1985 making it a punishable offense to deny or whitewash the extent of the Holocaust. To me, that comes perilously close to infringement of free speech. There is also no statute of limitations for war crimes, the only such exception in the penal code.

Our most demanding appearances, both for the listeners and for us, are before predominantly Jewish audiences but there have been only a handful of these. While the average student may be fascinated with the Nazi era, it's seldom a painful, personal experience that can reach the dimension of a catharsis. In August of 1982, we spoke to about 300 Jewish women at the Brandeis--Bardin Institute near Los Angeles. Several of the survivors in the audience were visibly distressed when they saw me, but apart from some skeptical observations about the degree of my rehabilitation, the level of hostility remained icily polite. The same was true when we lectured in the synagogues of Palm Springs, California, and Spokane, Washington. Perhaps the sanctuary atmosphere helped, although an elderly, retired cantor in Spokane who had lost all of his family in a camp, began to intone a Nazi storm trooper song in German, yelling at me to ask if I were still happy seeing "Jewish blood drip off my knife." Somebody led him gently outside.

I faced my toughest audience on April 10, 1983. We had been invited to participate in a commemoration service for victims of the Holocaust, a first. When I sat amid three rabbis on the dais before 500 people, many of them survivors, and listened to the words of the *Kaddish*, the Hebrew prayer for the dead, my palms began to sweat. I looked beyond the six lighted candles, each symbolizing one million victims, trying to read the emotions behind the stony faces. The community had been told of my participation, but a dozen or more people still walked out spontaneously when I was introduced. They couldn't bear the presence of a former Nazi, even one, as the rabbi emphasized, who acknowledged the guilt of the regime. I wondered if I had made the right decision coming here. But I was aware that this was a watershed, my moment of truth. I didn't dare tell this audience that I felt we had also been victimized, and that there should be a seventh candle for the adolescents who had gone to their deaths believing in Hitler. I did make a short plea for understanding if not forgiveness; despite their indifference, most Germans had not wanted to harm Jews. Their faces remained set; it sounded wooden and unconvincing.

After the ceremony, an elderly lady walking with a cane came up and held out her thin hand. "I'm the only one of my family who left Bergen-Belsen alive," she said in German. "I thought I'd never see the day a Nazi would admit to me what happened. Now, I can die in peace. Thank you." Deeply touched, I thought this might be the turning point, that the burden both sides shared might be lifted. Several others shook my hand and thanked me for coming, but Helen brought me quickly down to earth. One of the men who had praised me for my honesty with an especially hearty handshake, had berated her for being friends with a fanatic who would have killed her without a second thought 40 years ago.

On the campuses, I learned that students can be much different than adults who have learned to mask their feelings. Some frankly admitted that the prospect of meeting me had aroused strong thoughts of antagonism, which were quickly diffused by my air of openness. "I wish you weren't so damn nice," blurted one bewildered young man. He had sworn the day before my arrival that he wouldn't shake my hand, and I was glad that he could joke about it when he did. He laughed when I confided I had similar apprehensions and never held out my hand to any Jew unless he or she offered first.

I had been rebuffed several times, once by an intense young rabbi with whom I later got into a discussion about the issue of mass guilt. He made the astonishing statement that he considered every German above the age of six guilty. I asked him if that included my cousin Gisela who had been nine when the war ended and never had been inducted into the junior branch of the Hitler Youth. She, her husband Jack, and their son Bradford had attended our lecture at St. John's University in Minnesota. I was extremely interested in Gisela's reaction, for she and her family were very knowledgeable on the Nazi era. Hitler's flags had waved when she was an infant on our farm. Gisela thought Helen and I had tried to paint an honest picture of the past, but she herself had not the slightest feeling of personal moral involvement. Surely, I queried the rabbi, her age would absolve her of any blame.

"No," he said. "She bears an abstract guilt because she was an eyewitness. A child of six can sense injustice being done to others." I don't know of any child, no matter how precocious, that has any grasp of the abstract political system under which it lives. But I was stung by his absurd theory. My defense of the Hitler Youth is that even at 16, few of my comrades had any inkling that they were pawns of an evil empire. Bombarded by incessant indoctrination from kindergarten on, and surrounded by adults who were either captivated themselves or lacked the suicidal courage to tell the truth, they never had the luxury of any choice. To expect a child to be that discerning was ridiculous!

I decided to broach the controversial and widely surpressed issue of the thousands of Nazi prisoners who had worked for their masters--especially the *Kapos*, who often treated their fellow inmates with wanton brutality. Some were sadists, but most tried to prolong their lives by fawning to their oppressors, even if it meant selecting others to die. Were they blameless, despite their option of refusal? Nobody *had* to become a *Kapo*--there were scores of eager volunteers in every camp--but everybody *had* to join the Hitler Youth or risk imprisonment and death.

"It's the same," asserted the rabbi in the safety of the California college sunshine. "I would have chosen to die rather than betray my humanity or serve such a monstrous cause." Perhaps he was one of the rare who possessed that extreme courage, but I doubted it. He did shake my hand when we said good-bye, indicating, as I remarked ironically, that he already had changed his mind within 24 hours.

The innocents most burdened by the past are the children of survivors and the children of former Nazi officials or war veterans. To see how disturbingly the past can intrude into the future, a person need not look beyond these two groups. The word "survivor" has become an encomium for the children of Nazi terror survivors, but a curse for the children of former Nazis, creating in both, sometimes severe psychological problems.

After our lecture at the University of California at Davis, a German exchange student broke down in front of nearly a thousand students when he confessed that his grandfather, an ex-*SS* officer, had refused to tell him what he had done during the war, except that he had served Germany honorably against Bolshevism. The boy felt that he himself was somehow implicated in whatever crimes his grandfather might have committed. This situation illustrated perfectly what repression can do. Very likely the grandfather was not a war criminal (he had been cleared by a de-Nazification commission) but was still attached to the Nazi ideology. His grandson could have accepted that easier than silence, but nobody talked. His parents not only shunned the subject of their father, but became Jehovah's Witnesses because of their abhorrence of war. My open admission of my former allegiance broke the dam of the boy's emotions, but it was Helen Waterford who helped him more than I. Like his grandfather, I would always be tainted, but when she, the victim of the *SS*, assured him that he was in no way responsible for any but his own sins, it was an absolution.

There were a number of less dramatic confessions by German students at other lectures. Remarkably, not one of them harbored any pro-Nazi feelings but, perhaps because they were better educated, nearly all complained that their fathers hadn't told them enough about their existence under Hitler. Presumably this was not because of sinister reasons, but because they hadn't come to terms with it themselves. This remains the pattern in West Germany today, although the Nazi era is extensively studied in most schools.

Many children of Jewish survivors are so influenced by their parents' bitterness that it perpetuates a hatred which seems learned rather than developed through personal experience. It seems an inevitable part of growing up, a rite of passage in the shadows of such a cruel past. Helen Waterford's hardest moments are when we encounter children of survivors who apparently hate her more passionately than me. The worst occurrence was at a supposedly "quiet" university, Rensselaer Polytechnic Institute in Troy, New York, which justly prides itself on its high scholastic level. In a group of non-students, two women identified themselves as children of survivors and began to shout explicit obscenities at Helen, mainly because she dared to sit next to me. They contended that that still "arrogant, smug Nazi should be dead like all Nazis." There was no physical danger, but I felt deeply sorry for my partner. She didn't deserve this gratuitous verbal violence, but it demonstrated how deeply ingrained is the hostility.

Despite my acceptance of enmity toward me (I had, after all, chosen to expose my past and was therefore prepared to risk danger) I wasn't prepared for what happened when we arrived in Albany, New York, on November 4, 1987, to lecture at the State University of New York that evening. We were met at the airport by young man who introduced himself as "Joe." He was a member of the university's lecture committee which had contracted our presentation six months previously. Deeply embarrassed, Joe told us that our lecture had been cancelled after an emergency meeting of the committee the night before.

"What do you mean cancelled?" I demanded. According to Joe, 500 to 800 Jewish students of the university were threatening to appear at our lecture and shout us down. "It's going to be a riot," said Joe, "and our committee felt it would be better to cancel since we can't guarantee an unhindered presentation, let

alone your safety." This was a memorable first: what the Ku
Klux Klan hadn't been able to do had happened at a renowned
university, a bastion of learning and enlightenment. We weren't
even given the chance to be heard, but were summarily silenced.
If ever there were a parallel to the surpression of free speech
under Hitler, this was it. Just like his storm trooper rowdies who
silenced the opposition, these Jewish students had succeeded in
cowing the university. But this wasn't Nazi Germany in 1933; it
was the United States in 1987. Ironically, the wrath of the
students wasn't directed primarily at me, the former Nazi, but at
Helen Waterford. According to Joe, these young Jews were
incensed by her association with me as well as by her assertion
that she never hated the Germans. There was, apparently, a
direct link to the incident at Rensselaer Polytechnic Institute
the year before. Joe told us that Jewish students from that
institution had influenced the Jewish student groups at Albany.
"They feel Mrs. Waterford makes Auschwitz seem like a
vacation."

Joe brought us to our hotel and handed me nine dollars for
the taxi fare to return to the airport the next morning. He had
tears in his eyes when he left. It wasn't he who should have
cried, but the university officials who gave in to a mob. Not one
of them bothered to pick up the telephone to give us an
explanation. While we weren't eager to confront hundreds of
agitated students, the university should have guaranteed our
right to do so. I believe we might have received a fair hearing
from most of the students despite their hostility, once they
understood that far from denigrating the importance of the
Holocaust, the purpose of our lecture is to keep it alive. While it
is their loss that we were denied the right to free speech, it is a
burning shame for their university to have allowed it. Had this
university and its students forgotten that the Holocaust did not
begin with murder but with acquiescence and silence?

After the years that Helen Waterford and I have lectured
together as the "odd couple" (as one New York magazine
described us) not much remains hidden. We have developed
more than trust on our monumental mission of remembrance. A
reporter once described our joint lectures as "a plea for
tolerance." That remains a utopian goal, although I have been
treated fairly by every reporter who either covered our lectures
or commented on my writings. Jewish writers in particular have

not allowed their personal feelings (and some admittedly had strong anti-Nazi sentiments) to interfere with their objectivity, so all is not bleak. I admire Helen's tenacity; despite her advancing years she continues to push herself at an untiring pace. A major goal is to reach that one vital segment of our society, the young. We have written off most members of our own generation as unreachable. Whether victims or perpetrators, Jews or Germans, they remain locked in and captured by their prejudices. Her commitment to the dead runs parallel to mine: an obsession to teach the living.

Astonishingly, she has retained a belief in the goodness of humanity which I don't share. Beneath the veneer of my geniality hides a thick layer of cynical pessimism. While I enjoy the stimulation of meeting many different people, even those who have mixed emotions about me, I have no desire to get close to any of them. I just don't care enough about individual fates. That coldness is likely attributable to the Hitler Youth dogma which held that any single person is only important in his service to the group.

Former Chancellor Helmut Schmidt called Auschwitz the moral watershed of our generation. Unfortunately, little has improved since then. Only the threat of mutual extinction keeps the major opponents at bay. More than four decades later, most Jews still regard most Germans with suspicious hostility, aptly demonstrated during President Reagan's visit to the Bitburg cemetery in the spring of 1985: "We shall never forgive and we shall never forget."

As a former Hitler Youth defender of Bitburg, I was interviewed on the "Today" show for my reaction to this drum fire of condemnation. My contention that it was both sad and wildly out of proportion was derided by many Jews, but was applauded by a handful. Ironically, Bitburg was not an *SS* cemetery. The two dozen *SS* soldiers buried there among hundreds of other military casualties were not war criminals. But the President was roundly condemned for this act of compassion. Could sane people believe that the President of the United States would actually pray for dead *SS* troopers? But in a possible lapse of political good sense he had expressed a shocking sentiment--that these young, dead Germans were also victims of Nazism. That was deemed unforgivable, because his sweeping statement put them on the same level with victims of the Holocaust. I'm neither that brave nor that casual. There *is* a degree of difference between dead German soldiers who fought for Hitler and those who died as his captives. While Mr. Reagan's attempted reconciliation was laudable, (if perhaps motivated by the fact that the *Bundesrepublik* is the staunchest NATO partner of the United States), his timing was off by a century. It will be at least that long before a U.S. President can pay his respects at a German World War II cemetery without being vilified.

When Chaim Herzog, the President of Israel, came to the Federal Republic of West Germany in April of 1987 for an historic first state visit by an Israeli head of state, he was warmly received by his counterpart, President Richard von Weizsäcker, a former captain of the *Wehrmacht* and the son of a convicted war criminal. The four-day visit was conducted with fitting dignity and no disturbances occurred, despite some controversy it caused in Israel. The two men appeared to like each other, and although the Israeli statesman didn't mention forgiveness in his final address, he did offer understanding. "There is no doubt that the past has erected an invisible wall between our peoples," he said, "before which we can only stand in silent contemplation."

And then he cited von Weizsäcker's eloquent warning to the *Bundestag* on the occasion of the fortieth anniversary of Germany's unconditional surrender, which took place on May 8, 1945. "He who closes his eyes to the past will be blind to the present." No one could sum up the legacy of the Third Reich or its burden better. In a few years we, the eyewitnesses, will be dust, but the infamy of our era will be remembered for as long as men record history. The disclosure of my own past is neither an apologia nor a plea for mercy. It is primarily intended as a warning to America's young, who never fail to ask at every lecture: "Could this happen here, in *our* United States?" Their implied assertion is that despite America's shortcomings, a dictatorship on the scale of Hitler's could never happen here, in the melting pot of humanity, the heartland of democracy. Dead wrong.

Few would deny that despite the progress this nation has made in 200-plus years, its foremost promise--equality for all--remains an elusive goal. Prejudice is still a pervasive ingredient of our social fabric, despite all the laws guarding individual freedom. What began under Hitler in 1933 and ended in a world afire 12 years and 50 million casualties later, was the result of acquiescence in the discrimination against less than one percent of our population--the 550,000 Jews of Germany. A highly cultural nation with a model system of education went on an irrational binge of xenophobic nationalism in its search for a scapegoat for the injustices inflicted on it by the Treaty of Versailles and by years of economic misery. Anti-Semitism again became not only respectable, but mandated by the state in a spate of laws.

Surely Americans with their innate sense of fairness and healthy distrust of government could never fall for such blatant injustice? Wrong again. We are not immune to such national hysteria, and neither are our elected officials. President Roosevelt signed an executive order sending more than 110,000 Japanese Americans to internment camps after the Japanese attacked Pearl Harbor on December 7, 1941. While a camp like Manzanar was benign compared to Dachau, it was nevertheless a political prison for entire families deprived of freedom and property not by a court of law but by executive order. Not one interned Japanese-American was ever found guilty of treason or even disloyalty to the United States. The wartime hysteria responsible for this outrage was just as irrational as Germans' fear of the Jews. In contrast to the Nazis, of course, sanity eventually prevailed and injustice did not lead to annihilation.

Just a few years later in the early '50s, using the tensions of the Cold War, Senator Joe McCarthy again created national hysteria in his witch hunt against domestic Communists, real and imagined. Shockingly the American free press, watch dog of freedom, was slow to awaken to the injustice, and in many cases fuelled the furor. It's not difficult to imagine what might have happened had a charismatic American leader been able to muzzle the media as effectively as Hitler; there would have been mass persecution of any who dared to deviate from government policy.

But this was the distant, regrettable past one might argue, and reason soon prevailed. Today, by law at least, aren't all citizens equal? So were the Jews of Germany in 1933; in fact they were prominent in more professions than any other segment of German society. Far from being denigrated as the economic underdog, they were envied for their achievements, and their very success was labeled a crime.

Is there a parallel to that in the United States? Are the Jews seen here, also, as the cunning power brokers? Certainly by most extreme right wing elements. But the American target of mass persecution likely will not be the Jews; it will be the masses who are denied access to the American dream. Millions of Americans are becoming increasingly frustrated in this, the most violent of all industrialized countries, where large sections of most major cities have become crime-ridden no-man's lands. How are we to deal with the thousands of unsalvageable adolescents, possessed of a smoldering resentment to all forms of authority? What are we to do when our cities are again aflame in riots? Are we going to open concentration camps to protect ourselves from the steadily rising wave of criminals? The undeniable moral decline of the United States in the past 20 years parallels the despair that seized so many Germans during the '20s and allowed them to fall prey to Adolf Hitler's promise of stability and protection. In this country, with its shocking indifference to domestic policies, where half of all eligible citizens don't vote, a demagogue of Hitler's hypnotic charisma could easily set citizen against citizen or minority against majority, with the promise of easy solutions. Perhaps more dangerous than the threat of a Soviet ballistic missile may be the fear and frustration developed during a steep economic slide, as was the case in Germany.

The enormity of the Holocaust awakened the conscience of the world, just as the atomic destruction of Hiroshima and Nagasaki has, thus far, prevented nuclear war. Although I believe that genocide such as occurred in Cambodia, needs the cover of war to proceed unhindered and unnoticed as did Hitler's, we must never assume it can't happen here. The enigma of why it happened in Germany, the enlightened land of the "poets and thinkers," should be a constant reminder to Americans that we must never forget--not primarily in respect for the dead but to guard our own future. While Hitler's legacy may well be my own personal burden, it should remain a lasting warning to the world.

Reactions from a sixth grade class at Rosebank School in Chula Vista, California to Alfons Heck's *A CHILD OF HITLER*

Feelings
I know you feel awful
That some of your friends have died.
But why did everyone hate the Jews?
I am Jewish and that is very hard to know
That Jewish people are dead.

Death at the Eastern Front
This is the place where Jews and Jypsies and
other Caucasians disappear. They never come
back and never regain their respect. I wonder if
the death of Christ meant anything to the SS?
This is the place where kids are never children.
Where kids would turn their relatives and lie
about their parents. All because of one man. The
man who killed and brainwashed all of
Germany. The man called Adolph Hitler. Should
this be how life should end like........

The Hitler Youth
The Hitler Youth sounds like a terrible group.
The SS men remind me of destruction.
All the violence you can hear around you.
11,000,000 fall to the ground.
The ground is red from the blood of the bullet shots.
Achtung!
I hear a watch ticking,
Ticking, ticking, ticking........

Why?
Why did it happen like that?
Couldn't it be some other way
Or not happen at all?
Why did it happen?
If you know please tell me.

Hitler
Hitler, Hitler, Hitler
Take him away.
Yes, take him away
And will make him pay.
But that's not right.
We shouldn't fight
Now I see the light.
Hitler
Hitler
Hitler
Sweat covered my forehead
As I lay there,
Thank God it was
Only a dream.

Chapter Twelve:

FACING THE PUBLIC

During my first seven years on the lecture circuit, I recorded many questions and my answers from audiences at more than 150 colleges and universities. In addition, I have done media interviews, call-in talk shows and addressed special groups such as Holocaust survivors, Rotarians and Lions. Many questions repeat from audience to audience, and a selection of those is offered first. I conclude with examples of the more unusual questions from specific audiences.

"Do you receive threats on your life? By whom?"

> "Occasionally, but thus far never at lectures. Usually the threats are a result of my articles, made by extreme right wing radicals, although they are always anonymous."

"Are you afraid somebody might kill you?"

> "No, although the thought has crossed my mind a number of times."

"Do you get tired hearing about the Holocaust from Mrs. Waterford?"

> "Not from Mrs. Waterford, even after all of our joint lectures, because she tries to see the Holocaust in a wider perspective and acknowledges that most Germans were not actively implicated in it."

"Did you tell your wife you had been a Hitler Youth leader when you first met her?"

"I was engaged before I told her about my life in Nazi Germany in some detail. I felt she was entitled to know about that part of my past."

"Do you have Jewish friends today?"

"Only Mrs. Waterford, although I remain friendly with some Jews I have met over the years."

"Do you *really* consider yourself also a victim?"

"I do, mainly because I was raised in the Nazi ideology as a child, and my love for Germany was misused. I consider it an obligation to speak for my comrades who died for a regime whose evil they never had an opportunity to grasp."

"Did you know of the concentration camps?"

"Yes. The first one was Dachau, established in 1933 when Hitler came to power. Its purpose was not to imprison Jews, but to contain the regime's political enemies, especially the Communists and Social Democrats in those early years. Later, other opponents of the Nazis, as well as criminals, conscientious objectors and homosexuals were sent to concentration camps."

"Where was Auschwitz located, and why didn't you know what was done there?"

"Auschwitz was one of the six extermination camps, all of which were located in remote rural areas of Poland. Their sole purpose was to kill masses of people as efficiently as possible, usually by gas. Their existence was top secret, kept from the German masses. I never heard the word Auschwitz until after the war. By contrast, the hundreds of concentration camps inside Germany were not only known to all of us, but used as a deterrent to any opposition. I grew up regarding them as political prisons, more frightening than any jail, since incarceration in a concentration camp could last from a few days to many years, or it could end in sudden execution."

"Do you regret Germany lost the war?"

"I did for several years after our defeat, partly because I was treated pretty roughly by the French occupation authorities."

"How were Hitler Youth leaders chosen?"

"Usually for their enthusiasm and, to a lesser degree, for their intellectual and physical abilities."

"Did you really believe the United States would join the Nazis in fighting the Soviets in 1945?"

"That was the last great delusion for many of us, especially since communism and capitalism are natural adversaries. It seemed in the best interests of the United States to finish off both Hitler and Stalin. In light of the Cold War, one could argue that the United States missed its chance to become the sole global power."

"Was anti-Semitism a factor in the indifference of the German people toward the fate of the Jews?"

"Without a doubt, but indifference is not the same as mass murder. Not even fanatic members of the Hitler Youth would have advocated genocide."

"Why didn't the churches oppose Hitler?"

"Partly for self-serving reasons--Hitler's government was the legal authority which, among other things, collected church taxes, the main income of both Protestant and Catholic churches. Many remained unopposed because their priests and ministers approved of the stability Hitler had brought to the nation."

"Are you still a Catholic?"

"In name only; but I do believe in some form of a higher power."

"How many Jews live in West Germany today?"

About 30,000, as compared with 550,000 in 1933."

"Do you believe the two Germanies will be reunited one day?"

"It's inevitable, but not in the foreseeable future or in my lifetime. Sooner or later in the long cycle of history, it's bound to happen, since we share many centuries of a common heritage."

"Do most Germans feel guilty about the past?"

"I don't think so, although they regret what happened. It's exceedingly rare to find expressions of individual remorse. The destruction of Germany, the loss of territory and the savage punishment inflicted on millions are seen as an excessive punishment for the sins of the past. The Germans, after all, paid a terrible price for their infatuation with Hitler."

"Have the Germans changed?"

"They have indeed. Their allegiance to Hitler died with him, and the West Germans of today bear no comparison to the intoxicated masses who hailed the *Führer*. The postwar generation in particular, doesn't deserve to be tainted with the Nazi past. Unfortunately, it will remain the dark side of its heritage for many generations."

"If you had been an adult during the war, do you think you would have been as forthright with young people as you wish adults had been with you?"

"I doubt very much that I would have been. My youth and my immaturity are the extenuating factors which make the admission of my fanaticism possible. Implied in this is a silent plea for understanding if not forgiveness."

What follows are some of the more unusual questions I have been asked by specific audiences:

Female student at Cabrini College, 1982

"Were you more fanatic than most other members of the Hitler Youth? If so, was it because your family consisted of Nazis?"

"As I rose in the ranks of the Hitler Youth, I did become more of a fanatic than most, primarily because of my leadership position and not because of family influence. On the contrary, not one other member of my family became a card-carrying Nazi. In fact my grandmother,

Margaret Heck, often privately criticized the regime to me."

"Wasn't that dangerous?"

"I was more afraid of my grandmother's wrath than of the *Gestapo*. I also loved her more than any other member of my family, which is why she didn't have to fear that I would ever denounce her."

"Would you have turned over your father to the *Gestapo*?"

"Although I knew he didn't care for Hitler, I was unaware of his deep hatred toward him and the regime. It's conceivable I would have turned him in, especially since I didn't like my father then, but only if he had persisted in denouncing Hitler and his regime, despite my warning to refrain. Fortunately for him, we had very little contact with each other during the Nazi era. I was raised by my grandmother and my aunt. My parents and my brother lived 200 miles away."

A Jewish student at a four-hour symposium about Nazism at the Cafe del Rey in San Diego in 1983

"I have a strong feeling of hatred for you because my paternal grandparents were killed by Nazis in Poland in 1939. Could you have been one of the killers?"

"No. I was 11 years old when Germany invaded Poland, and lived about 600 miles away in the Rhineland of Germany."

"I still hate you because you, the Nazi, survived and they didn't. How can I deal with this hatred?"

"Although I deeply regret what happened to your family, your hatred toward me is harder on you than on me." (I received several calls from this young woman, who later retained a psychiatrist to help her deal with what had, in her own words, become an "obsession" that focused on me.)

A middle-aged Jewish woman at the U.S. Merchant Marine Academy, May 1985

"I was chased through the streets of Munich in 1938 by teenagers of the Hitler Youth. They were just as vicious as the

SA (storm trooper) adults. Nobody who was raised like that can change, and I don't believe for a moment that you have. The only thing you are sorry for is that you lost. Isn't that the real truth? If you get paid for this, don't you think you should turn this blood money over to the people you harmed?"

> "Whether you believe me or not, I am sorry for what happened to you. I don't dispute that Hitler Youth members in various instances harrassed Jews, but that was the exception. These teenagers you mentioned were almost certainly off duty. I concede also that there was a time when I dearly wished we had won the war. I was, after all, not in a very good position in the hands of the French. As far as the money goes, that is not my first priority, and I do believe that I give a unique insight into the Nazi era that can't be matched by the average history professor. I have no intention of turning over the money to any cause, although I do, on occasion, waive my fee. Since you inquired about my finances, may I ask if you receive a check from the West German government--a restitution check as a Nazi victim?"

"That has nothing to do with it. I'm entitled to that money. We lost all we had under the Nazis and what I get is little enough, you smug, arrogant Nazi."

A male student at the University of California at Davis, 1985
"I'm gay, and I would like to know why the Nazis persecuted and killed gays?"

> "One of the mainstays of Nazi ideology was the sanctity of the German family, coupled with the aim to produce as many children as possible. Homosexuals were seen as a deterrent to that goal, and their life style was branded as perverted."

"Do you still think we are perverts?"

> "No. Although your sexual preference is unnatural to me, you have every right to engage in it with consenting adults."

Biola University, California, 1985

"Could you have sex with Jewish girls?"

"No. Under the Nuremberg Racial Laws of 1935, sex between Aryans and Jews was a felony. From that time, no Aryan German female servant under the age of 45 could work in a Jewish household."

Bucknell University, 1987

"Have you ever felt a need to atone for your crimes, and would you do penance on a Kibbutz?"

"If you class fanaticism as a 'crime', I have indeed atoned, but that was the only charge of which I was accused by French authorities. What lies on my conscience are my comrades who died needlessly for an evil regime. No, I would not do penance on a Kibbutz, particularly since I never laid a hand on any Jew. By the time I was 12, the Jews of my hometown had already been forced to emigrate, and the remaining 80 or so were deported in 1940."

"But didn't you kill anybody? Allied soldiers?"

"Yes. We shot down an American B 17 Flying Fortress on the Western Front and we engaged in a firefight with American troops near Bitburg in February of 1945, in which several Americans were killed along with a couple of our men. That's legitimate warfare for which I have no feeling of guilt."

An Irish Catholic professor at the University of Northern Michigan

"Can you explain to my students why you are not still in prison, in light of the horrendous Nazi crimes of which you were a part?"

"Since *Reichsjugendführer* Baldur von Schirach received 20 years, and since his successor Artur Axmann wasn't even indicted by the Allies, your question makes no sense. Although I served an evil regime, I don't consider myself a war criminal, and neither did the harshest occupation authorities."

"Nazis never change."

"You are entitled to your opinion."

A rabbi professor at Carnegie-Mellon University, 1985

"I had deep misgivings about your coming here, but your testimony has done more for the enlightenment of our students than any number of survivors, notwithstanding their suffering. I applaud your courage, but have you totally overcome all remnants of your past?"

> "I have refuted the Nazi ideology unreservedly, but some memories of my past remain pleasant. I loved the flying, the camaraderie and also the power I wielded, as well as the challenge of being confronted with often difficult tasks. Our enthusiasm was both naive and genuine. We thought we were serving a noble Germany, not a murderous regime. Jarring as it may sound, we also became the victims of Nazism."

Male student, University of San Diego

"Was Hitler's hatred of the Jews not merely a ploy, a propaganda hook? Wasn't he half-Jewish?"

> "Hitler's abiding hatred of the Jews was genuine. Its origins stem from his early Vienna years when, as an adolescent, he was influenced by the virulently anti-Semitic feeling that permeated the city. In his book *Mein Kampf* he later claimed that he became a dedicated anti-Semite upon his discovery that 'the Jew was the cold-hearted, calculated director of prostitution,' and that both the art world and the Social Democratic press were 'controlled' by the Jews. Undoubtedly the failed and shiftless Hitler of Vienna days found, in the hatred of the Jews, an outlet for his own deep sense of frustration. From there to the idea of a Master Race seemed an almost natural transition, especially since it was a notion appealing to millions. There is, however, no credible evidence in Hitler's family history to indicate he was part Jewish. Hitler didn't invent anti-Semitism; he merely used it more effectively than any other politician to hoodwink the masses into believing they needed a savior. That, though, doesn't detract from his own genuine obsession with what he considered the 'Jewish danger,' which eventually became so compulsive that he deprived the German war machine of bitterly needed trains in order to

transport Jews to death camps."

"Why did you hate Jews, with the exception of your kindergarten friend?"

"Despite all efforts at indoctrination, I never did hate Jews as individuals, partly because the ones I saw were deeply frightened. I did, however, fear them as a larger group, as a world-wide movement to gain power not only over Germany but over much of the world. In that respect, I did fall for the Nazi line."

"What happened to your friend Heinz?"

"I was told late in 1945, about six months after the war, that Heinz and his family had been gassed in Auschwitz. However, in December 1987, Walter Kahn, a Jewish citizen of Wittlich now residing in Florida, notified me that Heinz had obtained a visa to Peru before the outbreak of World War II and thus became the only member of his immediate family to survive. He never made any attempt to contact me, which is not surprising since he left Wittlich as a child, outcast by a hostile community. He died of a heart attack several years ago in Switzerland, depriving me of a chance to make amends for the era that victimized both of us."

"Did that make you feel guilty?"

"Yes."

Female student at Penn State University, 1987

"Do you believe Mrs. Waterford is racially inferior to you?"

"I believe Mrs. Waterford would object violently to being classed as inferior by anybody, racially or otherwise! If I held any such notion--absurd as early as 1945--we certainly would not be friends."

Professor at Baptist College of Newhall, California, 1982

"You say if Hitler had died in 1938, he would have been hailed as one of the greatest German statesmen of all time, despite the increasing persecution of the Jews. What was his appeal to the Germans?"

"Hitler succeeded in restoring pride to a defeated nation which had been punished excessively by the Treaty of

Versailles in 1919. He speedily restored full employment and with it a sense of order and stability, gaining him quick acceptance with the masses."

"And for that the people apparently tolerated abuses of the Jews, their fellow citizens?"

"Yes, and not only the common people. The hierarchies of both Catholic and Protestant churches did nothing to protest; neither did our famous universities."

"This could never happen here, in the United States. Our people wouldn't stand for it."

"You are mistaken. May I remind you of the treatment of the Indians? And in a modern parallel to the Nazi racial laws, scarcely two decades ago, interracial marriages were unlawful in a number of southern states, only one indicator of America's inferior treatment of Blacks."

A male student at the University of Alaska, Fairbanks, 1984

"Do you feel awkward sitting next to Mrs. Waterford when she says that you Germans murdered six million Jews, and do you accept that number as correct?"

"I don't feel awkward sitting next to Mrs. Waterford because we have become friends, but the enormity of what she says still strikes me on occasion. Although no exact figures are available, I accept the number of six million Jewish victims as correct, based on the evidence presented at the Nuremberg Trials. Every postwar German government, by the way, has agreed with the number of at least 5,700,000."

"Has Mrs. Waterford forgiven you?"

"You'd better ask her that."

Mrs. Waterford's reply: "There was nothing to forgive. Mr. Heck was raised into the Nazi system as a child. He wasn't an adult with mature judgment. I don't blame him."

"I still wouldn't sit next to him."

Mrs. Waterford: "You don't have to."

A Polish survivor who was a member of the studio audience when I was a guest on WBZ-TV Boston in 1982

"How did a Nazi like you become a U.S. citizen? Did you lie about your past? And why did you become a citizen? You can't tell me you believe in democracy."

"Membership in the Hitler Youth was not classed as belonging to a criminal organization. If I had been a member of the SS, I would not even have received a visa for permanent entry into the United States, although exceptions were made. Rocket scientist Wernher von Braun, who was a major of the SS, was so useful to this country that his Nazi background was ignored; he became a citizen. I remind you that I passed several intensive background checks and was cleared of having committed any war crimes. I never lied about my Hitler Youth career, although I didn't make it public until recently. When I became a citizen in June of 1969, I was again thoroughly questioned. Two American citizens who had known me for at least five years--which was the requirement--testified to my character and voiced their opinions that I was no longer a Nazi. The decision to relinquish my German citizenship wasn't easy, for I still love Germany as the country of my birth. Because of my Nazi past, I appreciate the freedom of a democracy much more than the majority of Americans who simply take it for granted. Can't you, a victim yourself, see that people are able to change?"

"Nazis don't change, and I think it's a disgrace they let you into this country; you fooled them. The only thing you are sorry for is that you lost."

Interviewer on the same show: "While we can accept that you didn't commit any war crimes, such as murdering civilians, isn't it true that you would have taken part in an execution if you had been ordered by your superior officers?"

"Yes. I couldn't conceive of disobeying a direct order."

Female Jehovah's Witness on the same show: "Why did the Nazis imprison and kill Jehovah's Witnesses?"

"Because of their refusal to bear arms for Germany. That's the reason fewer of their women were arrested, since women didn't have to serve in the Armed Forces. During the war, male Jehovah's Witnesses were given the chance to be released from concentration camps if they 'volunteered' to go to the front."

Female student at Syracuse University, 1987

"Did the Nazis have a program to produce a super race by special breeding?"

"Yes. The so-called *Lebensborn* (Fountain of Life) program, largely the brainchild of *SS* Leader Himmler, produced an estimated 200,000 blue-eyed, blond infants, whose parents were selected not only because of their "ideal" Nordic looks, but also because of their intelligence as well as total dedication to the Nazi ideology. Usually they were not married and their liaison seldom lasted more than several weekends together at special resorts. The males were often members of elite *SS* units or Hitler Youth leaders, and the young women nearly always belonged to the Hitler Youth. Their offspring were, as a rule, raised by dedicated Nazi families. As a result, most of the children never knew or were told about their biological parents. It was envisioned that by such selected breeding, the transformed Master Race would evolve over a span of four generations or about 120 years. The whole issue was not as important as it sounds; it has been sensationalized out of proportion to the facts."

"I suppose you weren't selected because of your dark hair and brown eyes?"

"True. But even if I had qualified, I was too young. One had to be at least 18, although we were freely encouraged near the end of the war to have sex in order to produce children for the Fatherland--one directive we liked immensely."

Male student at the University of Alabama, Huntsville, 1985

"Here in Huntsville, we are aware of the work of German rocket scientists, especially that of Wernher von Braun. Do you think Hitler would have used an atomic warhead to destroy New York, and do you think President Truman was justified in dropping atomic bombs on Hiroshima and Nagasaki?"

"Yes to both questions. Truman's decision shortened the war with Japan thus saving many lives that might have been lost."

Veteran of the U.S. 99th Infantry Division
"Who had the best generals in World War II, and what were their names?"

"The consensus of military historians is that despite our defeat and despite Hitler's often irrational interference in the military conduct of the war, Germany had the most capable generals. Our best tactician was Field Marshal Erich von Manstein, followed by such popular battlefield commanders as Field Marshals Walther Model, Gerd von Rundstedt, Hans von Kluge, Ewald von Kleist, Albert Kesselring, and Colonel-Generals Heinz Guderian, Sepp Dietrich, Hasso von Manteuffel and Juergen von Arnim. Field Marshal Erwin Rommel, the 'Desert Fox' was held in the highest esteem by Germans and foes alike, but he wasn't in the class of von Manstein as a strategist. Hitler's military operations chief of staff was the able but unfortunate General Alfred Jodl who, together with his medio-cre superior, Field Marshal Wilhelm Keitel, was hanged at Nuremberg in 1946. The best *Luftwaffe* general of the fighter arm was Adolf Galland; the chief of the *Luftwaffe*, Reich Marshal Hermann Göring, was a mediocre wartime leader although he had developed the prewar *Luftwaffe* into the best in the world. On the Allied side, the most widely known and respected field general was George Patton, Commander of the U.S. Third Army. General Eisenhower was seen as a 'political' general, but Chief of Staff General George Marshall was highly regarded as a tactician. It was he who directed Eisenhower, although Eisenhower himself made the tough decision of when to land on the beaches of Normandy, June 6, 1944. On the Russian side, Marshal Konstantin Rokossovsky was perhaps his nation's best field commander, followed by Marshals Semyon Timoshenko, who took the brunt of the German invasion in June of 1941, and Marshal Georgi Zhukov. On the British side, Field Marshal Bernard Montgomery was best-known, but despite his victory over Rommel at El Alamein, his reputation was overrated, and couldn't begin to match the drive of his later rival General Patton. In any war, only the top commanders have an overall picture of the various operations on all fronts, and even then they commit costly mistakes. A glaring example on our side was misreading the site of the D-Day landings. Among major British errors was the mid-September landing by Field Marshal Bernard Montgomery of nearly 10,000 men near Arnhem in Holland, in an effort to seize the bridges and open a shortcut into the Ruhr, our industrial heartland. The egomaniacal Montgomery, who resented General Eisenhower's authority, disregarded American intelligence warnings about German strength in Holland and landed his unit in an area held by a major *SS* division, thereby sacrificing more than 7,000 men with his Operation Market Garden."

"What about General MacArthur?"

"Since he commanded the Pacific war for the United States, he seemed far removed from us. We pictured him as flamboyant and popular, although his subordinates such as Admirals Chester Nimitz and 'Bull' Halsey provided much of his glory. His enlightened role in treating postwar Japan humanely was perhaps his best achievement. It certainly bound Japan to the United States."

"I agree with what you say about our generals, but weren't our infantry men better fighters than your *SS* troops?"

"Taken unit by unit, the *Waffen SS* was superior to the infantry of any of the Allied nations."

Male student at Northwestern University, Chicago, 1985

"When did you first find out about the extermination of the Jews, and what difference did it make in your loyalty to Germany?"

"In the fall of 1944, my friend *Oberleutnant* Leiwitz told me about a mass execution he himself had witnessed. He stressed that this wasn't an isolated incident but organized mass murder. I didn't accept the truth then, because it seemed preposterous. We needed labor badly. Why would we kill people who could work for us? But even if I had believed it, there would have been no difference in my loyalty. By then, our cities were sinking into rubble, and we were literally fighting for our survival. More than anything, I feared the defeat of Germany, since I fully expected I would, at best, become a slave. If anything, the knowledge of such atrocities would have been an added incentive to keep fighting, since we could hardly expect mercy."

"That means, then, that you would have remained a Nazi even if you had known of the exterminations and Germany had won the war?"

"I'm afraid the answer has to be yes."

"I think you got off too easy."

Female student at Grand Rapids Baptist College, 1983

"Aren't the abortions we allow in this country the same as the genocide perpetrated by the Nazis on pregnant Jewish and gypsy women?"

"No. Abortion in the United States is nearly always performed by choice. Where do you see the parallel?"

"Don't you agree that abortion is murder of the innocent unborn?"

"I'm afraid not. I think it should be the choice of the informed woman."

"You haven't learned anything from your Nazi experience."

Male student at Fordham University, 1986

"How can you convince me you no longer hate Jews? Do you have any Jewish friends?"

"If you don't take our joint lecture as proof that I don't hate Jews, I have no way of convincing you. Apart from Mrs. Waterford, who is my friend, I know a number of Jews, but I still feel uneasy with the past and I can't call them my friends. It's emotionally too difficult for them to form a true friendship with me. The only exception is Mrs. Waterford. We paid our dues together."

A rabbi at Tufts University, 1984

"Do you think the Jews will ever forgive the Germans for the extermination of their European brothers and sisters?"

"Not in my lifetime, and likely not for generations to
come. The best we can hope for is a measure of
understanding."

"Understanding for what? The guilt is quite clear."

"Despite the enormity of what was done, the fact remains
that the majority of the Germans had nothing to do with
the killings. It was done under the cover and turmoil of
war and largely outside of Germany. While you may argue
that all of us knew of the persecution, and that most of us
stood by, this still doesn't add up to compliance in mass
murder."

"Nevertheless, that callous indifference led to it, and as far as
I'm concerned no German of your generation has the right to
ask for forgiveness."

"I didn't ask."

On the Today Show, April 1985, John Palmer asked

"What do you think of President Reagan's visit to the Bitburg
cemetery?"

"As a former enemy, I was gratified that the President
extended a hand of conciliation and recognized that there
were victims on both sides. That view, however, is not yet
widely accepted, as the vehement reaction to his visit
proves. We haven't learned much since 1945."

And this question is asked by nearly every audience:

"What do you see as the solution to prevent anything like a Nazi
regime from taking hold again?"

"Education, as important as it may be, is not the only
answer. We had an excellent system of education in Nazi
Germany, and it was subverted by the state. The only
hope is to maintain unrestricted, unlimited freedom of
speech, especially for those who don't share our beliefs."

A *Jungvolk* honor guard stands death watch for fallen Hitler Youth, likely those killed in air raids. The line above the names reads:

YOU ARE STILL VICTORIOUS

BIBLIOGRAPHY

Arbeitskreis Eifeler Museen. *Notjahre Der Eifel 1944-1949*. Warlich Verlag, 1983.

Bekker, Cajus. *Angriffshöhe 4000 (The Luftwaffe War Diaries)*. Gerhard Stalling Verlag, 1964.

Botting, Douglas. *From the Ruins of the Reich 1945-1949*. Crown Publishers, 1985.

Brett-Smith, Richard. *Hitler's Generals*. Osprey Publishing, 1976.

Dawidowics, Lucy S. *The War Against the Jews 1933-1945*. Holt, Rinehart and Winston, 1975.

Galland, Adolf. *Die Ersten Und Die Letzten*. Wilhelm Heyne Verlag, 1976.

Haupt, Werner. *Das Ende Im Westen*. Podzun Verlag, 1972.

Jackson, Robert H. (Chief U.S. Prosecutor at the Nuremberg Trials). *Report of the United States Representative to the International Conference on Military Tribunals*. U.S. Department of State, 1949.

McMillan, James. *Five Men at Nuremberg*. Harrap Limited, 1985.

Miller, Russel. *The Resistance*. Time-Life Books Inc., 1979.

Naumann, Bernd. *Auschwitz: The 1963 Trial in Frankfurt*. Athenäum Verlag, 1965.

Nosbüsch, Johannes. *Bis Zum Bitteren Ende*. Paulinus Druckerei, 1978.

Schaaf, Erwin. *Neubeginn Aus Dem Chaos - Die Geschichte Des Landkreises Bernkastel-Wittlich 1945-1950.* Weiss-Druck Verlag, 1985.

Shirer, William L. *The Rise and Fall of the Third Reich.* Simon and Schuster, 1960.

Taylor, Telford. *Munich - The Price of Peace.* Random House, 1979.

Toland, John. *Adolf Hitler.* Random House, 1976.

Wistrich, Robert. *Who's Who in Nazi Germany.* Macmillan, 1982.

Wyman, David S. *The Abandonment of the Jews.* Pantheon, 1984.

Young, Peter. *The World Almanac Book of World War II.* Bison Books, 1981.

ACKNOWLEDGMENTS

I owe a special debt of gratitude to my close friend and former *Cusanus Gymnasium* colleague Rudolf Hein. His help in obtaining research material and his recollection of a past we shared were invaluable. The numerous conversations with my brother Rudolf Heck were equally important in recalling accurately the events of 40 and 50 years ago, in particular in reconstructing dialogue as truthfully as possible. Other former colleagues who assisted were Hermann Henkel, his wife Elfriede, and my childhood friend Wolfgang Knopp. Sincere appreciation to His Honor *Herr* Helmut Hagedorn, Mayor of Wittlich, to the Tourist Office of the City of Wittlich for its photos, and to the efficient staff of the *Bundesarchiv* in Koblenz, for locating and processing period photographs of particular subjects requested. And to my cousins Gisela Lee, Marika Klein, and Margaret Heck for eliminating superfluous correspondence.

Following are some of the many friends and well-wishers who encouraged me throughout the writing of *The Burden of Hitler's Legacy*: Homer Rydell and the "Thursday Night Meeting," Linda and Douglas Johnson, Curtis and Veturia Ingram, Pat Katka and Jean Hughes of the Palomar Chapter of the California Library Association, which honored me with a membership, my Canadian friends Ken and Connie Appleby, and my former history teacher, *Frau* Dr. Hella Fein.

I would be remiss in not mentioning several comrades with whom I shared not only the war but the bitterness and hope of post-war Germany: Hans Josef Fabry, Wolfgang Friderichs, Norbert Hess, Josef Hubert, Alois Kranz, Heinz Kranz, Josef Kremer, Monika Möhn, Hans Peter Petri, Fred Stein, and the entire *Cusanus* class of 1949, whose collective experience is reflected in these pages.

A special "well done" is due my friend and publisher, Eleanor H. Ayer and her able staff, who again made my task so much easier.

And finally, this book would not have been written without the devotion of my wife June--who, unlike my dachshund Elfie-- left me no choice.